The Fundamentals of Content Analytics

A Practical Guide for Marketing and Communications Professionals

Russ Bahorsky

The Fundamentals of Content Analytics: A Practical Guide for Marketing and Communications Professionals

Russ Bahorsky
Zion Crossroads, VA, USA

ISBN-13 (pbk): 979-8-8688-2600-9
https://doi.org/10.1007/979-8-8688-2601-6

ISBN-13 (electronic): 979-8-8688-2601-6

Managing Director, Apress Media LLC: Welmoed Spahr
Acquisitions Editor: Shivangi Ramachandran
Development Editor: James Markham
Coordinating Editor: Jessica Vakili

Cover image by eStudioCalamar

Distributed to the book trade worldwide by Springer Science+Business Media New York, 1 New York Plaza, New York, NY 10004. Phone 1-800-SPRINGER, fax (201) 348-4505, e-mail orders-ny@springer-sbm.com, or visit www.springeronline.com. Apress Media, LLC is a Delaware LLC and the sole member (owner) is Springer Science + Business Media Finance Inc (SSBM Finance Inc). SSBM Finance Inc is a **Delaware** corporation.

For information on translations, please e-mail booktranslations@springernature.com; for reprint, paperback, or audio rights, please e-mail bookpermissions@springernature.com.

Apress titles may be purchased in bulk for academic, corporate, or promotional use. eBook versions and licenses are also available for most titles. For more information, reference our Print and eBook Bulk Sales web page at http://www.apress.com/bulk-sales.

Any source code or other supplementary material referenced by the author in this book is available to readers on GitHub (https://github.com/Apress). For more detailed information, please visit https://www.apress.com/gp/services/source-code.

If disposing of this product, please recycle the paper

To my wife, whose creativity, entrepreneurial spirit, and pursuit of purpose are my inspiration.

Table of Contents

Chapter 3: Mapping Content Journeys **51**

Chapter 4: Data Collection and Preparation **79**

About the Author

Russ Bahorsky is a communications professional with more than 20 years of experience in strategic marketing communications for the higher education, publishing, and the nonprofit sectors. He has led creative teams and developed print and digital content for the University of Virginia, National Geographic, the American Psychological Association, and others with a strong focus on using analytics to improve engagement and impact. He holds an MBA in marketing management from Johns Hopkins University, an MFA in creative writing from Arizona State University, and a BA in English literature from Virginia Commonwealth University, along with certifications in UX design and research from the Nielsen Norman Group and direct marketing from the American Marketing Association. He is also the principal consultant for *Crosswalk* Analytics, LLC, and author of the Substack newsletter *The Crosswalk Report* at crosswalkreport. substack.com.

About the Technical Reviewer

Karen M. Schmidt, PhD, has 41 years of experience in research, statistical analysis, test and scale design, and modern measurement techniques. She has worked on many cognitive, personality, developmental, and health data analysis projects. She has an MA in human development and was awarded a PhD in quantitative methods from the University of Kansas in 1997. She has been a professor at the University of Virginia for 28 years, where she teaches courses in advanced statistical methods and item response theory, co-directs the College Science Scholars program, and is Director of Recruitment for the +1MA program in Accelerated Research Methods in the Department of Psychology. She has been a consultant and co-investigator on many technical research projects in social, educational, and health science internal and external research grants and has published articles in a wide variety of psychology, measurement, and health journals. In her various teaching, mentoring, and research roles, she has reviewed many grant proposals, articles, theses, dissertations, presentations, and projects for technical quality, statistical methodological strength, writing clarity, and cohesiveness.

Acknowledgments

This book would not have been possible without the support, guidance, and encouragement of many people. Special thanks go to Lorenzo Perez, Editorial Director for the College and Graduate School of Arts & Sciences at the University of Virginia, for reviewing early drafts and for his exceptional editorial judgment. His insights made this work stronger.

I am also profoundly grateful to Karen M. Schmidt, professor of psychology at the University of Virginia, whose expertise in analytics methodology has informed and sharpened this book. Her advice has been invaluable.

Thanks also to my colleagues over the years—writers, designers, editors, analysts, and developers—who have taught me the value of maintaining high standards and that creative work is never a solitary pursuit; to my wife, Kelly Feltault, for her patience and input throughout the process of research, writing, and revision; and to my mother, for her encouragement and her eye for detail and for making books an important part of my life.

Finally, to the readers of this book: thank you for your interest in taking the art of content creation to a new level. I hope this book helps you tell more powerful stories and find more meaning in the work that you do.

Introduction

How many clicks does it take for your online content to be successful? A thousand? A million? One?

Let's look at the question another way: Imagine you own a brick-and-mortar store on a busy city street. Your store is often crowded, but your sales are lower than those of your competitor whose store always looks empty. If you equate clicks with customers, you can see the problem. Can you really call someone a customer just because they walk through the front door, and is one customer just as good as another?

In today's data-centric world, content developers have access to mountains of data and incredibly powerful tools designed to help them understand how consumers are engaging with their content. But at the end of the day, if they're not helping you understand who's buying and why, those tools are just wasting your time—and maybe even your money.

If you create or curate content for your organization or manage those who do, and you find yourself with more questions than answers about the impact that content is having on your customers and on your bottom line, chances are your attempts at content analytics are falling short.

More than just an exercise in counting clicks, effective content analytics is the structured and purposeful practice of measuring, interpreting, and improving how individual pieces of content contribute to your organization's most important objectives. Its focus spans formats (articles, videos, landing pages), channels (web, email, social), metrics (engagement, conversion, perception), and tools (Google Analytics, Salesforce, Sprout Social) while helping teams answer the most important questions in digital communications:

Is our content working or not?

How do we know?

What do we do next?

What's more, content today isn't just the supporting player it once was. It's often your organization's product, its mission, and its primary tool for creating relationships. Organizations publish and communicate across a variety of platforms every day: newsletters to donors, explainers for students, campaigns to customers, statements to the public. Yet, most teams still struggle to see the impact of that content in a way that goes beyond clicks or page views.

If you're ready to take the next step, it's important to understand, first, what content analytics is and what it isn't. For starters, it's not the same as web analytics, which is typically focused on website performance. It's not exactly marketing analytics either, which takes a much broader view of its organization's assets and their impacts. It's also not just a matter of assuming that because one video got 1,000 likes or shares it's better than one that only got 100.

Practical content analytics is about understanding effective communication: how to tell a good story, how to hook your audience, and how to recognize when it's having real influence. It's also a scientific pursuit, one that makes it possible to ask smarter questions and make evidence-informed decisions that lead to creating the kind of content that has measurable impact and genuine value.

As a science, content analytics involves a wide variety of disciplines: computer science, statistics, marketing, psychology, linguistics, and even sociology. To be a content analyst, however, or to manage an effective content analytics effort, you don't need to be an expert in any of those disciplines. You just need to understand what you might be missing and how all the pieces fit together. You also need to be able to speak the language—to know, for example, what a regression model is and what it's good for, even if you don't know how to build one.

Ultimately, content analytics offers a number of critical advantages to today's content managers who are looking to harness data to maximize the value of their content.

- **It Improves Audience Insight**: Content analytics helps identify what resonates with and engages your audience by examining metrics like page views, engagement times, and conversion rates, which allows you to create content that has real, measurable impact for your organization.

- **It Enhances Content Strategy**: By analyzing high-performing content and pinpointing areas for improvement, content managers can refine their content strategies, use their resources more effectively, make more effective decisions, and identify opportunities to create strategic advantages.

- **It Makes Trend Identification Possible**: Content analytics helps in identifying meaningful trends and changes in audience behavior, keeping content creation and marketing strategies relevant and effective over time.

- **It Helps Optimize Content Performance**: Regular content analysis allows for the continuous improvement of your content. By understanding which pieces perform best and why, content managers can replicate successful elements and improve underperforming content.

Who This Book Is For

This book is written for marketers, content strategists, communications professionals, nonprofit storytellers, and higher education teams—anyone who creates online content that plays a role in advancing their organization's mission.

You might be part of a small nonprofit communications team juggling content production, campaign planning, and stakeholder reporting and are looking to have a bigger impact with the resources available. Or you might be part of a large corporation that already has the analytics experts you need in-house—if you only knew how to ask for their help. You might also be someone who is comfortable writing or designing content but less confident translating numbers into the kind of insight you need to make your work better, more effective, or more valuable to your employer.

Ultimately, if you've ever wondered whether a blog post helped drive donations or questioned whether a newsletter made any impact at all, this book is for you.

It's also important to stress that this book is not written for data scientists. You won't need to know R or Python or have a degree in data science. It's also extremely important to make a distinction between the practice or methods of content analytics and the tools needed to put those methods into use. One term you'll encounter in this book is "content analytics program," which is simply a systematic approach to collecting and analyzing data about your content in a way that allows you to make better business decisions, regardless of which tools you use to do the work. Think of it this way: statistical models, databases, and analytics apps and platforms are like the tools you need to build a house, and your content analytics program is the blueprint. Without a plan, the tools are useless.

And while you'll find some very basic information about how to use platforms like Google Analytics or how to do some simple statistics, the point of the book is not to recommend any of those tools but to show you the part they play in the bigger picture, underscoring why simply counting clicks is no basis for effective decision-making.

Instead, you'll learn how to

- Frame the kinds of business questions that are fundamental to making content analytics essential to your organization's strategic objectives.

- Collect and prepare the right kinds of data for analysis.

- Test your ideas and your assumptions and understand what the data is telling you.

- Simplify complex datasets and communicate your findings to stakeholders.

- Build a content analytics process that supports your team and your organization's goals.

- Develop a team-oriented approach to creating content that inspires engagement and gets real results.

Essentially, you'll learn everything you need to know to be able to effectively manage and grow your organization's content analytics efforts. You'll also learn when it's time to bring in a data expert or partner to help you take your insights to the next level and how to make that partnership a successful one.

How the Book Works

The chapters you'll encounter in the book are designed to be self-contained units of a comprehensive process of building a fully functioning content analytics program. You can move through the book linearly or jump into the sections most relevant to your current needs. Whether you're launching a new content strategy or refining an existing program, you'll find tools and insights you can apply immediately.

Most chapters include

- Case studies from higher education, nonprofit, media, and business settings

- Workbook exercises to help you apply the concepts to your own organization

- Practical tips for managers on a budget

- Management guidance to help you collaborate across teams and roles

- Supporting material and resources to help you get your own analytics efforts off the ground right away

It's also important to note that there may be other ways to approach the subject of content analytics. However, this one is intended to be practical and scalable—whether you work for a small business or a large corporation—and it's meant to be the kind of approach that can be implemented, managed, and championed by someone who knows more about marketing, communications, graphic design, or videography than someone who can build a behavioral model or a relational database. Most importantly, it's an approach meant to produce clear, actionable results that help you make better business decisions and produce more effective content.

The Content Analytics Mindset

Finally, you might think that you need mountains of data and the latest tools that promise to do all the hard work for you, but the most important ingredient in an effective content analytics program is a mindset that values evidence, clarity, and curiosity.

That means

- Asking not just *what* but *why*

- Treating data as a means, not an end

- Seeing patterns without jumping to conclusions

- Knowing the limits of your metrics and the value of human interpretation

- Staying open to the idea that the content you love might not be the content that performs

It also means being willing to test your assumptions, share your findings, and adjust your strategy, because it makes your work better.

Most importantly, it means not asking "What is our data telling us?" before asking "What is it that we need to know?"—a critical distinction that separates a leader with purpose and vision from one who's just groping in the dark.

Throughout this book, you'll also see that the most successful content analytics programs aren't always the ones with the biggest budgets or the most complex systems. They're the ones that approach the work with a spirit of inquiry and use that mindset to build trust, clarity, and momentum across their organization.

So, if you're ready to look beyond the clicks, let's get started. Chapter 1 walks you through the most critical step in the process: identifying your destination before you start the journey.

PART I

Strategic Foundations of Content Analytics

Aligning Content Analytics with Business Goals

Why does one piece of online content get a thousand views while another on the very same subject gets only ten? If only there were some way to know before you invest your time and resources in writing a story or a newsletter or posting a video, right? Without understanding what resonates with your audience and why, the best you can do is make a good guess. If that's one of the challenges you face as a content manager or producer, the solution is to recognize that the real value of that content isn't just in its quality but in the insights it generates. That way even the story, the podcast, or the video that fails to connect with your audience can still be a goldmine of insight.

That's where content analytics comes in. By turning data about how your audience responds to your content into useful strategic intelligence, analytics reveals not just what users do, but why they do it, and that can provide you with essential clues to understanding the role that content plays in the success of your organization. As organizations pour more and more resources into blogs, videos, podcasts, and social media, that kind of intelligence becomes the essential feedback loop that connects creative effort to real-world impact. It can also answer the question,

© Russ Bahorsky 2026
R. Bahorsky, *The Fundamentals of Content Analytics,*
https://doi.org/10.1007/979-8-8688-2601-6_1

"Why does it matter if my blog or my feature got a thousand views?" which is the first step in transforming your creative work into assets with tangible economic value.

Too often, firms apply analytics tools solely as a rear-view mirror: a set of dashboards showing page views or click-through rates (CTRs) for past campaigns. Such descriptive data may answer the question, "What happened?" and is a necessary foundation for a content analytics program. But it's far from being enough. Today's leading organizations are shifting from descriptive reporting to a full analytics lifecycle—asking comparative, correlational, causal, and predictive questions—to optimize their content strategies often in near real time. By embedding this kind of analytics into their content planning, production, and distribution, teams move from reactive insights ("Our video did well last month") to proactive decision-making ("Testing thumbnail variants could lift watch time by 20% or raise subscription rates by 4% next quarter"), a shift in thinking that takes you from mere reporting to playing a significant role in the success of your organization.

This chapter lays the groundwork for that transformation by showing you how to align your content with your organization's fundamental business objectives. Because when analytics is tied to strategic goals—whether that's increasing subscriptions, reducing churn or attrition, or driving ecommerce revenue—it becomes a powerful tool for deciding how to prioritize your time and resources and measure your performance in ways that really matter to your organization. Along the way, we'll look at why starting with clear objectives isn't just best practice; it's the only way to ensure your analytics efforts translate into tangible business outcomes rather than just produce vanity metrics that confuse or mislead stakeholders and squander your budget.

> **WHAT ARE VANITY METRICS?**
>
> Vanity metrics are numbers that look impressive but don't directly translate into strategic impact. Think page views, likes, or follower counts. They may suggest reach but rarely show behavior change or drive business outcomes.

What Happens When You Start with Metrics Instead of Goals?

To illustrate how easily teams can miss the mark when they skip this first, critical step, consider these examples from two different sectors, one corporate, one from higher education.

Problem #1: Analytics Without Alignment

A software company launches a major rebrand, redesigns its homepage, and launches new paid ads. The marketing team focuses on boosting site traffic, and the metrics look great—click-throughs are up 40%, bounce rates are down, and social shares are climbing. But revenue doesn't budge, and sales teams report that none of the new leads are converting.

In a way, the campaign "worked"—just not in a way that served the business.

The problem? No one clearly defined what success looked like. The analytics team chased metrics that were easy to track instead of outcomes that mattered.

Problem #2: Grad School Recruitment Gone Sideways

A university communications office is asked to support recruitment for a struggling graduate program. The admissions team wants "more visibility," so the content team launches blog posts, paid search ads, and a faculty Q&A series.

Applications tick up slightly, but many new leads are unqualified and yield drops.

Eventually, the team hits pause and asks: *"What's the real business goal?"*

It turns out the program doesn't just want more applications. It wants more enrollments from working professionals in the region. That changes everything. The content team narrows its focus to employer partnerships, highlights hybrid scheduling, and targets local metro areas with tailored testimonials.

The campaign relaunches. Fewer people click, but more of the right people apply. And enrollments rise.

Redefining the Objectives

Both teams succeeded *only after* stepping back to define a clear, measurable business objective. The revised strategies included

- **Clarifying the Outcome:** Not "getting more clicks," but "increasing qualified applications from X audience"

- **Aligning Metrics with Decisions:** Choosing data points that inform content instead of impressing stakeholders

- **Designing for Impact:** Creating content that solves a business problem instead of just making you more visible to the wrong people.

Analytics can measure *anything,* but it can't tell you what matters. Before you begin thinking about analytics, you need to clearly define what success looks like from a business point of view.

If your team is struggling to make data actionable, stop and ask: Do we even know what we're trying to achieve?

Understanding Your Business Objectives

Before diving into the data you've collected, or for that matter, before you even begin developing content, it's essential to articulate the business objectives that your content efforts need to support. Unless you've taken that critical step, poorly defined goals lead to misaligned analytics, fragmented reporting, wasted effort, and missed opportunities. To avoid this mistake and to make sure your definition of a goal is an actionable one, apply the **SMART** criteria developed by corporate planning guru George Doran.[1] His approach involves ensuring that business objectives are **S**pecific, **M**easurable, **A**chievable, **R**elevant, and **T**ime-bound (Table 1-1).

---

[1] George T. Doran, "There's a S.M.A.R.T. Way to Write Management's Goals and Objectives," *Management Review* 70, no. 11 (1981): 35–36.

Table 1-1. *SMART criteria*

SMART Element	Definition	Example
Specific	Clear and unambiguous	"Increase monthly newsletter sign-ups."
Measurable	Quantifiable so progress can be tracked	"Grow sign-up rate from 2% to 3%."
Achievable	Realistic given resources and constraints	"Allocate budget for two new landing page tests."
Relevant	Aligned with broader business priorities	"Supports our Q3 goal of expanding email reach."
Time-bound	Defined by a clear deadline	"By the end of Q3 2025."

Here are a few examples of common content-driven objectives included to get you thinking about the possibilities:

- **Lead Generation:** Driving whitepaper downloads, webinar registrations, or demo requests that feed into the sales funnel

- **Audience Growth:** Expanding reach via social shares, referral traffic, and organic search rankings

- **Engagement and Retention:** Increasing metrics like average time on page, scroll depth, and repeat visits to nurture loyalty

- **Revenue and Conversions:** Directly linking content interactions to purchase behavior, subscription sign-ups, or ad revenue

- **Brand Awareness and Thought Leadership:**
  Establishing authority through qualitative measures
  like share of voice, sentiment analysis, and qualitative
  feedback

Once your business objectives are clearly defined, the next step is
to map your content metrics to these goals. For example, if your aim is
to boost lead generation, your primary metric might be "content-driven
demo requests," supported by secondary metrics like "click-through rate
on call-to-action (CTA) buttons" and "drop-off rate on registration forms."
This kind of functional mapping ensures that when you review dashboards
or plan A/B tests, you're always also asking, *"How does this impact our key
objective?"*

By grounding your analytics program in well-defined, SMART
objectives, you create a clear target for your efforts—ensuring that every
question you ask, every data pipeline you build, and every test you run
propels you toward a quantifiable business objective and gives your
content measurable value.

USING SMART GOAL ALIGNMENT IN HIGHER ED

A university wants to increase applications to its graduate program.

- **SMART Goal**: Grow applications by 15% by the end of the next
  admissions cycle.

- **Primary Metric**: Application form completions.

- **Supporting Metrics**: Program page dwell time, CTA button
  clicks, bounce rate from recruitment emails.

Mapping Content Metrics to Business Goals

With clear business objectives in place, the next step is to translate those goals into the specific content metrics you'll track, that is, the kinds of quantifiable measures that reflect how a piece of content performs— such as time on page, scroll depth, or CTA click-through rate. Too often, content teams default to "vanity metrics" like page views or "likes" without considering whether those measures truly align with or serve your organization's strategic priorities. Instead, use the content objectives you defined earlier in this chapter to guide you in selecting the metrics that translate content into value (Table 1-2).

Table 1-2. *Mapping business goals to content metrics*

Business Objective	Primary Content Metric	Supporting Metrics
Lead generation	Content-attributed demo requests	Call-to-action (CTA) click-through rate; form completion rate
Audience growth	Organic search sessions	Social shares; new vs. returning visitor ratio
Engagement and retention	Average time on page	Scroll depth; pages per session; repeat visit rate
Revenue and conversions	Content-driven sales or subscription rate	Click-to-purchase rate; cart additions from content pages
Brand awareness	Share of voice (mentions across channels)	Sentiment score; referral traffic from third-party sites

Let's look at an example. Suppose your goal is audience growth. A high-level descriptive question might be:

> *"What channels drove the greatest growth in organic sessions last quarter?"*

To answer it, you'd rely on Google Analytics to pull organic search traffic by landing page (descriptive). Then you can drill into comparative metrics:

"Which blog category (e.g., 'how-to' vs. 'thought leadership') saw the larger month-over-month increase in search sessions?"

If you see that "how-to" articles grew by 18% vs. 5% for thought leadership, you've uncovered a comparative insight that directly informs your editorial focus. You might then ask a causal question:

"Did increasing adding video to how-to articles drive that 18% growth, or did external factors like a social campaign contribute?"

By building a simple statistical model called a regression, you can establish whether your optimization efforts truly caused the uplift (don't worry …we'll explore later how regression models can help you rank the factors that affect your content's success).

Avoiding Metric Misalignment

A common mistake in thinking about tying content to business objectives is tracking a metric because it's *available*, not because it *matters*. For instance, monitoring page views without understanding bounce rate or time on page can leave you in the dark about what users are thinking when they encounter your content. Likewise, celebrating social shares while ignoring whether those clicks lead to downstream conversions undermines the true goal of a revenue-and-conversions objective.

Ultimately, the process of mapping your metrics to your organization's objectives is a four-step process. You'll need to

1. Identify a specific business outcome.

2. Select the single primary metric that best measures progress toward that outcome.

3. Add two to three secondary metrics that provide context or diagnostic insight or validation.

4. Ensure that your data collection system (GA4 (Google Analytics 4), CMS (content management system) tags, CRM (customer relationship management) integrations) accurately captures these measures.

This way you turn every glance at your dashboard into a strategic check-in—*Are we on track to meet our SMART goal?*—rather than an exercise in collecting data for data's sake.

Table 1-3 maps common analytics platforms to where you can find specific content metrics.

Table 1-3. *Common analytics platforms and their metrics capabilities*

Platform	Metrics	Location
Google Analytics 4 (GA4)	Engagement, page views, user behavior	Engagement reports, real-time reports
HubSpot	Conversions, lead generation, email metrics	Analytics tools, campaigns dashboard
Facebook Insights	Shares, likes, comments, reach	Insights tab on Facebook page
Twitter/X Analytics	Retweets, likes, impressions, engagement rate	Analytics dashboard
LinkedIn Analytics	Shares, likes, comments, clicks	Analytics tab on LinkedIn page
Instagram Insights	Likes, comments, saves, reach	Insights tab on Instagram profile
YouTube Analytics	Views, watch time, engagement, subscribers	Analytics dashboard

Frameworks for Organizational Alignment

In the short run, your analytics efforts may not need to focus on anything more than making incremental improvements in your content that make you and your team more productive and more effective at meeting the day-to-day goals you're already tasked with, but a full-fledged content analytics program is most effective when it's fully aligned with your organization's strategic objectives.

One way to ensure that you maintain a consistent and comprehensive alignment between the two is to adopt a structured framework that makes analytics a key ingredient in your organizational planning. Two proven approaches are the Balanced Scorecard and Objectives and Key Results (OKRs).

The Balanced Scorecard

Originally developed by former Harvard Business School professor Robert S. Kaplan and David P. Norton, former CEO of the global consulting firm the Palladium Group, the "Balanced Scorecard" framework translates high-level strategy into a holistic four-tiered set of performance measures.[2]

Traditionally used for organizational performance management, the framework is an ideal tool for aligning a web content analytics program with broader strategic goals. Instead of only focusing on content-level variables and metrics, it takes a more comprehensive approach to integrating metrics into your organization's strategic planning efforts by applying metrics to four interrelated perspectives: Financial, Customer, Internal Process, and Learning and Growth.

---

[2] Kaplan, R. S., and David P. Norton. *The Balanced Scorecard: Translating Strategy into Action.* Boston: Harvard Business School Press, 1996.

By applying relevant content metrics to each of the four perspectives, organizations can balance their focus and avoid prioritizing short-term financial gains at the expense of audience satisfaction or internal capabilities. For example, the Customer perspective might track average session duration and social sentiment, while the Learning and Growth perspective measures your team's progress toward developing new skills—a leading indicator of the organization's ability to evolve toward more advanced predictive and causal questions. Applied thoughtfully, the framework challenges content teams to shift their thinking from dashboard maintenance to value creation.

Financial Perspective

For most organizations, the aim of developing expertise in web content analytics is to support revenue growth and cost efficiency. In this dimension, web content is evaluated based on its measurable impact on the business's bottom line by focusing on lead conversions attributed to specific content, revenue per content cluster, or cost per acquisition via organic channels.

Analytics Objectives:

- Measure content-driven revenue uplift (e.g., form fills, conversions).

- Evaluate ROI of high-performing content clusters.

- Track cost per acquisition from content vs. other channels.

Example Key Performance Indicators (KPIs):

- Strategic lift (e.g., increase in impact over a baseline)

- Cost per qualified lead from content

- Customer lifetime value tied to content engagement

Customer Perspective

In addition to being a revenue or lead driver, your content may also be critical to developing a relationship with your organization's customers or prospects. Consequently, analytics might focus on personalized engagement, satisfaction proxies (such as scroll depth or engagement duration), or segmentation by customer type. Satisfaction surveys that generate Net Promoter Scores (NPSs), or similar feedback mechanisms that measure customer satisfaction or their intent to promote or recommend your organization, can be tied directly to content touchpoints, enabling organizations to understand which materials foster trust, loyalty, or just confusion. Additionally, this domain provides you with the opportunity to validate the "why" behind user behavior, not just the "what."

Analytics Objectives:

- Understand content preferences across personas or segments.

- Assess Net Promoter Score (NPS) post-content touchpoint.

- Diagnose drop-off points or content friction in user journeys.

Example Key Performance Indicators (KPIs):

- Percentage of visitors engaging with key decision-enabling content

- Content satisfaction scores (survey or behavior-based proxies)

- Return visit rate or "scroll depth" by audience segment

Internal Process Perspective

Content analytics may also help you better understand how efficiently your team produces, optimizes, and governs content. From an operational standpoint, this lens focuses on the systems behind content delivery—editorial workflows, optimization cadence, and content repurposing efficiency—and might measure time-to-value for new content or how successful your efforts are at reworking existing content for new purposes. A predictive content analytics program can enhance how efficiently your team is working and highlight where to invest effort—what to update, what to retire, and what to double down on.

Analytics Objectives:

- Track content production-to-performance lag.

- Identify repeatable traits of "evergreen" or high-performing content.

- Monitor usage of predictive tools in editorial decision-making.

Example Key Performance Indicators (KPIs):

- Average time to optimize underperforming content

- Percentage of content audited with your predictive relevance framework

- Ratio of repurposed vs. new content

Learning and Growth Perspective

Finally, content analytics can also provide a measure of your team's internal development and its capacity to scale and adapt to new challenges. This might involve measuring how many team members are trained in interpreting strategic metrics or how often insights are shared cross-functionally. Adoption of proprietary frameworks, integration of analytics into planning rituals, and even internal feedback loops all signal readiness for growth. This is where analytics evolve from side project to core value.

Analytics Objectives:

- Educate stakeholders on how to interpret metrics that matter (i.e., beyond page views).

- Track upskilling of content teams in analytics literacy.

- Embed strategic metrics into tooling and culture.

Example Key Performance Indicators (KPIs):

- Number of team members trained in interpreting predictive content scores

- Internal usage rate of your diagnostic frameworks

- Number of strategic insights shared cross-functionally per quarter

Objectives and Key Results (OKRs)

A more streamlined approach to strategic alignment, OKRs pair ambitious organizational objectives with measurable key results that may be shared across departmental or divisional lines. An example for a content team might be as follows:

- **Objective:** Establish our brand as a thought leader in digital marketing.

- **KR1:** Increase average time on "thought leadership" articles from two minutes to three minutes.

- **KR2:** Achieve a 25% growth in LinkedIn shares of our whitepapers.

- **KR3:** Grow webinar attendance from 200 to 500 registrants per event.

OKRs force a direct link between qualitative aspirations (the objective) and quantitative measures (the key results). By reviewing OKRs quarterly, teams can assess which content initiatives move the needle and then pivot away from low-impact efforts. Moreover, mapping OKRs to a research question (we'll explore this in more detail in the next chapter) ensures that your approach has a sound methodological foundation.

Ultimately, Google's adoption of OKRs helped that organization popularize the framework as a model for setting transparent and trackable objectives.[3]

Tip   To avoid OKR bloat, limit each objective to two to four meaningful key results. More than that can dilute focus and create reporting fatigue.

Implementing the Framework

Most likely, implementing one of these frameworks will require a certain amount of change in organizational culture, so it's essential that you approach the process in a way that maximizes your chance of success. Follow these steps to integrate the framework in a way that creates lasting change with minimal pushback:

---

[3] Doerr, J. *Measure What Matters: How Google, Bono, and the Gates Foundation Rock the World with OKRs*. New York: Portfolio, 2018.

1. **Executive Kickoff:** Secure leadership buy-in by presenting the chosen framework, linking it to corporate strategy.

2. **Workshop Sessions:** Facilitate cross-functional workshops to define perspectives (Balanced Scorecard) or draft OKRs, ensuring clarity and consensus.

3. **Metric Mapping:** Populate framework fields with your SMART-aligned metrics from the section "Understanding Your Business Objectives."

4. **Regular Check-Ins:** Schedule monthly or quarterly reviews to update scorecards or OKR progress, leveraging dashboards that automatically pull in the relevant measures.

5. **Continuous Improvement:** After each cycle, meet with your team to review which metrics drove the most actionable insights and where the framework revealed gaps.

Organizations that rigorously apply these frameworks typically report higher strategy execution rates. For example, PricewaterhouseCoopers found that companies using Balanced Scorecards are 12% more likely to meet performance targets,[4] while Google's own use of OKRs has been credited with aligning teams on audacious goals from Gmail to Google Maps.[5] By embedding your content analytics program within a robust strategic framework, you ensure that every data point serves a larger purpose and that your analytics efforts drive meaningful business results.

---

[4] PwC. "Strategic Performance Measurement: Creating a Common Language to Drive Execution." Strategy&. Accessed May 27, 2025. `https://www.strategyand.pwc.com/gx/en/insights/2017/strategic-performance-measurement/strategic-performance-measurement.pdf`

[5] Google. "Google re:Work - Guides: Set Goals with OKRs." Accessed May 27, 2025. `https://rework.withgoogle.com/en/guides/set-goals-with-okrs`

Case Study: From Vanity Metrics to Strategic Alignment

A nonprofit focused on urban sustainability invested heavily in its content strategy—publishing weekly blog posts, social campaigns, and quarterly video case studies. Their goal: increase community engagement and attract new donors. But despite producing high volumes of content, the executive director noted flat growth in donations and low engagement with their newsletters.

The Challenge

The organization's reporting centered on surface-level metrics: blog page views, video completions, and social shares. Yet those numbers didn't correlate with email list growth, volunteer sign-ups, or donations—core business goals. The communications team realized that although they were tracking *activity*, they weren't measuring *impact*.

The Turning Point

A newly hired content strategist introduced an alignment workshop, starting with SMART business objectives. The team redefined their primary goal as follows:

Objective: Increase individual donor conversions from 2% to 4% within six months.

Using this goal as an anchor, they mapped the following metrics:

- **Primary:** Donation form completions attributed to blog or video traffic

- **Supporting:** Click-through rate on donation CTAs; scroll depth on donor stories; bounce rate from social media

They also adopted an OKR framework:

- **Objective:** Improve donation storytelling effectiveness

- **KR1:** Increase CTA click-through from 1.2% to 2.5%.

- **KR2:** Raise average scroll depth on donor stories by 20%.

- **KR3:** Add 500 new subscribers from donation-content landing pages.

Actions Taken

- A/B tested donation CTAs on blog posts

- Adjusted content length and structure for mobile readability

- Used GA4 event tagging to track scroll depth and CTA interaction

- Segmented content performance by traffic source and audience type

Results

Within five months

- CTA click-through rose to 2.8%.

- Average scroll depth increased by 23% on donation-related pages.

- Individual donor conversions hit 4.2%, surpassing their SMART goal.

Takeaway

By shifting from disconnected performance indicators to a strategic analytics framework tied directly to business outcomes, the nonprofit not only improved its KPIs—it also built internal confidence that its content investments were paying off.

Workbook Exercise: Aligning Your Content Strategy with Business Goals

Use this guided exercise to clarify how your content analytics can serve a measurable business objective.

Step 1: Identify one strategic objective

Write a single SMART goal for your organization or team (Specific, Measurable, Achievable, Relevant, Time-bound).

Example: Increase newsletter subscriptions from 10,000 to 12,500 by Q4.

Your SMART Goal: ____

Step 2: Define one primary content metric

What single metric would best indicate progress toward that goal?

Example: Number of newsletter sign-up completions per month

Primary Metric: ____

Step 3: Select two supporting metrics

Choose secondary metrics that add context or show leading indicators of success.

Example:

1.   Click-through rate on blog post sign-up banners

2.   Bounce rate on the newsletter landing page

Supporting Metrics:

1.

2.

Step 4: Choose a framework

Select either OKRs or a Balanced Scorecard model. Write two to three key results or performance indicators that support your SMART goal.

Example (OKRs):

- **KR1**: Increase blog-to-newsletter CTR from 1.5% to 3%.

- **KR2**: Reduce newsletter landing page bounce rate from 65% to 50%.

Your KR1:

Your KR2:

(Optional) **Your KR3:**

Once you've completed the workbook exercise, you'll have a clear analytics roadmap that ties content metrics directly to a business outcome—ensuring your reporting remains focused, actionable, and meaningful. Save this document as your alignment baseline and revisit it quarterly to update based on evolving business needs.

Incorporating the Team

Aligning content analytics with business goals is not a solo act. It requires the coordinated efforts of a cross-functional team, each bringing a different lens to how success is defined, measured, and pursued. When alignment becomes a shared responsibility, teams work smarter to avoid redundant efforts or conflicting priorities.

Who Should Be Involved?

Even if you don't have a user experience (UX) designer or a search engine optimization (SEO) specialist on your team or whether or not you have the resources to hire people to do those jobs, you'll want to consider how your existing team members might develop new areas of expertise to be able to play more than one critical role. Use Table 1-4 to consider how that expertise factors into an effective analytics program.

Table 1-4. *Team member roles for effective collaboration*

Team Member	Role in Alignment
Content strategist	Connects content goals to business objectives and defines key performance indicators
Marketing manager	Identifies campaign-level goals and provides insight into acquisition and conversion
Data analyst	Designs the metrics framework and ensures data accuracy and availability
UX designer	Ensures content experiences support user journeys that reflect strategic priorities
SEO specialist	Aligns content visibility efforts with growth objectives and search intent
Executive stakeholder	Provides strategic clarity and ensures analytics efforts align with broader goals

How to Collaborate

Develop new processes that reinforce the importance of collaboration for your team and give them the greatest chance of success:

- **Host Alignment Workshops:** Host regular quarterly or kickoff workshops where stakeholders articulate business objectives and co-define supporting content KPIs.

- **Develop Shared Dashboards:** Build dashboards with sections tailored to each stakeholder's interest (e.g., conversion rates for marketing, audience engagement for editorial).

- **Hold Weekly or Biweekly Syncs**: Keep goals top of mind by revisiting top-level metrics in regular team meetings. Even a ten-minute review helps maintain focus.

- **Encourage Cross-Functional Testing**: Let analytics fuel experimentation. For example, if marketing wants to test CTA copy, the content strategist can support messaging, and the analyst can guide measurement.

When goals are clear and roles are defined, the team can prioritize content projects more confidently. Instead of debating what to publish next, they clarify the problem by helping you focus on which initiative moves you closer to your goal.

Budget-Friendly Strategies for Alignment

If you're working with a lean team or limited tools, aligning content analytics with business goals can still be done effectively. Successful strategic alignment isn't a matter of how much you have to spend; it's about clarity, focus, and process.

Start Simple with Free Tools

- **Google Analytics 4 (GA4)**: Track content engagement and conversions using event-based data and user flows.

- **Looker Studio (Formerly Data Studio)**: Create customizable dashboards to visualize key performance indicators.

- **Google Sheets**: Log SMART goals, OKRs, and key metrics in a shared spreadsheet to track progress over time.

- **Miro or FigJam**: Use these free online collaborative whiteboard tools for collaborative alignment workshops or content planning sessions.

Prioritize What to Measure

Don't try to track everything. Choose three to five core metrics tied directly to your goals. For example:

- Lead generation? Track form submissions.

- Brand awareness? Focus on referral traffic and social shares.

- Engagement? Use scroll depth and return visit rate.

Repurpose Existing Content

Rather than creating new reports from scratch, repurpose what's already available:

- Convert campaign briefs into OKR tracking documents.

- Transform editorial calendars into roadmap tools.

- Update old blog posts with aligned CTAs and new measurement tags.

Encourage DIY Data Literacy

Upgrade your team's skill set with low-cost or free resources:

- YouTube tutorials on Google Analytics and Looker Studio

- Free courses from HubSpot, Coursera, or Moz on content and analytics

- Internal "lunch and learn" sessions led by team members with analytics experience

By focusing on clarity of purpose and alignment over tool sophistication, even small or resource-constrained teams can build a powerful analytics foundation that serves the business without overextending their budget.

Final Thoughts

When you anchor your content analytics program in the organization's strategic priorities, you create more than just dashboards and meaningless metrics—you create direction. After all, you can't lead if you don't know where you're going.

This chapter has laid the foundation for everything that follows— how to ask the right questions, how to collect the right data, and how to understand what to do with it—but none of that matters if you don't have a good reason for doing it.

A well-aligned analytics program helps your team focus on outcomes, not just outputs, and it helps you understand how to prioritize the opportunities in front of you and allocate the resources you have more effectively.

More than just a technical discipline, analytics is a strategic dialogue—one that brings together creators, marketers, analysts, and executives in pursuit of measurable progress toward a shared objective.

As you move through the rest of this book, return to this chapter often. Ask yourself: *"Are our analytics still aligned with our goals? Are our goals still relevant? Are our metrics still meaningful?"* The answers to those questions will keep your content analytics efforts grounded, purposeful, and powerful.

In the next chapter, we'll take the first step in the process of using analytics to reach a business objective: defining a research question.

CHAPTER 2

Formulating Research Questions

If you've stared at a dashboard filled with charts, graphs, and KPIs and still found yourself wondering what to do next or how it gets you any closer to a meaningful objective, you're not alone. You may be swimming in data, but if all that information doesn't help you understand how to make effective business decisions, you might as well be drowning.

That's because insight doesn't begin with data. It begins with a question.

Strong research questions are the foundation of any content analytics program. They give structure to analysis, align teams around a common objective, and ensure that your data gives you the power to make real-world decisions. Without a clear question, even the most sophisticated tools can lead to misinterpretation, paralysis, or just more confusion.

Consider two teams launching the same content campaign: one team tracks page views; the other starts with a question like, *"Which type of testimonial video is most likely to drive email sign-ups from first-time visitors?"* Articulating a clear research question allows the second team to develop

1. **A Clear Hypothesis**: Three-minute testimonials are more effective than videos under 1:30 minutes.

R. Bahorsky, *The Fundamentals of Content Analytics*,
https://doi.org/10.1007/979-8-8688-2601-6_2

2.   **A Measurable Goal**: Evaluate first-time sign-ups per landing page visit over a two-week period.

3.   **A Testable Structure**: A/B test variant A vs. variant B.

The difference gives the second team a much higher chance of understanding the impact of their campaign's assets and how they contribute to actionable insights.

This chapter will show you how to formulate high-quality research questions that give your content analytics purpose and the power you need to drive your organization forward.

Connecting Business Objectives to Research Questions

Good research questions don't appear out of thin air—they emerge from business needs. As you learned in Chapter 1, the process starts by identifying your organization's objectives. The next step is to translate them into questions that can be answered with data.

Let's say you work on a university admissions office's communications unit and your team wants to increase applications from out-of-state students. That's your business objective. Now consider how content might support that goal. You might already be publishing campus tour videos, student stories, or explainers on academic programs, so a clear research question would follow:

"Which types of videos lead to the highest engagement among prospective out-of-state students?"

That's a focused, practical question—narrow enough to explore with data, but broad enough to inform editorial strategy.

Here's a helpful formula for turning objectives into research questions:

To **[optimize/improve/understand] [metric or behavior]** for **[audience or platform]**, what is the effect of **[content variable]**?

Depending on your industry, Table 2-1 offers examples of the kind of challenges that could produce effective research questions.

Table 2-1. *Research questions rooted in business challenges*

Business Objective	Research Question
Boost newsletter sign-ups.	What content categories on our blog lead to the most email sign-ups?
Improve engagement among new users.	How long do first-time visitors spend engaging with videos vs. articles?
Increase donations from mobile users.	Does mobile-optimized content lead to higher donation rates among smartphone users?
Reduce bounce rate.	What's the relationship between homepage layout and bounce rate for desktop visitors?
Increase subscriber loyalty.	Which authors or series are most associated with repeat visits among subscribers?

Whatever challenges you face, the key is to identify a specific problem that can be solved by changing or improving the content you create or by being more intentional about when, where, and how your audience sees it. Once you've identified that question, you can be sure your analytics efforts are rooted in a purpose—not just curiosity.

Characteristics of a Good Research Question

To be sure you're on the right track as you identify a practical purpose for your research, keep in mind that a good research question in content analytics has five key characteristics:

1. **Clarity**: It's stated plainly and unambiguously. Avoid vague terms like "better" or "successful" unless they're clearly defined.

   X *What kind of content works best?*

   ✓ *Which content types result in average time on page exceeding three minutes?*

2. **Specificity**: The question focuses on a single behavior, audience, or outcome—making it easier to measure and act on.

   X *How do people use our blog?*

   ✓ *How do returning users interact with articles tagged as "case studies" compared with news updates?*

3. **Actionability**: It leads directly to potential decisions or changes in strategy, messaging, or distribution.

   X *What's our bounce rate?*

   ✓ *Which landing page elements are most associated with higher bounce rates?*

4. **Relevance**: The question should reflect a current challenge or opportunity facing your team or organization.

   ✓ *Is there a relationship between an increase in free subscriptions and an increase in paid subscriptions?*

5.   **Time-Bound (When Appropriate)**: Many questions benefit from being grounded in a time frame, especially when evaluating trends or the effect of a campaign.

     ✓ *How did average watch time change after the newsletter redesign in Q2?*

Here's a useful trick to asking better questions. Ask yourself two things:

1.   *"Can I list all the possible answers to this question?"*

2.   *"What would I do in each case?"*

If you're unable to answer these questions, you probably need to revise. Otherwise, you're likely to end up with information that has no practical value.

When you're forming content analytics research questions, it also helps to understand what drives user actions. According to the Theory of Planned Behavior, a person's intention to perform an action—like downloading a guide or signing up for a webinar—is influenced by three factors: their attitude toward the action, social pressures or norms, and whether they feel capable of completing it easily.[1]

The concept reminds us that user behavior is influenced not just by your content but by the internal attitudes and perceived effort of those engaging with it. When formulating questions, especially causal ones, considering behavioral factors—like how difficult it is to reach the content or how much personal information a user might have to give up to get it— can sharpen both the question and its implications.

By keeping these factors in mind when drafting research questions (e.g., "What perceptions might prevent users from completing this form?"), you can design better questions that ultimately lead to more actionable insights.

---

[1] Icek Ajzen. "The Theory of Planned Behavior," *Organizational Behavior and Human Decision Processes* 50, no. 2 (1991): 179–211.

EXAMPLE: A VAGUE RESEARCH QUESTION LEADS TO WASTED EFFORT

A nonprofit organization wants to increase donations from its year-end giving campaign.

At the campaign planning meeting, a team member suggests the research question:

"How is our content doing?"

The Problem:

- The question is too broad. It doesn't specify what "content" (articles, videos, emails?) or what "doing" means (page views, donations, shares?).

- Different team members interpret it differently:

    - One analyst measures page views.

    - Another looks at time on page.

    - The fundraising lead looks at donation form starts.

- Because the question wasn't specific, each team member collects different data, and they can't agree on what the data says.

The Result:

- Reporting is fragmented and confusing.

- Leadership feels uncertain about which content efforts were successful.

- The team misses the opportunity to learn clear lessons for next year's campaign.

Bottom Line:

A vague research question led to scattered analysis, wasted time, and weaker insights.

Asking a better question—*"Which types of year-end blog posts led to the highest donation page clicks?""*—would have focused the team's effort and made findings actionable.

Takeaway:

Good research questions save time, focus energy, and lead to insights that can actually improve content strategy.

Common Types of Research Questions in Content Analytics

Research questions can take many forms, depending on what you're trying to learn. Here are five types that show up often in content analytics, along with examples and the tools most often used to explore them.

1. **Descriptive: *What happened?***

    These questions summarize content performance using available data.

    -   *Which videos received the most views last month?*

    -   *How many email sign-ups came from the blog in Q1?*

2. **Comparative: *What performed better?***

    Used when testing two or more versions of content, such as headlines, layouts, or formats.

- *Did the redesigned landing page lead to more downloads than the original?*

- *Which subject line performed better in our last newsletter A/B test?*

3. **Correlational: *What patterns or relationships exist?***

Looks at how different content features or audience behaviors relate to each other.

- *Is there a correlation between article length and average scroll depth?*

- *Do longer video descriptions lead to higher watch times?*

4. **Causal (Experimental): *What impact did X have on Y?***

Explores cause-and-effect relationships, often through controlled experiments.

- *Did featuring testimonials on the homepage increase donations?*

- *Does changing the call-to-action text affect sign-up rates?*

5. **Predictive: *What's likely to happen?***

Uses historical data and modeling to forecast user behavior or performance outcomes.

- *Which users are most likely to click a case study after reading a blog post?*

- *Can we predict the likelihood of donation based on visit patterns?*

A single business goal can also generate more than one type of question. For example, if your objective is to increase lead generation, you might ask:

- **Descriptive**: How many leads came from blog content last quarter?

- **Comparative**: Which blog category produced the most leads?

- **Causal**: Did adding testimonials to case studies increase conversions?

- **Predictive**: What types of content are likely to produce leads in the future?

However, it should be said that it's best to focus on keeping things simple at first. A content analytics program can quickly become complicated, so if you're just starting out, make sure you can demonstrate your team's skills and capacity to tackle one question effectively before you take on more than that.

Closed vs. Open Audiences: A Strategic Distinction

Before you can frame strong research questions, it's also important to understand what kind of audience you're working with. One of the most fundamental—but often overlooked—distinctions in content analytics is whether your audience is closed or open. This difference affects what kinds of questions you can ask, what data you can access, and how you interpret results.

A closed audience refers to a defined group of users: email subscribers, donor lists, enrolled students, customers in your CRM, or users behind a login. You already know something about them—their contact information, their past behavior, their preferences—and you often have the ability to build on that relationship.

Ideal tools for working with these audiences include tools that help you follow known users over time, better understand who they are, and track how they interact with your content across different platforms. These tools include

- **CRM platforms** like Salesforce, HubSpot, Slate, or Blackbaud, which store user profiles and allow you to analyze behavior over time or by segment

- **Email marketing systems** like Mailchimp, Campaign Monitor, or ActiveCampaign, which track opens, clicks, and conversions tied to specific users or groups

- **Marketing automation platforms** such as Marketo, Eloqua, or Pardot, which integrate content and behavior tracking across campaigns and customer journeys

- **Product or platform analytics tools** like Mixpanel or Amplitude, which allow you to track logged-in user behavior across multiple touchpoints

- **Data warehouses or customer data platforms (CDPs)**, which centralize and unify data across systems, making more sophisticated queries and models possible

An open audience, by contrast, consists of users who find your content through public channels like organic search, social media, or third-party referrals. They're often anonymous, and their interactions are harder to trace across sessions or platforms. Your insights come from aggregated data, not user-level detail.

Open-audience analytics rely more heavily on tools that track session-based behavior, often anonymously. You're usually working with browser-based identifiers or referral paths, not individual user records. Common tools include

- **Web analytics platforms** such as Google Analytics 4 (GA4), Adobe Analytics, or Matomo, which track page views, traffic sources, bounce rates, and content engagement for anonymous visitors

- **SEO tools** like Ahrefs, SEMrush, or Google Search Console, which help you evaluate how your content performs in search and what keywords drive new traffic

- **Social media analytics** provided by platforms like LinkedIn or Facebook, which offer insights into engagement, impressions, and reach but rarely connect that behavior to deeper outcomes

- **Heatmapping and session recording tools** like Hotjar, Microsoft Clarity, or Crazy Egg, which help visualize how users navigate content and where they drop off

- **A/B testing tools** like Visual Website Optimizer (VWO) or Optimizely, which help you test content changes on public-facing pages with anonymous users

Because open-audience tools retain user data for only a short time, you often make decisions using proxy metrics: scroll depth instead of time spent, bounce rate instead of intent, and Urchin Tracking Module (UTM) codes instead of user profiles (we'll explore these more later).

Ultimately, the distinction between open and close audiences shouldn't just shape your tactics; it should directly influence your analytics strategy.

When you're working with a closed audience, your research questions can be more precise. You can compare how different user segments respond to the same message, track behavior over time, and test personalization strategies. You might ask, *"Which newsletter subject lines drive the highest open rates among repeat donors?"* or *"Does adding a student testimonial increase scholarship form completions among admitted students in our CRM?"*

With an open audience, your questions tend to focus more on behavior patterns at scale. You're looking for signals that help you make decisions in a more variable, less controlled environment. You might ask, *"Which blog topics attract the most organic traffic from new users?"* or *"Does average scroll depth differ between mobile and desktop users on our program pages?"*

The difference also affects what kinds of research question types are realistic. With closed audiences, it's often possible to explore correlational and even causal questions, especially if you have the ability to run controlled tests. With open audiences, you're more likely to rely on descriptive or comparative analysis, using session-level data to identify trends and opportunities.

Understanding whether you're working with a closed or open audience ensures that you're asking questions your data can answer and that your findings reflect the reality of how your content is experienced.

Thematic Areas and Industry Examples

Table 2-2 illustrates how different sectors frame research questions according to their goals and audience.

Table 2-2. *Research questions relevant to specific industries*

Sector	Objective	Example Research Question
Higher education	Increase prospective student engagement.	*Which video formats lead to longer watch times among prospective undergrads?*
Nonprofit	Boost donations from email campaigns.	*Which stories result in the highest email open-to-donate conversion rate?*
Corporate marketing	Generate qualified leads.	*What percentage of whitepaper downloads lead to demo requests within seven days?*
News and publishing	Grow subscriber base.	*Which article categories result in trial subscription sign-ups?*
Government agency	Inform and educate public.	*What topics have the highest full-video completion rate across age groups?*
Digital marketing agency	Optimize ad campaign ROI.	*Which creative formats lead to the lowest cost per acquisition on LinkedIn?*

Each of these questions is tightly linked to a business objective, measurable through data, and actionable based on the results.

From Question to Answer: Selecting the Right Tools and Methods

Once you have a solid research question, the next step is selecting the right method—and the right tool—to answer it.

Think of your research question like a diagnostic: each type of question calls for a different approach to analysis. Table 2-3 offers suggestions for matching common question types with appropriate tools and methods.

Table 2-3. *Matching research questions with analytical methods and tools*

Question Type	Prompt Question	Goal	Analytical Method	Common Tools
Descriptive	What is happening?	Measure, characterize, or describe a behavior.	Trend reports, data tables	Google Analytics, social media dashboards
Comparative	Which one is better?	Compare two versions or options.	A/B testing, cohort analysis	Optimizely, HubSpot, email platforms
Correlational	How are these related?	Identify patterns or connections between variables.	Cross-tabulation, scatter plots, correlation matrices	Excel, Tableau, R, Python
Causal	Why did this happen?	Identify cause-and-effect relationships.	Experiments, regression models	Google Analytics 4 with event tagging, statistical tools
Predictive	What will happen next?	Forecast future outcomes based on past data.	Machine learning, predictive scoring	CRM systems, machine learning tools, Python/R scripts

Here's a quick decision tree to help guide tool selection:

- **Is your question about change over time?** Try time-series analysis or dashboards with historical filters.

- **Are you comparing multiple versions of content?** Use A/B testing or multivariate testing platforms.

- **Do you want to see if a behavior *causes* an outcome?** Consider tagging, experiments, or regression models.

- **Are you trying to predict future behavior?** Use machine learning, logistic regression, or pre-built scoring tools in your CRM.

Choosing the right method ensures you don't overinterpret your results—or use a tool that can't provide a valid answer to your question.

Pitfalls to Avoid

Even when your research questions are good, there are a number of common mistakes that can derail your analysis. Here are a few common problems and traps you might encounter as you explore the kinds of questions you'd like your content analysis program to answer:

Vague Questions

- **Asking:** *"How's our content doing?"*

- **Try:** *"Which content formats produced the most repeat traffic in the last 30 days?"*

Confusing Correlation with Causation[2]

- Seeing a relationship doesn't mean one thing caused the other. Time of day might correlate with higher engagement—but it could be a proxy for audience type.

Ignoring Context

- A spike in views might look like a win, but if bounce rate and unsubscribe rate also rose, there's more to the story.

Not Aligning with Stakeholders

- A question might be interesting to you but irrelevant to leadership or disconnected from business needs.

Chasing Vanity Metrics

- Focusing on views or likes alone without tying them to downstream behaviors (like sign-ups, purchases, or shares).

Keep in mind that the way you ask a question is important too. A question that suggests an answer creates a red flag known as *confirmation bias.* For example, instead of asking, *"How does our new feature improve engagement?"* ask, *"What effect does our new feature have on engagement—and why?"* This subtle shift in the way the question is asked opens the door to real insight, rather than steering the analysis toward a "positive" result. Make sure your question is open-ended enough to discover something new—not just confirming what you think or hope is true.

---

[2] Note that while analytics often aims to understand patterns and relationships in human behavior, it usually can't prove cause and effect with certainty. This is because researchers often study people in real-world settings, where many factors (known or unknown) can influence outcomes. While analytics may show that two things are related or even strongly related, that doesn't always mean one necessarily causes the other. Analysts sometimes suggest that a strong correlation is the equivalent of causality, but it's important to keep in mind that what they're referring to is a strong probability and never a certainty.

Case Study: Building a Question in Practice

Let's look at how a nonprofit might go from goal to research question …and from question to insight.

Background

A mid-sized environmental nonprofit wants to increase donations from first-time website visitors. They publish short explainer videos about conservation efforts and long-form impact stories about community partners. Here are the steps they took to go from research question to results.

Step 1: Define the goal

Increase first-time visitor donations.

Step 2: Understand user behavior

Review past analytics: new visitors tend to engage most with video content, but they rarely click the donation button.

Step 3: Draft a research question

"Does featuring a donation button directly below video content increase donation conversions among first-time visitors?"

Step 4: Choose a method

Run an A/B test: one version with the button directly under the video, one version with the button at the bottom of the page.

Step 5: Analyze and interpret

Results: Version A (button under video) saw a 32% higher donation rate among new visitors.

Step 6: Act on insights

Redesign the layout of all explainer pages and prioritize video content on donation landing pages.

This simple experiment resulted in higher conversions, and it proved the value of targeted, structured research.

Workbook Exercise: Draft Your Own Research Question

Use this space to apply what you've learned to a real-world scenario at your organization or within a project you're planning.

Instructions

Pick one content-related goal you're trying to reach. Then work through the prompts in Table 2-4.

Table 2-4. *Research question worksheet*

Step	Prompt	Your Answer
1	What's your objective?	(e.g., Increase app downloads from blog readers)
2	What audience or user group are you focused on?	(e.g., Returning mobile users)
3	What content behavior do you want to improve or understand?	(e.g., Clicks on in-article app banners)
4	Draft a research question based on your answers above.	(e.g., What blog topics result in the highest app banner click-through rate?)

Integrating the Team: Roles in Formulating Research Questions

Creating strong, actionable research questions for content analytics isn't a solo effort; it requires collaboration across multiple team roles.

Each team member brings a different lens to identifying what matters, how it can be measured, and why it supports business goals.

Table 2-5 explains how each role can contribute to the research question development process.

Table 2-5. *Team member roles in developing effective research questions*

Role	Potential Responsibilities
Content analyst	Analyze past content performance; suggest trends or gaps worth investigating with new research questions.
Content strategist	Align research questions with organizational goals and overall content strategy; prioritize questions based on strategic importance.
SEO specialist	Propose research questions related to search behavior, keyword performance, and organic visibility (how often and how prominently your content appears in unpaid search results).
Data analyst	Help frame research questions in measurable, testable terms; advise on data requirements and feasibility.
Content writer/ editor	Provide audience insights based on direct experience; suggest questions related to engagement, readability, and messaging.
Graphic designer/ videographer	Raise questions around how visual elements (infographics, video thumbnails) impact user engagement or conversion.

(continued)

Table 2-5. (*continued*)

Role	Potential Responsibilities
Social media manager	Suggest research questions focused on audience interaction, content shareability, and channel-specific performance.
Project manager	Coordinate the research question development process, ensuring input from all stakeholders and clarity on next steps.
UX/user experience designer	Identify questions about user behaviors, interaction flows, and friction points related to content consumption.
Analytics manager	Oversee the full analytics framework; ensure that research questions align with existing tracking setups and reporting capabilities.

Budget-Friendly Ideas for Generating Smart Research Questions

You don't need 20 research questions to build an effective content analytics effort. Three or four well-chosen, measurable questions can transform how your team plans and evaluates content and makes it easy to act on the results in a meaningful and manageable way.

- **Start with content teams first.** Writers and editors often have the best intuition about audience behavior. Empower them to brainstorm initial research questions based on their goals and challenges.

- **Involve data experts selectively.** Bring in an analyst or consultant once a rough list of questions exists. Their job is to shape and refine questions for measurability— not to invent them from scratch.

- **Use existing data first.** Before commissioning new tools or tracking setups, explore what your web analytics, CRM, or social platforms already offer. You may already have enough information to answer important questions.

- **Prioritize questions that drive action.** Focus your first analytics efforts on research questions that tie directly to content planning, resourcing decisions, or business KPIs.

- **Template the process.** Create a simple research question worksheet for your team to fill out:

  Goal➤Hypothesis➤Proposed Research Question➤Potential Metric Sources

Final Thoughts

Content analytics becomes exponentially more valuable when anchored in well-defined research questions, questions that

- Translate vague goals into focused, testable problems.

- Help teams prioritize data collection and choose the right tools.

- Provide clarity and purpose when interpreting content metrics.

- Bridge the gap between curiosity and business impact.

Whenever you feel overwhelmed by dashboards or paralyzed by reports, return to this question:

"What am I trying to learn, and why does it matter?"

In the next chapter we'll focus on seeing your content from the audience's point of view, an exercise that could help you form better and more effective research questions or fine-tune the ones you already have.

CHAPTER 3

Mapping Content Journeys

The path that a customer takes from the moment they learn about a new product to the time they make their first purchase is rarely a straight line. The more expensive a product or service is (like a college education), the more commitment it requires (like a year-long subscription), or the more intangible the benefit (like a donation to a good cause), the more circuitous the route can become as consumers interact with multiple content channels, formats, and experiences before finally taking action.

Content journey mapping—originally popularized by customer experience (CX) designers—is the process of plotting these interactions graphically, revealing where users discover, evaluate, and ultimately engage with your content. In fact, research shows that brands that use journey maps typically report improvements in customer satisfaction and loyalty.[1] By visualizing the stages of awareness, consideration, decision, and advocacy, the practice of journey mapping helps you

---

[1] Contentsquare. "Benefits of Customer Journey Mapping." Accessed May 21, 2025. https://contentsquare.com/guides/customer-journey-map/benefits/?utm_source=chatgpt.com

R. Bahorsky, *The Fundamentals of Content Analytics*,
https://doi.org/10.1007/979-8-8688-2601-6_3

- **Identify data blind spots.** You'll see exactly where analytics may be missing key touchpoints (e.g., video drop-off points or social referrals) so you can adjust your tracking strategy accordingly.

- **Prioritize optimizations.** Rather than guess which pages or formats matter most, journey maps highlight high-impact moments—such as the first email click or product demo—where small changes can yield big returns.

- **Align cross-functional teams.** A clear visual serves as a shared artifact that brings content, UX, analytics, and leadership onto the same page about user needs and strategic priorities.

When you map your content journey, you begin to gain insight into how your content influences your market (or doesn't) and how it supports the kind of consumer decision-making that impacts your bottom line (or doesn't). You'll also begin to translate dashboards into user stories—a practice that will open up new avenues of insight that we'll explore in the chapters to come—and you'll discover opportunities to ask more meaningful research questions.

What's more, research suggests that brands that use journey maps typically report higher conversion rates and improved alignment between content delivery and user needs.[2]

---

[2] Forrester Research. *The Customer Journey Mapping Playbook for 2020.* Forrester, 2020.

Defining the Content Journey

A content journey map is more than just a funnel chart: it's a narrative timeline of every touchpoint a user experiences as they move toward a goal. According to the UX research and design firm the Nielsen Norman Group, journey mapping "compiles a series of user actions into a timeline" and then layers on observations of user thoughts and emotions to create a coherent story of intent and friction.[3] Unlike a simple decision funnel, which often counts drop-off rates between generic stages, a journey map calls out specific channels (blog, email, social, webinars), content formats (articles, videos, whitepapers), and moments of frustration or fanaticism. The journey may also include touchpoints after the initial goal, including efforts to upsell or renew or to earn referrals or positive reviews.

Stages of a Content Journey

As they develop their content journey maps, most B2B and higher education organizations find that their consumers' journeys share four primary phases:

1. **Awareness**: Users are first exposed to your brand or topic—often via SEO-optimized articles, social posts, or paid search ads. This phase focuses on broad discovery and education.

2. **Consideration**: Prospects engage more deeply— signing up for newsletters, watching explainer videos, or reading case studies—to evaluate solutions or programs.

---

[3] Nielsen Norman Group. "Journey Mapping 101." Accessed May 21, 2025. `https://www.nngroup.com/articles/journey-mapping-101/?utm_source=chatgpt.com`

3. **Decision**: At this point, content like comparison guides, pricing pages, and demo invitations aims to convert prospects into leads or customers.

4. **Advocacy**: After conversion, content such as user communities, alumni newsletters, or loyalty programs fosters retention and encourages referrals.

Research conducted by Salesforce, a leader in cloud-based customer relationship management (CRM) solutions, to improve customer relationships, emphasizes that aligning content to these phases ensures each piece serves a clear purpose and can be measured against stage-specific metrics (e.g., scroll depth in awareness, click-through rate in consideration, form completion in decision).[4]

However, as you gain a deeper understanding of your users, you may see opportunities to develop a more complex map. Here are additional (or alternative) stages that can be integrated into a more comprehensive or flexible content journey framework:

1. **Discovery**

   - In some content journey models, this step precedes the awareness stage and focuses on identifying the ways users arrive at an awareness of your organization.

   - When users aren't actively searching but stumble upon your content through search engines, social media, or recommendations.

   - **Relevant Content**: SEO-optimized explainers, infographics, social snippets, listicles.

---

[4] Salesforce. "Customer Journey Mapping: A Complete Guide." Accessed May 21, 2025. `https://www.salesforce.com/marketing/engagement/journey-orchestration/customer-journey-mapping/?utm_source=chatgpt.com`

2. **Education/Exploration**

   - A deeper phase of early engagement before full consideration.

   - The user is gathering information, not yet comparing options.

   - **Relevant Content**: How-to's, beginner's guides, webinars, FAQs, glossaries.

3. **Evaluation**

   - Often a more detailed sub-stage of consideration.

   - The user is actively comparing choices, weighing trade-offs.

   - **Relevant Content**: Comparison charts, ROI calculators, customer testimonials, case studies.

4. **Activation/Trial**

   - Particularly important in SaaS (Software as a Service) or subscription models.

   - This is where the user takes a low-commitment action (e.g., signs up for a free trial, downloads a sample).

   - **Relevant Content**: Onboarding flows, email nurtures, walk-throughs, demo videos.

5. **Adoption**

   - This comes after decision but before advocacy.

   - The user is using your product or content consistently and forming habits.

- **Relevant Content**: Success tips, advanced use cases, onboarding series, feedback prompts.

6. **Satisfaction/Loyalty**

   - A key post-conversion phase.

   - This is where retention and long-term value are built.

   - **Relevant Content**: Insider content, customer-exclusive resources, loyalty program materials.

7. **Re-engagement/Renewal**

   - For cyclical or subscription-based offerings.

   - The user is at risk of churn or disengagement.

   - **Relevant Content**: "What you've missed" emails, account summaries, upgrade offers, loyalty campaigns.

8. **Influence/Co-creation**

   - Beyond advocacy, when the user becomes part of your extended brand presence.

   - Think of brand ambassadors, beta testers, or user-generated content contributors.

   - **Relevant Content**: Collaboration invitations, branded templates, influencer spotlights.

Ultimately, mapping your content to an expanded journey helps identify gaps (e.g., you may have lots of decision content but little for adoption), clarify what success looks like at each phase, and design better experiments and personalize analytics dashboards.

HOW B2B AND B2C CONTENT JOURNEYS DIFFER

- B2B often includes longer evaluation stages, more touchpoints, and decision-makers.

- B2C may rely more on emotion and impulse, especially in discovery and decision.

Tailor your map based on user type and buying behavior.

Table 3-1 offers a more comprehensive look at the stages, the content and metrics aligned with each, and some of the research questions you'll need to gain insight into each. You can also use this as a template to audit your current content library to see which of the stages relevant to your users' content journey are well-covered or which might be neglected.

Expanded Content Journey Framework

Table 3-1. *Expanded content journey framework*

Stage	Content Types	Key Metrics	Sample Analytics Questions
Discovery	SEO blog posts, infographics, social snippets, listicles	Organic impressions, click-through rate (CTR), bounce rate	What keywords or platforms drive first-time visits?
Awareness	Brand stories, explainer videos, introductory webinars, landing pages	New users, page views, session duration, traffic source mix	Which top-of-funnel content attracts the most qualified traffic?

(continued)

Table 3-1. (*continued*)

Stage	Content Types	Key Metrics	Sample Analytics Questions
Education/ exploration	How-to's, beginner's guides, FAQs, glossaries, email series	Scroll depth, video completions, return visits, time on page	Are visitors engaging deeply with educational content? What topics keep them exploring?
Consideration	Product features, detailed blog posts, white papers, use cases	Downloads, return visits, CTA clicks, lead magnet completions	Which formats lead to high-value engagement (e.g., downloads or email sign-ups)?
Evaluation	Comparison charts, calculators, testimonials, demos	Comparison page exits, demo requests, conversion assist rate	What content moves users from interest to decision? Which assets correlate with conversions?
Decision	Pricing pages, checkout flows, contact forms	Conversions, form completions, assisted conversions	What content paths lead to conversion? Where are users dropping off before decision points?
Activation/trial	Free trials, onboarding flows, welcome videos	Activation rate, time to first action, email open rate	Are trial users engaging with onboarding materials? What content shortens time-to-value?
Adoption	Pro tips, advanced tutorials, customer education blogs	Feature usage, return frequency, help center traffic	What content supports long-term use? Where are users seeking help post-decision?

(continued)

Table 3-1. (*continued*)

Stage	Content Types	Key Metrics	Sample Analytics Questions
Satisfaction/ loyalty	Loyalty newsletters, product updates, user-only perks	Net Promoter Score (NPS), churn rate, repeat usage	What content retains users? Does NPS vary by content interaction type?
Re-engagement/ renewal	"We miss you" campaigns, usage summaries, upsell offers	Revisit rate, renewal rate, reactivation clicks	What brings back dormant users? Which content increases renewal conversions?
Advocacy	Case study invitations, user-generated content, referral programs	Reviews submitted, social shares, referrals	What types of content prompt users to refer others or leave positive feedback?
Influence/Co-creation	Ambassador programs, community blogs, beta programs	Contribution rate, mentions, influencer conversions	Who are your top content collaborators? What motivates their ongoing participation?

Finally, as you begin to segment your audiences into groups like prospective buyers or current buyers, students or parents (for universities), subscribers or non-subscribers (for publishers), or donors or prospects (for nonprofits), you may want to develop unique maps for each.

Keep things simple at first, though. As you can imagine, you can easily overcomplicate this process, and that complexity snowballs as you begin to collect and analyze data at each waypoint on your map or maps.

> **Tip** A journey is not a campaign. A campaign is time-bound and goal-specific. A content journey is ongoing and behavior-driven. Campaigns may fit into the journey, but your analytics strategy should reflect the full path—not just isolated events.

How Users Find Content: Common Discovery Channels

One of the most useful steps in the content-mapping process is making sure you know how your users typically discover content in the first place, whether through intentional or incidental pathways or a mix of both. Before your users begin a journey, they need to know you exist. Table 3-2 suggests some of the ways users might find your content.

Table 3-2. *Pathways to content discovery*

Discovery Channel	Examples	Intent Level
Organic search	Google, Bing, YouTube searches	High (explicit query)
Social media	Twitter, LinkedIn, Facebook, TikTok shares	Low–Medium (passive to active)
Email and newsletters	Campaigns, drip series, alerts	Medium (opted in)
Internal site navigation	Related links, navigation menus, search bars	High (on-site exploration)

(continued)

Table 3-2. (*continued*)

Discovery Channel	Examples	Intent Level
Referral traffic	Links from partner sites, blogs, media articles	Medium (external endorsement)
Paid ads	Display, search, social ads	Low–High (depends on targeting)
Push notifications	App or browser alerts	Low–Medium (interruption-based)
Direct access	Users entering a URL or using a bookmark	High (brand familiarity)
Voice search/smart devices	Alexa, Siri, Google Assistant	Medium–High (spoken intent)

Each of these channels produces different behavioral patterns and analytic signatures (e.g., bounce rates, session duration, device usage) and often requires distinct content strategies. Understanding the pathways users are taking to your content is a rich source of research questions that you can explore as you build your program.

Why Distinguish Touchpoints and Emotions

As you develop these waypoints, it can also be useful to overlay user motivations and emotions—curiosity in awareness, trust-building in consideration, urgency in decision—to each stage in the content journey, which ultimately helps you tailor both content and analytics. In journey mapping, emotional overlays refer to documenting what users feel—such as curiosity, anxiety, or satisfaction—at each touchpoint. These insights help teams create empathetic, user-centered content.

The global consumer research company GWI notes that combining journey maps with consumer insights "moves you from assumptions to true understanding backed in data," enabling you to craft experiences that resonate at every step.[5] By defining these stages and touchpoints clearly, you lay the foundation for the data collection strategies detailed in Chapter 4 and the analysis techniques in Chapter 5.

Building Your First Journey Map

Creating your first content journey map is a collaborative exercise that combines user research, analytics data, and stakeholder insight. Follow these steps to craft a map that's both accurate and actionable:

1. **Gather Qualitative and Quantitative Inputs**

   - **Stakeholder Interviews:** Speak with marketing, sales, UX, and customer support teams to understand how they perceive user motivations and roadblocks—this "inside-out" view reveals assumptions you'll need to validate or challenge.

   - **Analytics Data:** Pull entry and exit pages, top referrers, and drop-off rates from GA4 or Adobe Analytics. Look for patterns in traffic sources and content performance that suggest key touchpoints.

   - **User Feedback:** Leverage survey comments, social media mentions, and on-site feedback (e.g., Hotjar polls) to capture real user sentiments—these anecdotes often uncover friction points that raw metrics miss.

---

[5] GWI. "Customer Journey Mapping: How Consumer Insights Drive Better Experiences." Accessed May 21, 2025. `https://www.gwi.com/blog/customer-journey-mapping?utm_source=chatgpt.com`

2. **Define Stages and Touchpoints**

- Start by outlining the major phases—awareness, consideration, decision, advocacy—and listing the content types and channels associated with each.

- For each touchpoint, note the primary user goal (e.g., "discover program benefits" at the awareness phase) and the metric you'll track (e.g., scroll depth on explainer articles).

3. **Map User Thoughts and Emotions**

- Overlay what users might be thinking or feeling (confused by jargon, excited by testimonials) at each step. The Nielsen Norman Group emphasizes that including "user thoughts and emotions" transforms a map from a funnel into a narrative that drives empathy and alignment.[6] If you have access to a UX expert, integrating user testing (observing users as they interact with your content) can be invaluable.

4. **Visualize the Journey**

- Use a simple horizontal timeline or swim-lane diagram (a diagram that uses parallel lanes to show how different user roles or systems interact with stages in the journey). Place stages on the x-axis and touchpoints on the lanes, and annotate emotions or barriers with icons or brief notes.

---

[6] Nielsen Norman Group. "Customer Journey Mapping." Accessed May 22, 2025. https://www.nngroup.com/articles/customer-journey-mapping

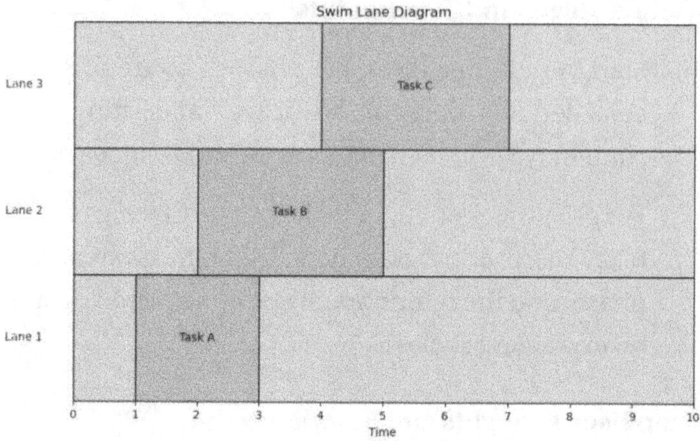

Figure 3-1. *An example of a simple swim-lane diagram offering a visual representation of three tasks and how they overlap or do not overlap in real time*

- Aim for clarity over complexity: a single page with five to seven touchpoints keeps teams focused.

5. **Validate and Refine**

- Review the draft map in a workshop with cross-functional stakeholders. Identify any missing steps or inconsistent data points.

- If possible, conduct three to five quick user interviews or contextual inquiries to confirm that the map reflects real behaviors.

By following this process, you create a shared artifact that not only guides your analytics setup in Chapter 4 but also serves as a strategic reference for content planning and optimization.

VISUALIZING JOURNEY MAPS

There are a variety of ways to create visual representations of user journeys. The choice of which to use depends on the complexity of the journey and who will need to use your map. Table 3-3 offers some suggestions.

Table 3-3. *Types of journey maps*

Format	Definition	Best For	Use Case Category
Timeline-based map	A linear map showing the user's journey across stages, touchpoints, and emotions.	Simple, clear storytelling	• Simpler journeys • Stakeholder communication
Swim-lane map	A horizontal map dividing the journey by roles (e.g., customer, staff, systems). See Figure 3-1.	Cross-functional collaboration	• Complex journeys • Operational planning
Service blueprint	A detailed map showing frontstage (customer-facing) and backstage and support processes (behind the scenes).	Operational alignment and service design	• omplex journeys • Strategic planning
Infographic-style map	A visually rich, stylized map using icons, colors, and illustrations.	Presentations, executive summaries	• Simpler journeys • Stakeholder communication

(continued)

Table 3-3. (*continued*)

Format	Definition	Best For	Use Case Category
Empathy map	A tool to capture what a user thinks, feels, says, and does.	Early-stage research and persona development	• Simpler journeys
Matrix/grid layout	A table comparing journey stages across personas, segments, or scenarios.	Comparative analysis	• Complex journeys
Storyboard	A narrative format using visuals to depict the user's experience.	Long-term planning and team alignment	• Strategic planning • Stakeholder communication
Circular/ spiral map	A nonlinear map showing cyclical or recurring journeys.	Subscription models, long-term engagement	• Complex journeys

Case Study: Mapping for a Higher Ed Recruitment Campaign

A mid-sized university aims to boost out-of-state undergraduate applications by 15% over the next admissions cycle.

Journey Map Highlights:

- **Awareness:** Prospective students often arrive via SEO-optimized blog posts on campus life. Analytics showed high bounce rates on these posts (65%) but no clear path to program pages.

- **Consideration:** Campus tour videos embedded in social ads generated longer watch times (average 2:30 minutes) but weren't tagged for downstream tracking, leaving the team blind to whether video viewers later visited application pages.

- **Decision:** The application form page had a 40% abandonment rate; exit page analytics suggested form length was a barrier.

- **Advocacy:** Accepted students received an alumni newsletter, but open rates (22%) and click-throughs (4%) were below the university average.

Actions Taken:

1. **Added Event Tagging:** Tagged video plays, social ad clicks, and form interactions in Google Analytics/GA4 to fill data gaps—enabling analysis of which videos led to application starts

2. **Redesigned Touchpoints:** Broke long blog posts into "top 5 reasons" listicles with clear CTAs, reducing bounce rates by 20%. Moved critical form fields "above the fold," cutting abandonment by 15%

3. **Aligned Content and Channels:** Created a follow-up email series for students who watched at least 50% of the tour video, improving newsletter open rates to 35%

Results:

- Applications from out-of-state prospects rose 18% year over year.

- Video-to-application conversion increased by 30%.

- Form abandonment dropped to 25%.

Key Takeaway:

Mapping the full journey exposed hidden drop-off points and data blind spots. By aligning tagging, content, and channel strategy to the map, the team turned fragmented metrics into a coordinated campaign that surpassed its goal and laid the foundation for ongoing analytics-driven improvements.

Aligning Data Collection to the Journey

Translating your journey map into measurable insights begins with defining what you'll track at each touchpoint and how you'll capture it. For each stage of the journey, take these steps:

1. **Specify the Key Actions and Metrics**

   - **Awareness:** Track page views on top-of-funnel assets (blog posts, social landing pages), bounce rate, and average scroll depth to gauge initial interest.

   - **Consideration:** Capture video plays, time watched percentages, whitepaper downloads, and email link clicks—signals that users are evaluating your offerings.

   - **Decision:** Monitor form starts and completions, demo request clicks, cart additions, or checkout steps. These are your conversion events.

   - **Advocacy:** Record repeat visits, referral link clicks, social shares, and survey responses to measure ongoing engagement and loyalty.

2. **Define Event Names and Parameters**

    - Establish a clear, consistent naming convention
      (e.g., video_start, download_whitepaper, form_
      submit) and include parameters for contextual
      details—source, content ID, user segment.

    - Document these in a shared tracking plan so
      everyone—from writers to developers—knows
      exactly how each event is implemented.

3. **Map Metadata and Content Attributes**

    - Alongside behavioral events, capture content
      attributes: format, topic tag, author, funnel stage.

    - Store these either in your CMS or as event
      parameters so you can evaluate performance
      according to your content characteristics (see
      Chapter 4 to learn more about how your content is
      also a form of data).

4. **Ensure Cross-Platform Consistency**

    - Use the same content IDs and campaign UTMs
      across website, email, ads, and social.

    - Stitch together sessions that may start on one
      channel and finish on another.

5. **Validate and Audit**

    - Before relying on this data, run through each journey
      step yourself and confirm that the events fire correctly or
      are captured accurately in your analytics platform.

    - Schedule a quarterly audit to catch any drift—new
      content types, changed URLs, or missing tags that
      erode data quality.

By systematically mapping events and metadata back to your journey stages, you guarantee that every user interaction feeds into a coherent analytics framework—turning your map into a source of actionable, data-driven insights. We'll look at this in more depth when we dive into data collection systems in the next chapter.

COMMON TRACKING MISTAKES

- Using generic event names like click1

- Forgetting to tag PDFs, videos, or outbound links

- Overwriting UTMs with every redirect

- Ignoring cross-device sessions

For more on tagging, see Chapter 4 and Appendix A.

Beyond the Content Journey

Preparing your team to build a content analytics program need not be an onerous task, but in addition to understanding the journeys your audience might be taking, there are other factors you might consider evaluating before getting started. Preparatory steps like auditing your content portfolio or studying your competition will all yield insights and opportunities to craft better research questions and identify prime targets for growth and improvement.

Table 3-4 suggests a few of the things you could consider as you take those first steps.

Table 3-4. *Preliminary journey-mapping tasks*

Task	Description and Purpose	Tools
Content inventory	Create a comprehensive list of all content assets, including blog posts, videos, infographics, and social media posts to understand the scope and variety of content available.	Spreadsheets, content management systems (CMSs)
SEO audit	Evaluate content for search engine optimization, including keyword usage, meta descriptions, and backlinks to ensure content is optimized for search engines to improve visibility and ranking.	SEMrush, Ahrefs, Moz
Content quality assessment	Review content for quality, including accuracy, relevance, readability, and consistency to ensure content meets the brand's standards and provides value to the audience.	Grammarly, Hemingway Editor
Audience analysis	Understand the target audience's preferences, behaviors, and feedback to tailor content to better meet audience needs and expectations and to establish a baseline of their opinions on your brand or organization.	Surveys, user personas, social listening tools
Competitor analysis	Evaluate competitors' content strategies and performance to identify gaps and opportunities in your own content strategy.	BuzzSumo, Similarweb

(continued)

Table 3-4. *(continued)*

Task	Description and Purpose	Tools
Content gap analysis	Identify topics or areas that are underrepresented in your content to help in planning future content to fill these gaps.	Keyword research tools, audience feedback
Content lifecycle analysis	Assess the lifecycle of content from creation to retirement to determine when content needs updating, repurposing, or retiring.	Content management systems, editorial calendars
User experience (UX) audit	Evaluate how users interact with your content, including navigation, layout, and design to ensure a seamless and engaging user experience.	Heatmaps, user testing tools
Content alignment check	Ensure content aligns with overall business goals and marketing strategies to confirm that content supports broader organizational objectives.	Strategic planning frameworks, alignment workshops
Content accessibility review	Check content for accessibility standards to ensure it is usable by all audiences, including those with disabilities, to promote inclusivity and compliance with accessibility regulations.	Accessibility checkers, screen readers
Content freshness check	Review content to ensure it is up-to-date and relevant to keep content current and valuable to the audience.	Content management systems, editorial calendars

Workbook Exercise: Create Your Own Content Journey Map

Table 3-5 offers a guided approach to drafting a journey map tailored to a specific objective in your organization.

Table 3-5. *Steps to developing a content journey map tied to a specific objective*

Step	Prompt	Your Notes
1	**Objective**: What is one business goal you're supporting?	(e.g., Increase trial sign-ups from blog readers)
2	**Audience**: Who are you mapping? Identify the user segment or persona.	(e.g., SMB marketing managers)
3	**Stages and Touchpoints**: List three to five steps this audience takes—from first contact to conversion or advocacy.	1. Awareness: SEO article → 2. Consideration: webinar sign-up → …
4	**User Intent and Metric**: For each touchpoint, state what the user wants and how you'll measure it.	(e.g., "Watch webinar" → track video_complete)
5	**Content Attributes**: Note the key metadata you'll capture (format, topic, author, funnel stage).	(e.g., format=webinar, topic=lead gen, stage–consideration)
6	**Data Gaps**: Where does your current setup lack events or metadata?	(e.g., "No tracking on PDF downloads")
7	**Next Actions**: List two to three steps to fill those gaps before your next analysis.	(e.g., "Implement PDF download event"; "Add content ID slug to UTM")

Once you've completed the table, sketch a simple flow diagram on a whiteboard or slide. Place your stages horizontally, annotate touchpoints and metrics, and highlight the gaps. This live document will guide your data collection planning (which we'll explore in the next chapter) and keep your team aligned around the journey you just mapped.

Common Pitfalls in Journey Mapping

Even the best-intentioned journey maps can falter if you're not careful. Here are the most frequent missteps and how to avoid them:

1. **No Clear Goals or Scope:** Without a defined objective—such as increasing demo requests or reducing form abandonment—your map becomes a "map to nowhere," collecting every possible touchpoint without focus. UXPin warns that building a journey "just for the sake of building it" leads to wasted effort and stakeholder disengagement.[7] Always start by answering: *"What decision(s) will this map inform?"*

2. **Relying on Assumptions Instead of Research:** Guessing user behaviors or skipping stakeholder and user interviews produces an inaccurate map. Xerago finds that "weak or no research" drives many failed initiatives, because the resulting map reflects internal opinions rather than actual user needs.[8] Use analytics data and direct feedback to ground your map in reality.

---

[7] UXPin. "Customer Journey Mapping Mistakes and How to Avoid Them." Accessed May 22, 2025. `https://www.uxpin.com/studio/blog/customer-journey-mapping-mistakes`

[8] Xerago. "Top Customer Journey Mapping Mistakes and How to Avoid Them." Accessed May 22, 2025.

3. **Focusing on the "Average" Customer:** A single, monolithic journey ignores key segment differences. LinkedIn contributors note that mapping only the "average" persona can oversimplify or exclude niche but high-value paths— like enterprise buyers who require more detailed content and multiple approvals.[9] Consider creating multiple maps for distinct personas when variation is high.

4. **Overcomplicating or Oversimplifying the Map:** Including too many stages, channels, or emotional states turns your one-page guide into a multi-pane maze. Overly detailed, static maps become desk ornaments rather than living tools, because teams never refer to or update them.[10] Aim for five to seven key touchpoints per journey, and keep annotations concise. On the other hand, some organizations fall short by producing one-size-fits-all maps, failing to connect touchpoints to measurable content outcomes.[11]

5. **Failing to Update and Maintain:** A journey map should evolve with your content strategy and user behavior. UX design firm Akendi notes that many organizations create maps once and never revisit them, missing shifts in channels or content formats that render the map obsolete.[12] Schedule quarterly "journey reviews" to validate and refresh your map.

---

[9] LinkedIn. "What are some common pitfalls to avoid when creating a customer journey map?" Accessed May 22, 2025. `https://www.linkedin.com/advice/3/what-some-common-pitfalls-avoid-when-creating-3f`

[10] Reddit. "I Thought Journey Maps Were Meant to Capture the Full Experience." Accessed May 22, 2025.

[11] Kalbach, J. *Mapping Experiences: A Complete Guide to Customer Alignment Through Journeys, Blueprints, and Diagrams.* Sebastopol: O'Reilly Media, 2020.

[12] Akendi. "12 Mistakes to Avoid When Journey Mapping." Accessed May 22, 2025. `https://www.akendi.com/blog/12-mistakes-to-avoid-when-journey-mapping`

Integrating the Team Around the Journey

Journey mapping is inherently cross-functional. Its success depends on clear roles, shared ownership, and ongoing collaboration:

- **Marketing and Content Strategists**

  Define business objectives, draft the map's scope, and ensure each touchpoint aligns with strategic priorities.

- **Analytics and Data Teams**

  Supply quantitative inputs (entry/exit pages, referral data) and validate tracking plans to ensure each touchpoint generates reliable metrics.

- **UX Designers and Researchers**

  Lead user interviews, usability tests on prototype touchpoints, and surface emotional insights that enrich the map's narrative.

- **Sales and Customer Success**

  Provide frontline perspectives on obstacles, questions, and friction encountered during decision and advocacy stages.

- **IT and Development**

  Implement event tagging, maintain tracking scripts, and troubleshoot technical barriers to data collection.

- **Project Managers**

  Coordinate workshops, document decisions, and keep the map and data collection plan on track.

According to industry experts, journey maps drive stronger collaboration when they're created in facilitated workshops that bring all these roles together, ensuring shared understanding and buy-in from day one.[13] By clarifying responsibilities at each stage and using the map as a living reference, teams move from siloed activities to synchronized workflows that improve both the user experience and analytical rigor.

Budget-Friendly Approaches to Journey Mapping

Even without dedicated journey-mapping software or large research teams, you can still build and maintain effective content journey maps:

- **Leverage Free or Familiar Tools**

  Use Google Slides, Miro's free tier, or even a shared spreadsheet to sketch and iterate your map. These platforms support real-time collaboration and version control without new licenses.

- **Run "Micro-workshops"**

  Instead of a full-day offsite, convene a 60-minute virtual session with two or three key stakeholders. Use a shared whiteboard to capture touchpoints and validate with a quick poll.

- **Start with Your Top Funnel**

  Focus on the single journey slice that delivers the most value (e.g., blog ➤ demo sign-up) rather than end to end. You can expand later once you've proved ROI.

---

[13] LinkedIn. "How Can Customer Journey Design Improve Cross-Functional Collaboration?" Accessed May 22, 2025.

- **Repurpose Existing Data**

  Pull simple flow reports from GA4 or your CMS to identify high-traffic landing and exit pages. Overlay these with even a hand-drawn journey to spot your biggest gaps.

- **Document Lightweight Updates**

  Keep a one-page "journey change-log" in your team space. When you add a touchpoint or fix a data gap, note it there. Quarterly reviews then become a five-minute check rather than a major project.

Final Thoughts

Mapping content journeys transforms scattered metrics into coherent user stories. By visualizing stages and touchpoints, you gain clarity on where to collect data, which metrics matter, and how to optimize each interaction. Remember that journey maps are living artifacts—update them whenever you launch a major campaign, redesign your site, or discover a new channel. When done right, these maps will guide your analytics strategy, inform your analysis, and provide you with clear opportunities to improve your content and its impact. Ultimately, they anchor your entire content analytics program in the real behaviors and needs of your audience, ensuring that every insight leads to a better experience and stronger business outcomes.

In the next chapter, we'll begin to lay the foundation for your analytics efforts by looking at how to collect the data you'll need to answer your research questions.

CHAPTER 4

Data Collection and Preparation

A content analytics program is only as good as the data behind it. No matter how sophisticated your dashboards, models, or reports, if your underlying data is incomplete, inconsistent, or disorganized, your insights will be dubious and your decisions risky.

For example, imagine you've launched a live webinar series to drive prospect engagement, but two weeks in, you discover that your analytics only tracked page views and not actual attendance or drop-offs. You can't tell whether people stayed for the whole session or left before the call to action. Now you're flying blind on your biggest content investment of the quarter.

That's why high-quality data collection isn't optional. Without knowing *exactly* what you're measuring and how, even your best content ideas can leave you with nothing to show for your efforts.

This chapter shows you how to set up strong, reliable content data pipelines: capturing the right information, keeping it clean, and structuring it for meaningful analysis.

You don't need to be a data engineer to get this right, but you will need to understand *what* to collect, *where* it comes from, and *how* to prepare it for the types of questions your team wants to answer.

To begin, Table 4-1 introduces the two types of data you'll be working with: structured data and unstructured data.

© Russ Bahorsky 2026
R. Bahorsky, *The Fundamentals of Content Analytics*,
https://doi.org/10.1007/979-8-8688-2601-6_4

Table 4-1. *Data types for analytics*

Type of Data	What It Includes	Examples
Structured data	Quantifiable, organized information about user behavior and performance	Page views, bounce rates, video completions, email clicks
Unstructured data	The raw content itself—text, audio, video, and image files	Article body text, video transcripts, podcast audio, infographic images

Think of it this way: you want visitors to your web pages, readers of your newsletter, etc. to do more of something, like clicking, sharing, or reading. And ultimately you want them to do more subscribing, applying, or buying. Your content is what makes that happen by persuading, influencing, and inspiring. Structured data, then, refers to the behaviors that we can observe, count, and compare, and unstructured data (what we typically think of as content with attributes that we can change, test, and improve) are your behavior modifiers.

Before you build any dashboard, database, or analysis plan, though, it's important to understand the two raw ingredients of content analytics: the behavior data that tells you what happened and the content data that helps you understand why and how.

Now, let's look at each type of data in more detail, what it is, and why it's important, as well as how to collect it and connect it.

Structured Data: Tracking User Behavior

Structured data captures *how* people interact with your content. It's usually captured using systems like Google Analytics (GA4), CRM tools, social media dashboards, and video hosting platforms.

Key structured metrics include

- **Page Views**: How many times a page was loaded

- **Click-Through Rates**: Percentage of users who clicked a call to action

- **Watch Time**: How much of a video users watched

- **Bounce Rates**: How often users leave without taking an action

- **Conversion Rates**: Percentage of users who complete a key action (sign-up, download, purchase)

To track specific actions beyond basic page views—such as video starts, form submissions, or content downloads—you'll also need to set up event tagging in your analytics platforms. Since these "events" are triggered by the coding of your digital content, this is something a web developer can help you do, but it's as simple as adding some additional elements, typically known as UTM codes that contain keywords or other identifying elements that you choose, to a link to help tools like GA4 to identify what users are doing with the content they find on your page.

To capture complex behaviors—like how many exposures lead to a conversion or where viewers drop off—event tagging gives you the additional insight you need to translate behaviors into useful insights (e.g., "Users who watched 75% of the video are 3× more likely to sign up") or to improve content design and UX decisions by showing where attention drops off.

EXAMPLES OF EVENTS THAT CAN BE TAGGED

- Clicking a specific CTA button (e.g., "Download Whitepaper" vs. "Request Demo")

- Playing, pausing, or completing a video

- Expanding an accordion or tabbed content section

- Scrolling 25%, 50%, 75%, or 100% down a page

- Hovering over or interacting with embedded elements (like tooltips or charts)

- Viewing a specific content block (e.g., reaching a pricing table or testimonial)

If you're having trouble identifying the events that need to be tagged, work with your UX expert to set up user testing sessions that will allow you to observe how users are engaging with your content.

User testing—also called usability testing—is a method used by UX experts to observe how real people interact with a product, website, or piece of content, to identify points of confusion, friction, or inefficiency. It typically involves asking a user to complete specific tasks (e.g., "Find and register for a webinar") while thinking out loud and watching where they struggle or where they succeed.

The exercise can be immensely useful in helping you identify which actions or events to collect, and it may also reveal obstacles and technical problems you didn't anticipate, like finding that a call-to-action button doesn't display correctly on a certain kind of browser or smart phone or that a photo or video takes too long to load. You'll also want to involve your web developer in these discussions to make sure they are aware of any technical issues with your content and to help you think through the practicalities of what you'd like to accomplish.

For more on setting up event tagging, see Appendix A.

Unstructured Data: Managing the Content Itself

While structured data helps you track what users do, unstructured data—your content itself—is what they experience. To draw meaningful conclusions, you need both: the behavior and the message that prompted it.

Unstructured data refers to content your team creates, including text content (blog posts, news articles, whitepapers) and audio/visual content (videos, webinars, podcasts), but it also includes the metadata assigned to those assets, their titles, descriptions, categories, and author tags.

Why is it important to think of your content as data? Ultimately, you'll want to be able to answer questions like *"What kinds of stories drive the most engagement?"* or *"Does article length affect conversion?"* or *"Do long headlines outperform short ones?"* To do that, you'll need to be able to link content attributes (e.g., format, topic, tone) to performance outcomes.

In fact, industry research suggests that unstructured content (text, images, video) now makes up as much as 80–90% of enterprise data—making it a vital but often under-leveraged resource in content analysis.[1]

In addition to ensuring that your structured data is accessible, manageable, and useful, you'll also want to have your unstructured data available for the same reasons. This means

- Archiving full content versions and not just URLs

- Creating clear guidelines for identifying categories of content, not just by type but by topic and even function (e.g., invitation to subscribe, first renewal request, second request, etc.)

---

[1] Amir Gandomi and Murtaza Haider, "Beyond the Hype: Big Data Concepts, Methods, and Analytics," *International Journal of Information Management* 35, no. 2 (2015): 137–144, https://doi.org/10.1016/j.ijinfomgt.2014.10.007

- Consistently applying metadata (titles, tags, themes)

- Storing transcripts or alt text when available for multimedia

As you begin the work of analyzing your content, you'll find that the more systematic you are in collecting and managing your unstructured data, its attributes, and its metadata, the more tools you'll have to help you understand how it's influencing those who engage with it.

Throughout this book, you generally see structured data referred to as, simply, data, while unstructured data will just be called content. However, it's worthwhile to understand the two terms insofar as they serve as a reminder that your content is a form of data in your effort to identify an equation for success.

Key Systems for Collecting Structured and Unstructured Data

Now that we've defined the types of content data, let's look at where they live and how to pull them together.

Collecting content data isn't about gathering information from just one place; it's about pulling together insights from multiple systems that track different aspects of user behavior and content performance.

Table 4-2 summarizes the most common sources of content data, what each system tracks, and examples of the kinds of metrics each provides.

Table 4-2. *Content sources and their uses*

Source	What It Tracks	Example Metrics
Web analytics tools (e.g., GA4, Matomo, Plausible)	Visitor behavior on your website	Page views, sessions, bounce rates, scroll depth, event completions
Content management systems (CMSs) (e.g., WordPress, Drupal)	Metadata about published content	Title, author, publish date, category, tags, content type
Customer relationship management (CRM) tools (e.g., HubSpot, Salesforce)	Leads and customer interactions linked to content	Lead form fills, content downloads, email clicks, deal progression
Social media platforms (e.g., Facebook, LinkedIn, Instagram)	External engagement with content	Impressions, likes, shares, comments, click-throughs
Video hosting platforms (e.g., YouTube, Vimeo, Wistia)	Viewer engagement with video content	Watch time, play rate, average percentage watched, drop-off points
Email marketing systems (e.g., Mailchimp, Marketo)	Campaign engagement metrics	Open rates, click rates, unsubscribe rates, conversion rates
Survey tools and feedback forms (e.g., Qualtrics, SurveyMonkey)	Direct feedback from users	User satisfaction, content relevance ratings, qualitative comments

Data Appends

It may also be useful to note that you're not limited to using just the data in your own organization's database, if that's the audience you're trying to reach. Third-party data enrichment platforms like Similarweb,

Apollo.io, and ZoomInfo, credit bureaus like Equifax and Experian, and data compilers like AppendSolutions and Innovative Data Services will help you augment your data by appending demographics, job titles, purchase histories, social media activity, email engagement, location data, and similar information collected from other sources. Data appends may provide you with a more robust picture of your audience and their interests, one that you can use to develop a better understanding of their needs and motivations.

Bringing It All Together

Now that you know where your structured and unstructured data lives, the next step is combining those sources into something usable, so you can begin making decisions based on complete, trustworthy information.

Having defined your key metrics, tagged events consistently, and archived content with rich metadata, the next, and most critical, step is to weave these structured and unstructured data streams into a single analytics engine. Fortunately, there are a variety of options if your team's skills or their resources aren't up to the task. Teams often use

1. **Data Warehouses**: (e.g., BigQuery) With scheduled ETL[2] jobs to load GA4, CMS exports, and CRM logs

2. **APIs and Middleware**: (e.g., Zapier, Stitch) For real-time syncs between platforms

3. **Manual Blends in BI Tools**: (e.g., Tableau Prep, Excel Power Query) For smaller teams
   Choose based on your volume, budget, and technical skill set.

---

[2] **Extract, Transform, Load**—a common process used to move data from various sources into a centralized system like a data warehouse.

Before you start pricing these services, have a conversation with your IT department to understand their capabilities and get their input on the kind of help you'll need. Include them in the conversation with the vendors you're considering.

WHEN BAD TAGGING BREAKS A CAMPAIGN ANALYSIS

A university's marketing team launches a major digital campaign to promote a new graduate program. They publish

- Blog posts

- Social media ads

- Webinars

- Email newsletters

The Goal

Track which content pieces drive the most applications to the new program.

The Problem

The campaign's content isn't tagged consistently:

- Some blog posts are tagged as "Graduate Admissions," others as "New Programs," and some have no tag at all.

- UTMs (tracking parameters on links) are set up differently by different team members—sometimes missing the campaign name entirely.

- Webinars aren't tagged with a specific event goal in Google Analytics.

The Result

When the team tries to run a performance report

- They can't group or compare similar blog posts easily.

- Some referral traffic looks like "direct traffic" because UTMs were missing, making it impossible to trace to the right campaign.

- They can't tell how many application form starts were influenced by the webinars.

Bottom Line

The campaign seems less successful than it really is, because the available data is fragmented, incomplete, and confusing. Worse, leadership questions the value of investing in future content campaigns because "The numbers don't show a return."

Takeaway

Poor data hygiene doesn't just waste analyst time; it erodes trust in your content strategy, your campaigns, and even your team's credibility.

From Data to Insight: Making It Actionable

Once your data sources are stitched together, your next job is to make sense of them—to connect performance patterns to business decisions. Connecting the dots this way isn't just about technical integration; it's about drawing meaning from the patterns, gaps, and relationships hidden in the data. This section helps you begin translating raw inputs into insights that serve your business goals.

For example:

1. Web analytics data tells you that a user visited your whitepaper landing page.

2. CMS metadata shows that the whitepaper topic is "AI in Education."

3. CRM records show that the visitor downloaded the whitepaper and later booked a consultation call.

Together, your datasets will allow you to connect your content with the actions you want your readers or viewers to take and the business outcomes these actions make possible (e.g., new applications, renewals, revenue, etc.).

Whenever possible, however, align your identifiers (e.g., URL structure, content ID, user ID) across platforms. This makes it much easier to stitch datasets together later for analysis. In other words, your marketing question should be your roadmap for how you're going to combine your structured and unstructured data, so make sure you and your team make sure it's clear how you're going to join your data points together.

HOW CONSISTENT IDENTIFIERS MAKE CAMPAIGN ANALYSIS POSSIBLE

A nonprofit launches a major fall campaign, producing content across multiple channels:

- Blog articles posted on their website

- Short videos shared on YouTube and embedded in newsletters

- Social media ads driving traffic to a downloadable guide

The marketing question they want to answer is: *"Which content formats and topics contributed most to guide downloads?"*

Table 4-3 illustrates how the nonprofit approaches aligning their identifiers.

Table 4-3. *Platform and identifier layout*

Platform	Identifier Used	Example
Website CMS	Content ID	/content/healthcare-innovation-2024 (URL structure includes clear, unique slug)
YouTube (video titles + UTM links)	Content ID embedded in UTM	utm_content=healthcare_innovation_video
Email marketing (Mailchimp)	Campaign name + UTM	utm_campaign=fall_campaign + utm_content=healthcare_innovation_email
CRM (form submissions)	Campaign ID field	Stores the UTM content or campaign name when someone downloads the guide

Why It Matters

- When downloads happened, the CRM recorded the UTM content value along with user info.

- GA4 captured page views and video starts, all tied to the content slugs (which match UTM content).

- YouTube analytics shows which videos with specific titles (mapped to content IDs) drive views and clicks.

Because the same content identifier (e.g., "healthcare_innovation") travels across all platforms, the team can easily stitch together

- Which blog post ➤ drove video views ➤ drove downloads

- Which email ➤ led to clicks ➤ led to downloads

Without Consistent Identifiers

- It would be a nightmare trying to figure out which video or blog contributes to results.

- They would need manual matching (guessing based on titles or dates).

- Key relationships might be missed entirely.

Takeaway

By aligning content IDs, URLs, UTM content parameters, and CRM fields *from the start*, the marketing team makes it easy to combine structured data (downloads, video clicks) with unstructured data (content topics, formats) to answer their strategic question.

How to Collect Structured Content Data Effectively

Structured content data—the clicks, scrolls, downloads, form fills, and more—is the backbone of performance measurement. But simply installing Google Analytics or another tracking tool isn't enough. To generate meaningful insights, you need to collect structured data intentionally and consistently.

While there are a variety of ways to connect data across systems by (1) using identifiers like user IDs or email addresses that two systems might share or (2) using time-based matching like aligning datasets by timestamp and session metadata (e.g., device type, campaign source, referrer) in cases where users aren't directly identifiable, tagging your content by adding labels or metadata to your content or user interactions so they can be tracked, grouped, and analyzed later is far and away the best practice for developing a robust content analytics system.

Tag Content Consistently

Every piece of content should be classified with clear, standardized metadata, so developing a system for doing this before you begin collecting data is essential. Without consistent tagging, it will be impossible to analyze the performance of your content by topic, format, or audience segment in a way that will provide you with valid results.

Common tagging fields include

- Content type (e.g., blog post, webinar, video)

- Primary topic or category

- Audience segment (if applicable)

- Author or creator

- Publish date

- Funnel stage (e.g., where the reader/viewer is in their decision-making process: awareness, consideration, decision, etc.)

Table 4-4 offers examples of tags that can be used for different types of content.

Table 4-4. *Tagging examples*

Field	Example Value
Content type	Blog post
Topic	Data privacy
Audience segment	Higher education IT leaders
Author	Jane Doe
Funnel stage	Awareness

Document your tagging rules in a shared content taxonomy guide and train your editorial, marketing, and content teams to use it consistently. Making sure your team is disciplined in applying tags consistently is essential to an effective analytics program.

Finally, if you haven't already taken stock of your content in a systematic way, tagging it can also be an important source of insight, identifying gaps and imbalances in your content portfolio.

Set Up Event Tracking Thoughtfully

As we've seen, in GA4 and other analytics platforms, you can track *events*—specific actions users take beyond just loading a page.

Common events to track for content analytics include

- Scroll depth (e.g., users scrolling 50% or 90% of the page)

- Video plays, pauses, and completions

- File downloads (e.g., PDFs, whitepapers)

- Button clicks (e.g., "Sign Up," "Download Now")

- Form submissions

Table 4-5 offers some examples of useful event setups.

Table 4-5. *Example event setups*

Event Name	Description
video_start	User started playing a video.
video_complete	User watched the entire video.
scroll_90_percent	User scrolled at least 90% down the page.
download_whitepaper	User clicked a whitepaper download link.

Proper event tracking allows you to measure true engagement—not just visits. It's an important step in the process of understanding not just what visitors are doing but why, so it's essential to make sure these are part of your data collection plan from the start.

You don't need to track everything, but make sure you identify the most important user actions on your site or app and ensure each is tracked as an event.

Ensure Cross-Platform Consistency

In today's digital-first world, your users interact with your content across various platforms, including websites, email, social media, and more. To gain a comprehensive understanding of their journey, your data collection should reflect these interactions seamlessly.

Here are a few of today's best practices in tracking your data across a variety of platforms:

1. **Consistent Use of UTM Parameters**

   - **Purpose**: UTM parameters help track the effectiveness of your marketing campaigns across different channels.

   - **Implementation**: Ensure that every link shared via email, social media, or other platforms includes UTM parameters. This consistency allows you to accurately attribute traffic and conversions to specific campaigns.

   - **Example**: Use parameters like utm_source, utm_medium, and utm_campaign to differentiate between sources and campaigns.

2. **Cross-Domain Tracking**

- **Purpose**: Users often navigate between multiple websites you control. Cross-domain tracking ensures that their journey is captured without interruption.

- **Implementation**: Set up cross-domain tracking in your analytics tools to maintain a unified view of user behavior across different domains.

- **Example**: Configure Google Analytics to track users across multiple domains by linking them with a common tracking ID.

3. **Clear Campaign Tagging**

- **Purpose**: Clear and descriptive campaign names facilitate easier analysis and reporting.

- **Implementation**: Tag your campaigns with meaningful names that reflect their purpose and timing. Avoid generic names like "campaign."

- **Example**: Use names like "spring_newsletter_signup" or "holiday_sale_2025" to provide context.

4. **Connecting User Identities Across Systems**

- **Purpose**: Integrating user identities across different systems helps create a holistic view of user interactions.

- **Implementation**: Use CRM IDs, email addresses, or other non-personally identifiable information (PII) such as device IDs, IP addresses, and cookies to link user data across platforms.

- **Example**: Sync user data from your CRM with your email marketing and web analytics tools to track interactions consistently.

Inevitably, you're going to face challenges as you work to build a fully integrated content data solution—especially if you don't have ownership over all the systems involved or if key datasets are siloed across teams, platforms, or vendors. The following tips can help you minimize friction and maintain data quality, even when you're working within those constraints:

- **Use Consistent Labels and IDs Across Platforms:** Even when tools like your CMS, email platform, and analytics suite don't integrate seamlessly, you can still design them to "speak the same language." Assign consistent naming conventions for content types, campaigns, user IDs, or tags.

  Example: Use the same campaign slug or content ID in your UTM parameters, email links, and CRM system. This makes it much easier to join datasets later during analysis.

- **Establish a Tagging and Parameter Strategy Early:** Define a shared document that outlines which UTM parameters, event labels, or content categories your team will use, and stick to it. This reduces ad hoc decisions that lead to messy, inconsistent data.

Tip   Schedule a 30-minute team alignment meeting each quarter to review new tags, outdated or obsolete parameters, and upcoming campaign needs.

- **Conduct Regular Audits and Spot Checks:** Make auditing part of your process. Review event tags, metadata, and tracking links regularly, especially before and after major campaigns. Spot missing or misfiring tags early to avoid analyzing incomplete or misleading data down the line. Even a lightweight monthly review can prevent weeks of troubleshooting later.

- **Document Everything—Even the Workarounds:** If you had to use a manual fix, spreadsheet merge, or API script to stitch together your data, write it down. Future team members (and future you) will thank you. Documentation helps preserve institutional knowledge and makes scaling easier over time.

- **Prioritize Privacy and Data Governance:** Always collect and store user data in ways that comply with privacy laws like the General Data Protection Regulation (GDPR), California Consumer Privacy Act (CCPA) (more on these later), and your own organization's data policies.

  - Don't collect more than you need.

  - Don't store personal data unless you have consent.

  - Make sure data use aligns with what users were told at the point of collection.

  - Remember that trust is hard to earn, but it' easy to lose.

- **Build Relationships with Data Gatekeepers:** Sometimes, the best integration strategy isn't technical, it's personal. Develop relationships with colleagues in IT, data science, CRM, or marketing operations. These partners can help you navigate roadblocks, access new datasets, and advocate for better systems.

Perfect integration may not be possible, but consistent planning, documentation, and communication can get you close enough to support reliable, actionable insights.

STRUCTURED DATA COLLECTION CHECKLIST

✓ Apply consistent tags and metadata to every content piece.

✓ Set up event tracking for key user actions.

✓ Maintain naming consistency across campaigns and platforms.

✓ Regularly audit your setup to find gaps, errors, or outdated tracking.

How to Collect and Prepare Unstructured Content Data

While structured data tells you *how* users behave, unstructured data helps you understand *what* they're interacting with. Analyzing the content itself—the articles, videos, images, and podcasts—gives critical context to your performance metrics. Good preparation of unstructured data makes it possible to answer questions like the following:

- What topics drive more downloads?

- Does video length affect watch completion rates?

- How does headline tone influence click-throughs?

Let's take a look at how to do this systematically.

Archive Your Content (Don't Rely on URLs Alone)

It's tempting to assume you can always "just pull the content later" from a website or CMS. But content changes over time—titles get updated, articles are retired, pages move.

As early as possible in the process of developing your program, create a structured archive that includes

- Full text of articles and blog posts

- Titles, subtitles, and author bylines

- Images or videos used within content

- Associated metadata (publish date, topic tags, campaign names)

- Transcripts for video and audio content when possible

Assign the task of creating this structured archive to your content manager (or senior content writer/editor). They bring

- **Organizational Chops:** Comfort defining and maintaining clear folder hierarchies, file-naming conventions, and version control

- **Metadata Fluency:** Experience tagging content with topics, dates, campaign names, and author info so nothing gets "lost"

- **CMS Know-How:** Familiarity with your publishing system (WordPress, Drupal, etc.) to export full texts, images, and assets

- **Attention to Detail:** Ensuring transcripts, thumbnails, and auxiliary files (PDFs, infographics) are correctly saved and linked to the parent item

In practice, your content manager sets up the archive structure and taxonomy standards, and then your writer/editor (or a dedicated content analyst) populates each folder with the text, media, and metadata, creating a "single source of truth" that makes analysis (and future audits) fast and reliable.

Tip   For video content, export both the media file (if possible) and the transcript. Text-based analysis of transcripts can reveal patterns you can't spot just from viewer stats.

Organize Content Attributes for Analysis

To analyze content meaningfully, you'll need to capture structured *descriptions* of the unstructured material.

Key content attributes to record are

- **Format** (e.g., article, infographic, explainer video, podcast episode)

- **Topic or theme** (e.g., AI in healthcare, alumni success stories)

- **Tone** (e.g., formal, conversational, humorous)

- **Length** (word count for text, minutes for audio/video)

- **Intended audience** (if known)

- **Purpose or funnel stage** (e.g., renewal solicitation, donor appreciation or awareness stage, decision stage, etc.)

Table 4-6 suggests ways to begin thinking about useful content attributes to record.

Table 4-6. *Examples of content attributes*

Content Title	Format	Topic	Tone	Length	Audience
"How AI Is Changing Classrooms"	Blog post	AI in education	Conversational	1,200 words	Educators
"Inside the Admissions Process"	Video	College admissions	Professional	5 minutes	Prospective students

Standardize and Clean Your Data

If you're manually tagging or categorizing content, standardization is crucial.

For example:

- Don't mix terms like "AI," "artificial intelligence," and "machine learning" interchangeably.

- Stick to pre-agreed tone labels (e.g., only "formal," "casual," "humorous," etc.)

- Define clear word count or time thresholds for classifying "short" vs. "long" content.

This makes later analysis—like grouping all "long-form articles" or "humorous social posts"—accurate and easy.

Tip   Document your definitions clearly. Create a mini "content coding manual" that anyone working with the data can understand.

UNSTRUCTURED DATA COLLECTION CHECKLIST

✓ Save full versions of published content, not just URLs.

✓ Record key attributes like format, topic, tone, and length.

✓ Standardize categories for consistent analysis.

✓ Maintain transcripts for video and audio content when possible.

Common Data Collection Challenges (and How to Fix Them)

Even with the best intentions, content teams often run into issues that make analysis harder later. Recognizing these challenges early—and setting up safeguards—can save major headaches down the line.

Table 4-7 lists some of the most common pitfalls in content data collection, along with practical ways to address them.

Table 4-7. *Common data collection challenges and solutions*

Challenge	What It Looks Like	How to Fix It
Inconsistent tagging	Content pieces categorized differently across teams or systems.	Create a shared taxonomy guide; require tagging before publishing.
Missing or incomplete tracking	Important actions (e.g., downloads, scrolls) aren't captured.	Conduct regular audits; add tracking tags where missing.
Outdated or conflicting metadata	Titles, topics, or audience tags are inconsistent or obsolete.	Standardize metadata fields and clean legacy records.

(continued)

Table 4-7. *(continued)*

Challenge	What It Looks Like	How to Fix It
Fragmented data across platforms	Web, social, email, and CRM data aren't linked.	Use consistent UTM parameters and IDs; integrate tools when possible.
Poor archiving of content	No access to historical versions of pages, videos, or text.	Archive content systematically at the time of publishing.
Lack of data ownership	No clear responsibility for maintaining data quality.	Assign a content data steward or QA owner.
Privacy and compliance risks	Collecting user data without consent or mishandling sensitive data.	Follow GDPR, CCPA, and FERPA (Family Educational Rights and Privacy Act) rules; anonymize or aggregate personal information.
JavaScript blocking and script errors	Analytics tags don't fire for users with ad blockers or page errors.	Implement server-side tracking fallbacks; use consent banners to explain analytics benefits.

A FOUR-STEP DATA HYGIENE CYCLE

1. **Plan** your tracking strategy around key user journeys.

2. **Implement** tags, metadata rules, and archiving workflows.

3. **Audit** regularly to spot missing events or mis-tags.

4. **Refine** your setup based on audit findings and new content types.

This cycle keeps data clean and your team aligned over time.

Additional Tips for Smoother Data Collection

A small investment in setting standards now prevents lost opportunities and costly cleanup efforts later. Here are a few more ideas to help you make sure your data is clean when you're ready to analyze it:

- **Plan tracking before launching content**, not after. It's easier to tag a landing page correctly up front than retroactively.

- **Use checklists for new campaigns** to confirm that all content and performance data will be captured.

- **Set quarterly reviews** to spot issues early, especially after big website redesigns or CMS migrations. Small data collection problems can quickly become overwhelming ones.

- **Collaborate across teams**—content creators, marketers, analysts, and IT all have a piece of the puzzle.

Research suggests that poor data quality has been shown to reduce decision-making effectiveness, inflate costs, and increase the risk of misinterpretation in analytics.[3] Spending time to do things right from the start will pay dividends later.

---

[3] Redman, T. C. *Data Quality: The Field Guide*. Digital Press, 2001.

Workbook Exercise: Content Data Collection Audit

Before you can optimize or analyze content performance, you need to know where you stand.

This audit exercise helps you take inventory of your current content data practices and spot easy wins for improvement.

Instructions

Fill out Table 4-8 based on your organization's current practices. Be honest! This exercise is meant to help you prioritize next steps. Ideally, make this a team exercise.

Table 4-8. *Content data collection audit table*

Area	Current Practice	Notes/Gaps Identified
Structured event tracking	(e.g., Are scrolls, downloads, and video plays tracked?)	
CMS metadata consistency	(e.g., Are all posts tagged with topic and format?)	
Content archiving practices	(e.g., Do you save full text and assets for all published pieces?)	
Social media content tracking	(e.g., Are UTM parameters used on all social links?)	
CRM/content integration	(e.g., Can you track content's influence on leads or conversions?)	
Privacy compliance	(e.g., Are you handling user data in a way that's compliant with the law, industry standards, and/ or company policies?)	
Ownership and maintenance	(e.g., Who maintains the data? Are audits scheduled?)	

Reflection Questions

Once your audit is complete, turn it into an opportunity to have an honest discussion with your team about your weaknesses and strengths as well as risks and opportunities. Use these questions to start the conversation:

- Which areas have the strongest coverage today?
- Which areas present the highest risk or present the greatest opportunity if improved?
- What small change could you implement this month to strengthen your data collection?
- Who needs to be involved to maintain and improve data quality across teams?

Use these if you want to take a deeper dive:

- What surprised you most during this inventory?
- Which gap would have the biggest impact if closed?
- Which single change could you implement this week?
- Who do you need to involve next to act on these findings?

Tip   Start with one quick win—like standardizing UTM parameters or updating your tagging guide. Building momentum early makes larger improvements easier later.

Integrating the Team

Effective data collection isn't just a technical challenge; it's a team effort.

Each role on a content team has a part to play in capturing accurate, usable data that fuels meaningful analytics and smart decision-making.

Strong data collection doesn't happen in isolation; it's the product of cross-functional collaboration. Table 4-9 lists the key roles and how they each ensure your data pipelines stay accurate, complete, and aligned with business needs.

Table 4-9. *Key roles in the data collection process*

Role	Potential Responsibilities
Content analyst	Define key content metrics; monitor day-to-day data accuracy and flag inconsistencies.
Content strategist	Set content taxonomy standards (topics, audience segments, funnel stages) that support strategic analysis.
SEO specialist	Ensure URLs, metadata, and tagging practices support SEO tracking and performance measurement.
Data analyst	Validate event tracking setup; clean and prepare structured data for analysis; advise on connecting disparate data sources.
Content writer/editor	Apply standardized tags and metadata when publishing; assist with consistent categorization of unstructured content.
Graphic designer/ videographer	Organize and archive visual assets properly; ensure video and multimedia files are labeled and tracked for performance.
Social media manager	Use consistent UTM tagging for campaign links; track engagement metrics across platforms; archive social posts tied to major campaigns.
Project manager	Maintain documentation of tagging standards, event tracking plans, and audit schedules; coordinate across content, IT, and analytics teams.

(continued)

Table 4-9. (*continued*)

Role	Potential Responsibilities
UX designer	Identify critical user interactions worth tracking (e.g., scroll depth, form interactions); collaborate on designing testable content experiences.
Analytics manager	Oversee the end-to-end data collection framework; ensure alignment with analytics strategy and business reporting needs.

Budget-Friendly Approaches to Data Collection and Preparation

Even with limited resources, you can build a robust content data program that drives reliable insights. These tips help you ensure data quality, maintain momentum, and prioritize investments where they matter most.

Focus on Your Most Important Journeys

- Track only the key content experiences tied to business goals (e.g., event sign-ups, downloads, applications).

- Resist the urge to "track everything" right away.

Use Free or Low-Cost Tools Smartly

- Google Analytics 4, Google Tag Manager (GTM), and free CRM tools (like HubSpot's free tier) offer strong out-of-the-box capabilities.

- Free surveys (like Google Forms or basic SurveyMonkey) can capture audience feedback.

- Consider running user tests to identify usability issues—no lab or expensive software required.

Cross-Train Internal Staff

- Writers and editors can learn basic tagging practices.

- Content managers can monitor dashboards with minimal technical skills.

- UX and IT staff can jointly design event tracking strategies.

Audit Quarterly; Improve Gradually

- Don't try to fix everything at once.

- Start by auditing one metric or platform (e.g., Are all downloads properly tracked?) and expand.

Consider Contract Help for Setups

- Hiring a freelance analytics consultant to set up your events properly can save more money long-term than struggling through an incomplete or broken setup.

Document As You Go

- Build lightweight guides for tagging, tracking, and reporting.

- Create clear documentation to prevent knowledge loss when teams change or grow.

Ideally, you might aspire to be able to track reader/viewer behavior down to the individual level, but if your budget doesn't allow for this level of focus, the capacity to see and evaluate changes in behavior in the aggregate may be enough. For example, having the ability to correlate increases in click-through rates in videos with a call to action to an increase in application rates or revenue may be all you need to justify an increase in your capacity to produce those videos—even if you don't know exactly *who* is clicking.

And finally, keep in mind that you don't have to solve every problem today. Start by collecting clean, consistent data for your top five to ten content types and improve over time.

Final Thoughts

Strong, well-planned data collection is the first step toward strong content analytics and a deeper analysis of who is using your content and why. When you capture structured and unstructured data consistently, you lay the groundwork for

- Answering better research questions

- Uncovering actionable insights

- Reporting clearly to stakeholders

- Planning future content with confidence

If you've done this kind of work before, you know that it's far easier to start with a clear plan that involves all your stakeholders and is audited on a regular basis than it is to go hunting for data only when you need to build a dashboard or write a report.

The key to an effective analytics program is to create a solid foundation for consistent, incremental growth and improvement, not something you turn to only when the alarm bells start ringing.

It's only when you've got a clear purpose in mind for your analytics program and a robust dataset that the analytics part of your content analytics program can begin. We'll turn our attention to that in the next chapter.

PART II

Building the Analytics Toolkit

CHAPTER 5

Analyzing Content Performance

You've gathered a wealth of data. You've meticulously tagged your content. Your dashboards are brimming with numbers. You've identified your key challenges, and you have clear research questions. Now what?

Data without interpretation is just noise. The true power of a content analytics program lies not in the data itself but in the insights and actions that you derive from it. In this chapter, you'll walk through the process of transforming raw metrics into meaningful insights by

- Making sense of structured content data

- Comparing performance in a fair and meaningful way

- Identifying patterns while avoiding the pitfalls of noise and vanity metrics

- Knowing when to seek the expertise of a data professional

You won't need to be a statistician to effectively analyze content performance, but you will need a clear objective, curiosity, and discipline to align insights with your business goals. However, if you do need a statistician, we'll explore that option too.

© Russ Bahorsky 2026
R. Bahorsky, *The Fundamentals of Content Analytics,*
https://doi.org/10.1007/979-8-8688-2601-6_5

Making Sense of Structured Content Data

Structured data that tells you about users' behaviors—page views, scroll depth, click-through rates, video completions—provides the raw material that you'll need for effective content analysis, but simply looking at numbers isn't enough. Good analysis starts with asking the kind of actionable framing questions we explored in Chapter 2 and understanding how to use the data you collect to answer them or to understand why users are behaving the way they do and what aspects of your content can influence those behaviors in a meaningful way:

- What are we measuring, and why?

- What content pieces or groups are we comparing?

- What behaviors signal success or a need for change?

Before diving into specifics, let's take another look at some of the data you'll need to make sense of how users are responding to your content.

Key Content Performance Metrics

Table 5-1 lists some of the most common (and useful) metrics you'll encounter.

Table 5-1. *Content metrics and what they measure*

Metric	What It Measures	Example
Page views	How often a page is loaded	10,000 views of a campaign landing page
Time on page	Average time users spend on a content page	3 minutes spent on a long-form article
Scroll depth	How far users scroll down a page	70% average scroll on an explainer piece
Click-through rate (CTR)	% of users who clicked a link or button	15% CTR on a "Download Now" button
Bounce rate	% of users who left without interacting further	60% bounce rate on a blog post
Conversion rate	% of users who completed a goal action (download, sign-up, etc.)	5% of visitors downloaded the brochure
Video completion rate	% of users who watched a video all the way through	40% completion for a 2-minute video

Keep in mind, however, that no single metric tells the whole story. You'll need to look at multiple metrics together to answer your research question and to understand what impact your content is having on your user. Relying on just one piece of the puzzle, like page views, can lead you to make assumptions about your users, your content, or even your team that are deeply flawed or serve no practical purpose.

Why Multiple Metrics Matter

Different metrics capture different aspects of user behavior. For instance, page views show how many people visited your content, while time on page indicates how engaged they were. Bounce rate reveals how many users left without interacting further, and conversion rate shows how many completed a desired action. By examining these metrics together, you can get a much clearer view of user engagement and their satisfaction with your content.

Metrics can also influence each other. A high bounce rate might seem negative, but if paired with a high conversion rate, it could indicate that users are quickly finding what they need and completing their goals. Conversely, a high time on page with low conversions might suggest that while users are engaged, they aren't taking the actions you need them to take to meet your objectives. Understanding these relationships helps you interpret data more accurately.

MINI CASE: ANALYTICS AS A DIAGNOSTIC TOOL

For one news site, page views were up 50%, but time on page fell 30%. An analysis by device type showed that mobile users were exhibiting a quick scroll-and-exit pattern, while desktop users were sticking around longer. By combining page views + time on page + device type, the team discovered a mobile formatting issue and fixed it, boosting mobile engagement by 25%.

Looking at multiple metrics can help pinpoint specific problems you need to address. For example, if you notice a drop in page views but an increase in time on page, it might indicate that fewer people are visiting, but those who do are more engaged. This could suggest that you need to do a better job of targeting your content to a specific segment of your market.

At this stage of the game, the objective is to understand *why* users behave the way they do. Page views, scroll depth, and conversions are just the by-products of consumers' interests, opinions, and decisions—shaped by emotion, timing, social influence, and habit. While some behaviors like conversion rates can be an indication that your content is doing its job, it's important to remember that a prospect's decision to purchase a product, apply, or donate to your organization is often a complex one. If you've read Chapter 3 on journey mapping, you're already thinking about that decision-making process as a funnel or a continuum along which your lead is presented with different content at a variety of stages in that process. The process can be complex, including invitations to connect with a chatbot or even a live human being, and it might even involve post-conversion phases intended to encourage a subsequent purchase or a renewal, but it could also be a simple three-step process that involves an awareness stage, a consideration stage, and a decision stage.

To understand *why* some users stick around and others bail out on relevant content, you need more than raw numbers. Take a look at "Rethinking Cognitive Load Theory" to get a better understanding of one theory of how people process information.

RETHINKING COGNITIVE LOAD THEORY: WHY SOME CONTENT KEEPS USERS ENGAGED AND SOME DOESN'T

Cognitive Load Theory explains that people have a limited capacity for processing information at any given time.[1]

If content is too complex, too dense, or poorly organized, users are more likely to disengage, leading to high bounce rates, low scroll depth, or abandoned videos.

When analyzing content performance

- Low engagement may not mean the topic was wrong; it could mean the presentation was overwhelming.

---

[1] John Sweller, "Cognitive Load During Problem Solving: Effects on Learning," *Cognitive Science* 12, no. 2 (1988): 257–285.

- Simplifying layouts, breaking blocks of text into smaller pieces, and reducing unnecessary distractions often lead to better content performance.

Marketing and content managers tend to interpret this idea as a less-is-more approach to keeping users engaged and to analyzing why users aren't engaging with content. However, this isn't exactly what Cognitive Load Theory suggests. The theory actually advocates for optimizing cognitive load or finding the right balance.

Caution   While less may be enough for most of the people seeing your content, it may not be true at all for your best customers or prospects. Your most motivated leads are likely to be a small percentage of the people your content reaches, and their appetite for the content you create may be substantially more robust. Even though it may seem counterintuitive, always consider testing content that is longer and more substantial. Engaging more effectively with your best prospects, who may be further along in their journey with you, may net far better results than trying to convert those who are just mildly interested.

Grouping Metrics Meaningfully

Keep in mind that it's not just structured data that can be grouped. You may also find it useful to group your content or unstructured data together rather than just analyzing one piece of content by itself. This approach allows you to see how individual pieces of content are working together, which will help uncover broader trends and lead to better strategic decisions.

Consider grouping your content by

- **Topic:** For example, compare cybersecurity tips with online learning strategies. This helps you understand which topics resonate more with your audience.

- **Format:** Analyze the performance of articles vs. videos vs. infographics. Different formats may engage users in unique ways, revealing preferences and effectiveness.

- **Audience Segment:** Examine how content performs among different segments of your audience, such as prospective students vs. alumni donors. Tailoring content to specific segments can dramatically enhance engagement and relevance.

- **Funnel Stage:** Assess content based on its role in the user journey, such as awareness, consideration, and decision stages. This helps you optimize content for each stage of the funnel by helping you address specific concerns a reader or viewer might have at each stage.

For example, instead of asking, "How did this one blog post do?", ask, "How did all our thought leadership articles on AI perform compared with our student success stories?" Grouping content in this manner allows you to see the bigger picture, allocate resources more effectively, and tailor strategies to different types of content or users.

BEHAVIORAL SEGMENTATION: WHEN ONE SIZE DOES NOT FIT ALL

Are your subscribers and non-subscribers seeing the same content? If you work for a university, are your prospective students seeing the same appeals you send to your alumni?

Audience segmentation is a powerful tool for gaining insight into your audience when you know that they're not all coming to your organization for the same reasons.

Even with basic tools like Google Analytics 4, your CMS, or email platform, you can segment your audience based on how users interact with your content. For example, you might filter by

- New vs. returning visitors

- Traffic source

- Users who visited more than three pages in a session

These behavioral segments help you understand which types of users are engaging most deeply—or dropping off early. If you're working with a CRM or marketing automation tool, consider layering in audience traits like industry, job title, or stage in the customer journey to make your insights even more targeted.

Additionally, a 2025 study suggests that Panasonic was able to improve responses to its ads by 30% after discovering that purchases often cluster around life events, which highlights how effective analytics can rely on an astute understanding of your user segments and their journeys.[2]

By grouping metrics meaningfully, you can gain deeper insights into your content's performance, identify areas for improvement, and make data-driven decisions that enhance your overall strategy.

---

[2] Google Marketing Platform. "Panasonic Improves Return on Advertising Spend by 30% with Google Analytics 360." Accessed July 14, 2025. `https://services.google.com/fh/files/misc/case-study-panasonic-improves-return-on-advertising-spend-with-google-analytics-360.pdf`

Reading Trends Over Time

Snapshot reports of moments in time are helpful for quick insights, but the most powerful revelations often come from analyzing trends over time. By examining how your data evolves, you can uncover deeper patterns and make more informed decisions.

Consider the following aspects when analyzing trends:

- **Month-Over-Month Changes:** Observe how engagement metrics shift from one month to the next. For example, did engagement rise after you introduced new calls to action (CTAs)? These changes can indicate the effectiveness of your strategies and help you refine them.

- **Seasonal Patterns:** Identify recurring trends that align with specific times of the year. Does your content traffic dip every summer? Recognizing these patterns can help you plan your content calendar more effectively and anticipate seasonal or cyclical fluctuations.

- **Campaign Timelines:** Track the impact of specific campaigns over time. Did webinar sign-ups spike after launching a particular blog series and for how long? Understanding the timeline of your campaigns can reveal which initiatives drive the most engagement and conversions and how to time follow-up efforts.

While small fluctuations day to day are normal, it's crucial to focus on longer-term patterns that suggest real shifts in user behavior. These trends provide a more reliable basis for strategic decisions and help you adapt to changing audience preferences.

You may also consider thinking of your lead-to-conversion process as a product of finding an optimum number of exposures. The "mere exposure effect" suggests that increased exposure to a product can positively influence a customer's likelihood of purchasing it.

Studies have shown that content like online reviews and customer engagement significantly impact purchase decisions. For instance, the Spiegel Research Center, a research group based at Northwestern University, found that the more customers interact with online reviews, the higher the likelihood of purchase. The effect is even more pronounced for higher-priced items.[3]

Thinking of your content as helping cultivate a relationship over time may be the key to understanding how it influences your target audience's behavior.

Comparing Content Performance

Once you've organized and reviewed your core metrics, the next step is to identify ways to compare them. In other words, you'll want to be able to understand how different content pieces, formats, or topics perform relative to each other. But comparison only works if you compare fairly.

How to Compare Content Meaningfully

Rather than comparing any two random content pieces, group them logically:

- Compare categories of content that share the same goal (e.g., blog posts meant to drive downloads).

- Compare similar time frames (e.g., content launched during the same quarter or campaign period).

---

[3] Spiegel Research Center, Northwestern University. *The Impact of Online Reviews on Consumer Purchasing.* Evanston, IL: Spiegel Research Center, Northwestern University, 2019. `https://example.org/online-reviewsreport`

- Normalize comparisons by audience exposure when necessary (e.g., a post emailed to 5,000 people can't be directly compared with a post emailed to 50,000 people without adjusting expectations). Get in the habit of thinking in terms of percentages and not raw numbers.

Table 5-2 offers some ideas for making better content comparisons.

Table 5-2. *Content comparison criteria*

Good Comparison	Poor Comparison
Blog post vs. blog post in the same series	Blog post vs. landing page targeting different audiences
Videos posted to the same social channel	Video posted on YouTube vs. article posted on LinkedIn
Content from the same campaign time frame	Content from two completely different seasons or promotions

Benchmarking vs. Internal Baselines

When evaluating your content performance—especially as you're beginning to get a content analytics program off the ground—you might wonder: "Should we use industry benchmarks?" While they can provide a helpful rough guide, your most valuable benchmark is your own historical performance. Keep in mind that there's a lot that an industry benchmark might not be telling you. The average email click-through rate may be about 2.4%, but that average can vary by industry, and what's far more important is how those CTRs differ for each of your own audience segments.

Better questions might be "What's the CTR of our most motivated customers and how many of them are there in our database?" Or you might ask, "At what response rate is it no longer profitable for us to continue to invest in converting a prospect who's mildly interested into one who's highly motivated?"

In other words, you might rely on your industry or competitors' benchmarks at first, but your goal should be to shift your focus to your organization's internal baselines as fast as possible, like a three- to six-month average of your key metrics, broken down by content type or channel. From there, you can track real improvements, which will create opportunities for

- **Generating Personalized Insights:** Industry benchmarks offer a general idea of what to expect, but they don't account for the unique aspects of your audience, content, and strategy. Your own historical data provides a more accurate and relevant point of comparison.

- **Marking Real Progress:** Tracking improvements against your own baselines allows you to celebrate genuine progress. For example, if your previous campaign videos averaged a 30% completion rate and your latest batch hits 45%, that's a significant improvement—even if industry averages suggest 50% is typical. This shows that your strategies are working and evolving in a meaningful way.

- **Diagnosing Unexpected Problems:** Comparing current performance with past results helps you identify real issues. If a metric suddenly drops, you can investigate what has changed and address it effectively. This approach is more actionable than relying solely on external benchmarks.

By prioritizing internal baselines, you can gain deeper insights into your content performance, celebrate real achievements, and make more informed decisions to drive continuous improvement.

Spotting Patterns, Outliers, and Trends

The bottom line is that raw numbers are just a starting point. Great analysts learn to spot the stories hidden within patterns, to see trends, and to recognize outliers and other anomalies. By identifying these elements, you can uncover valuable insights that will help you make more informed decisions and create meaningful change that you can offer your stakeholders.

How to Spot Meaningful Patterns

To find meaningful patterns in your data, consider the following:

- **Look for Consistency Across Formats**: Examine whether certain formats consistently outperform others. For example, are short videos consistently outperforming long articles? This can indicate user preferences and help you optimize your content strategy.

- **Spot Topic Trends**: Identify subjects that drive higher engagement, such as downloads or shares, regardless of format. Are certain topics consistently popular? Understanding these trends can guide your content creation and marketing efforts.

- **Monitor User Journey Milestones**: Track user behavior throughout their journey. Are users consistently dropping off after interacting with a certain type of page? Recognizing these milestones can help you pinpoint areas for improvement and enhance the user experience.

Pattern-Hunting Framework

Here are three practical strategies you (and your data analyst, if you have one) can use to surface meaningful content performance patterns without needing advanced tools or statistical expertise:

1. **Cluster:** Group your content by shared characteristics—like topic, format, or intended audience segment. Then compare performance across clusters using metrics like click-through rate (CTR), time on page, or conversion rate.

    Example: Do listicles consistently outperform deep-dive articles on mobile devices? Does "student success" content yield higher engagement than "policy updates"?

2. **Correlate:** Use a correlation matrix to spot which metrics tend to rise or fall together.
    Example: Does scroll depth strongly correlate with CTA clicks? Or does a longer time on page actually *decrease* downloads for certain formats?

    This kind of pattern can help you identify content types that are absorbing attention but not driving action—or vice versa.

3. **Visualize:** Create time-based heatmaps, line graphs, or bar charts to highlight when and where users are most active.

    Plot engagement by day of week, hour of day, or content publish date to uncover temporal trends.

    Example: Are explainer videos getting longer views when published midweek? Do readers abandon longer articles after three to four paragraphs regardless of topic?

For more help developing correlation matrices or visualizing data, see Appendix B.

Finally, when patterns start to emerge, ask: *Are these repeatable, meaningful, and tied to business goals?* If yes, they're worth turning into hypotheses for future content experiments.

Why Patterns Matter

Ultimately, patterns help you make content and distribution choices grounded in evidence, not guesses. By analyzing consistent trends, you can

- **Optimize Content Strategy:** Tailor your content formats and topics to match user preferences, increasing engagement and effectiveness.

- **Enhance User Experience**: Address drop-off points in the user journey to improve retention and satisfaction.

- **Allocate Resources Wisely:** Focus your efforts on areas that consistently perform well, ensuring efficient use of time and budget.

- **Make Effective Predictions**: Adjust your team's or your organization's capacity to meet changing demands.

Visualizing Patterns

When analyzing your data, don't underestimate the value of creating visualizations like graphs or heatmaps that highlight or reveal patterns. Develop a process and a schedule for creating and reviewing these visualizations consistently to spot trends. It's much easier to spot problems and opportunities with the help of a chart than it is to see them in a spreadsheet. They can also be helpful in identifying outliers, the numbers that seem to buck the trend.

Recognizing Outliers and What They Mean

Outliers are data points that behave very differently from the rest of your data. These anomalies can provide valuable insights into your content performance, revealing both opportunities and potential issues.

Examples of Outliers:

- **A Blog Post That Received 10× More Traffic Than Usual:** This could indicate that the topic resonated exceptionally well with your audience or that it was promoted more effectively.

- **A Video with an Unusually Low Completion Rate:** This might suggest that the content didn't engage viewers as expected or that there was an issue with the video's format or delivery.

What Outliers Can Signal:

- **Opportunities:** Outliers can highlight unexpected successes. For example, if a particular topic or format suddenly gains traction, it might be worth exploring further. This could lead to new content strategies that capitalize on these insights.

- **Problems:** Outliers can also indicate issues. For instance, a traffic spike followed by high bounce rates might be caused by misleading metadata or ineffective promotion. Identifying these problems allows you to address them and improve your content strategy.

Responding to Outliers:

Table 5-3 contrasts effective responses to outliers and common errors in interpreting unique data points.

Table 5-3. *Good vs. poor response to outliers*

Good Response to Outliers	Poor Response to Outliers
• **Investigate Causes**: Determine why the outlier occurred. Was it due to metadata, the topic, promotion, or another factor? Understanding the cause helps you make informed decisions.	• **Assume It's a Fluke and Ignore It**: Dismissing outliers as mere anomalies without investigation can lead to missed opportunities and unresolved issues.
• **Adjust Future Content**: If the cause is actionable, use the insights to refine your content strategy. For example, if a specific topic resonated well, consider creating more content around that theme.	• **Chase the Outlier Blindly**: Pursuing outliers without understanding why they occurred can result in ineffective strategies and wasted resources.

When you identify an outlier, take the time to analyze it thoroughly. Look at various factors such as metadata, topic relevance, promotion methods, and audience behavior. Use these insights to make data-driven adjustments to your content strategy, ensuring that you capitalize on opportunities and address any problems effectively. For example, direct marketers typically suppress customers who haven't paid for previous purchases from their mailing lists, but if you have flagged a group of "bad actors" from your own list of customers, have your UX expert take a closer look at what's going on. You may find that your website is difficult to navigate or doesn't address a common question or that an online form has a significant flaw. Any of these issues could turn an enthusiastic customer into a disgruntled one very quickly.

By recognizing and responding to outliers thoughtfully, you can enhance your content performance and improve your relationship with your audience or your customers.

Not every outlier demands action, but every outlier deserves *at least a second look.*

WHEN LOW-TRAFFIC CONTENT STILL MATTERS

Not all content is designed for mass appeal, and that's okay. Some pieces are intentionally created for a very small, high-value audience: a technical onboarding guide for enterprise clients, a letter from a university president to major donors, or a resource for journalists covering your industry.

These assets may generate little traffic, low engagement, or minimal conversions in your reports, but they can still be strategically essential.

Tip   Don't judge every piece of content by the same performance standards.

If content serves a non-scalable but high-impact purpose, consider excluding it from your general performance reports or flagging it as "strategic niche content."

Doing so helps your analytics tell a clearer story about what's working, without penalizing the content that's doing a different—but equally important—job.

Avoiding Analysis Traps

Outliers often highlight hidden problems or opportunities, and if they're misinterpreted, they can also lead you down the wrong analytical path. That's why it's important to stay alert to common traps.

Knowing what to watch for makes your insights sharper and protects your team from making decisions based on false signals.

Here are three of the biggest analysis traps to avoid:

1. **Chasing Vanity Metrics**

   Vanity metrics are numbers that *look* impressive but don't actually move your business forward.

   Examples of Vanity Metrics:

   - High page views but low conversion rates

   - Lots of video views with extremely short watch times

   - High email open rates with low click-through rates

   Ask yourself: *"Does this metric actually relate to a meaningful goal (like downloads, sign-ups, inquiries, or revenue)?"* If not, take a moment to celebrate if you like, but realize that you have a lot more work to do.

   Additionally, studies in marketing analytics have shown that overreliance on surface-level engagement metrics, like impressions or click-throughs, can lead teams to optimize for short-term attention rather than long-term conversion or trust.[4]

2. **Mistaking Correlation for Causation**

   Just because two things happen at the same time doesn't mean one caused the other.

---

[4] Davenport, T. H., and Jeanne G. Harris. *Competing on Analytics: The New Science of Winning.* Harvard Business Review Press, 2007.

Example:

Traffic to your blog rises sharply the same week a new ad campaign launches. Was it the ad campaign that caused the spike or something else (e.g., a trending news story about your sector)?

To avoid this error, always look for multiple pieces of evidence before claiming cause-and-effect relationships. Consider other potential factors and use statistical methods or controlled experiments to establish a more reliable connection between variables.

3. **Overinterpreting Small Data Samples**

Small datasets are especially vulnerable to random noise.

Example:

A whitepaper landing page gets two downloads one day, zero the next, and four the day after.

It's tempting to call this a "trend," but randomness likely plays a bigger role when sample sizes are small.

Use longer time frames or larger groups to identify real patterns.

What to Do When the Data Doesn't Add Up

Even in well-maintained systems, your content data will sometimes look wrong or just weird. A spike in conversions that doesn't match traffic, a dip in time on page without a change in content, or a missing metric for a whole campaign can all throw off your analysis.

If that's what you're seeing, here's what to do:

- **Double-Check Everything:** Don't jump to conclusions—or explain trends in meetings—until you've confirmed the data is complete.

- **Troubleshoot for Gaps in Tagging or Setup**: Was a tag removed? Was traffic filtered out by mistake? Did a campaign launch early or late? Was the content delivered correctly?

- **Compare Across Sources:** If something looks wrong in GA4, check your email platform, CMS logs, or CRM. One dataset may provide clarity.

- **Use Your Team:** This can be a big task that requires a focused approach. Break the job up into smaller parts and give your team permission to set everything else aside.

- **Document and Move On When Needed**: Not every gap can be filled. In those cases, flag the issue, document the limitation, and focus on the most trustworthy metrics available.

If a pattern seems too good—or too bad—to be true, it often is. Asking *"How confident are we in this number?"* is a leadership skill, not a technical one. In other words, there will always be some degree of uncertainty in the data you collect, so it's important to cultivate a sense of when to move ahead and when to raise a red flag.

MISLEADING SUCCESS: HIGH CLICKS, LOW CONVERSIONS

A company's marketing team ran a paid campaign promoting a free ebook download. They invested heavily in social ads with bold headlines like

"Download Our Free Guide to Skyrocket Your Sales!"

The campaign results initially looked impressive:

- Click-Through Rate (CTR): 6% (far above their usual 2–3%)

- Landing Page Traffic: 50,000 visitors over two weeks

The team celebrated, citing the high CTR as evidence that the content and promotion were highly effective.

The Problem

When they looked deeper into actual outcomes

- **Download Completion Rate:** Only 1.2% of visitors actually completed the download form.

- **Bounce Rate:** Over 70% of visitors left the page without interacting beyond the initial click.

- **Lead Quality:** Of the few who downloaded, most were not a fit for their product (wrong company size, wrong region).

Root Cause

The ads were *too broadly appealing*—designed for maximum clicks, not for attracting the *right* audience or setting the right expectations about the ebook's focus. The content didn't match the users' true needs once they clicked through. The result? Wasted ad spend and low lead quality.

Takeaway

High engagement at the first step (clicks) doesn't mean success if it doesn't lead to meaningful action (downloads, sign-ups, sales). Always connect top-of-funnel metrics to down-funnel outcomes before declaring a campaign successful.

Recognizing and Avoiding Common Biases in Content Analysis

Even when data is clean, human thinking can introduce bias. Your own thoughts about the product or service you're trying to sell or your relationship to the organization you're trying to promote can influence how you read the data showing you how your customers think and behave. It can lead you to draw conclusions too quickly or minimize the importance of test results that seem counterintuitive to you.

Table 5-4 lists some common cognitive biases to watch for and how to counter them when analyzing content.

Table 5-4. *Types of bias in content analytics*

Bias	What It Looks Like in Content Analysis	How to Counteract It
Confirmation bias	Only seeing evidence that supports your original belief ("Our blogs always work best!")	Assign a "devil's advocate" to question early assumptions.
Recency bias	Overemphasizing the latest content or campaign performance	Compare over longer periods (e.g., quarter-over-quarter).
Survivorship bias	Only analyzing successful content without reviewing failures	Examine both high and low performers.

(continued)

Table 5-4. *(continued)*

Bias	What It Looks Like in Content Analysis	How to Counteract It
Attribution bias	Misidentifying the cause of an outcome (blaming the copy on an underperforming landing page when a confusing layout may have been the cause)	Look at the whole user journey when possible or brainstorm all the possible variables with your team.
Anchoring bias	Letting early data overly influence conclusions ("The first webinar underperformed, so webinars don't work.")	Review cumulative data over time, not just initial results.

A robust analytics team that feels empowered to ask difficult questions can be your best ally in overcoming analytical bias.

Use team analysis sessions to ask simple questions like

- *"What data are we missing?"*

- *"What other explanations could fit this pattern?"*

Fighting bias isn't about being perfect; it's about staying aware and curious. And remember that going back to the drawing board with your content analysis program will always be easier on you than building a business plan based on faulty research.

Case Study: Using Content Analysis to Refine Strategy

A mid-sized healthcare publisher noticed something worrying: their long-form "Faculty Profile" articles, meant to highlight doctors and researchers at their institution, were getting decent page views but extremely low engagement.

Using GA4, they analyzed

- Scroll depth (how far readers scrolled through the articles)

- Time on page (how long users stayed)

- Call-to-action clicks (clicks to contact the featured faculty or learn more)

Findings

- **Average Scroll Depth**: Only 30%.

- **Average Time on Page**: Under 40 seconds (for articles averaging 1,500 words).

- Very few readers ever reached the embedded CTA buttons at the bottom of the articles.

Insight

Readers were abandoning the articles early, long before seeing the important calls to action.

Action Taken

The team redesigned the Faculty Profiles:

- Broke up long text into short sections with subheadings

- Added pull quotes and key facts at the top

- Moved CTAs into the first screen of the page ("above the fold")

- Shortened overall article length by 30% while preserving key information

Results (Measured Three Months After Relaunch)

- Scroll depth increased by 45%.

- Average time on page doubled.

- CTA clicks increased by 80%.

The data-driven redesign not only improved engagement but also supported business goals by generating more inquiries for partnerships and speaking engagements.

Key Takeaway

Insight without action is wasted effort. Analysis should always lead to a next step: changing strategy, optimizing formats, or reallocating resources based on evidence.

Workbook Exercise: Analyzing a Sample Content Dataset

Use the simple worksheet approach in Table 5-5 to practice turning data into insights and insights into action.

Table 5-5. *Content performance mini-audit worksheet*

Content Piece	Format (Blog, Video, etc.)	Three Metrics You Measured	Observations	Action Recommendation
Example: " The Future of AI in Healthcare"	Blog post	Page views, scroll depth, CTA clicks	High page views, but low scroll depth and low CTA clicks	Redesign for shorter paragraphs; move CTA higher on page.

Guided Prompts:

- Which content formats are performing best overall?

- Which specific metrics show strength or a problem?

- What is one small change you could make to optimize future content based on this data?

Tip   Pick one piece of content this month to optimize based on real data and track what happens next.

Integrating the Team

Content analysis isn't just the job of a data specialist. Each team member can (and should) contribute insights based on their expertise.

Table 5-6 lists the different roles that support a healthy, actionable content analysis process.

Table 5-6. *Team roles in content performance analytics*

Role	Responsibilities
Content analyst	Build reports, track core content metrics, flag trends or anomalies.
Content strategist	Connect insights to larger business goals; recommend strategic shifts based on data.
SEO specialist	Monitor search visibility trends; adjust optimization strategies based on organic performance.

(continued)

Table 5-6. (*continued*)

Role	Responsibilities
Data analyst	Perform deeper segmentation or predictive modeling if needed.
Content writer/editor	Review engagement patterns to refine content style, tone, and structure.
Graphic designer/videographer	Adjust visuals, thumbnails, or video formats based on user engagement data.
Social media manager	Analyze channel-specific content trends and recommend distribution adjustments.
Project manager	Coordinate reporting timelines, share insights across teams, maintain momentum.
UX designer	Analyze behavioral signals (scroll depth, bounce rate) and recommend content experience improvements.
Analytics manager	Oversee data integrity and reporting standards, and ensure insights tie back to key KPIs.

Tip   The best content analysis processes don't just stop at reporting; they feed insights back into the content creation, distribution, and UX design processes.

Budget-Friendly Ideas for Analyzing Content Performance

You don't need a full-time analyst or an expensive business intelligence tool to start analyzing content effectively. Here's how to make the most of limited resources:

- **Focus on a Few Key Metrics**

  Track the most important outcomes related to your business goals first, such as

  - Conversions

  - Engagement (scroll depth, time on page)

  - Shares or saves (for awareness campaigns)

  Don't overwhelm your team with 20 KPIs at the start.

- **Use Built-In Platform Dashboards**

  - Google Analytics 4 offers powerful built-in reports for engagement and conversions.

  - YouTube Studio provides excellent video engagement data.

  - LinkedIn, Facebook, and Instagram offer free, accessible post-level insights.

  You often don't need custom dashboards early on.

- **Hold Regular, Lightweight Insights Meetings**

  - Set up a recurring 30-minute meeting once a month or once a quarter.

  - Quickly review: What's working? What's not? What's next?

- Use simple charts or tables—no need for glossy decks unless you're pitching to the C-suite.

- **Document Small Wins**

  - Track even minor improvements (e.g., "Blog CTR improved by 8% after headline tests").

  - Create a simple "Content Wins" log to build momentum and justify future investment.

Tip   In early stages, momentum and learning matter more than perfect precision. Pick one metric that you want to impact and use your wins to demonstrate the value of further investment in meaningful analytics.

Final Thoughts

Collecting data is only the first half of the journey. The real impact comes when you analyze that data to

- Spot meaningful patterns.

- Recognize what's working and what's not.

- Tie actions back to business outcomes.

- Adapt your content strategy based on evidence.

Good content analysis turns dashboards into decisions. It helps your team create smarter, more engaging, and more effective content over time. It also keeps your research questions clear and your business goals in focus, and above all, it helps you use what you learn to make better decisions about how to move forward.

In the next chapter, we'll look at a powerful, but often overlooked, tool: qualitative analytics. Understanding how it fits into your toolkit can set the stage for profound improvement in your content development efforts.

CHAPTER 6

Qualitative Analytics

Content analytics has long leaned heavily on quantitative methods—page views, click-through rates, bounce rates, conversions—to give analysts insight into the minds of content consumers. These numbers do a good job of telling us *what* happened; however, they're rarely effective at telling us *why*. Why did visitors abandon that page halfway through? Why did an A/B test fail to yield significant results? Why did one article spark a viral conversation while another had no engagement whatsoever?

Qualitative analytics helps answer those "why" questions. By capturing and analyzing the language, emotion, and meaning embedded in user comments, survey responses, interviews, and chat logs, we gain a richer, more nuanced understanding of how content performs and how it's perceived. It's the difference between seeing that a video has low completion rates and hearing users say, "It felt too promotional" or "I didn't understand what the narrator was trying to explain."

Qualitative data helps fill the blind spots that structured metrics leave behind. It also builds empathy with content consumers, especially in situations where it's difficult to remember what it's like to encounter your organization and its brand for the very first time. Where charts and dashboards flatten the user into numbers, qualitative feedback shows you the human side of those users, a perspective that can reveal unmet needs, hidden frustrations, and powerful stories that numbers alone obscure.

© Russ Bahorsky 2026
R. Bahorsky, *The Fundamentals of Content Analytics,*
https://doi.org/10.1007/979-8-8688-2601-6_6

And keep in mind that qualitative analytics does not replace quantitative analysis; it complements it. The most effective content teams rely on both. For example:

- They use *structured* data to identify a drop in form completion rates.

- Then use *qualitative* analysis to understand user friction based on survey responses or chat transcripts.

This chapter will introduce the most common sources of qualitative content data, offer practical methods for analyzing it, and show how to combine these insights with structured data for a fuller picture of performance. You'll also explore real-world examples and get a chance to apply qualitative techniques using a guided workbook exercise.

By the end of this chapter, you'll be better equipped to listen more deeply to your audience, which will give you a clear strategic advantage over your competitors who routinely skip these methods.

Sources of Qualitative Content Feedback

To integrate qualitative analysis into your content analytics program, you first need to know where—and how—to collect open-ended feedback. As Table 6-1 suggests, many organizations already generate a wealth of qualitative data without fully recognizing or using it.

Table 6-1. *Common sources of qualitative feedback*

Source	What You Might Learn
Surveys (open-ended questions)	Pain points, suggestions, emotional tone, usability insights
Website comments	Real-time reactions, sentiment, recurring themes or questions
User interviews	Motivations, expectations, mental models, narrative framing
Chat logs/support tickets	Confusion, common complaints, content gaps
Social media replies	Public sentiment, user language, viral triggers, cultural cues
Usability testing notes	Observed frustration, hesitations, content comprehension issues

Of course, these sources vary in formality and depth. Some are structured (a survey with specific questions); others are opportunistic (comments left on an article). But both are valuable, especially when you think of them as tools to add depth to your analytics or to bring more nuance to your research questions. The key is to treat qualitative feedback as data—something you can systematically collect, analyze, and act on.

Tip   If you use tools like Intercom, Typeform, Google Forms, or any of a variety of social media platforms, you likely already have a growing database of unstructured user feedback. The challenge usually isn't getting the data; it's organizing and interpreting it.

Ethical Considerations

Before we begin exploring the mechanics of collecting qualitative data, it's important to address the ethical responsibility that requires. And if treating other people's data the way you'd like companies to treat yours isn't reason enough to take an ethical approach, remember that breaches of ethical conduct can be ruinous to your organization's reputation and its brand or, at the very least, harmful to your bottom line.

The Facebook–Cambridge Analytica scandal of 2018, for example, involving the improper use of the personal data of millions of Facebook users without their consent, led to a loss of trust, fines and legal fees, and increased oversight and regulatory scrutiny.[1]

That said, when collecting and analyzing qualitative data, especially if it includes personally identifiable information (PII) like names, addresses, and account numbers, it's crucial to follow ethical guidelines:

- Always inform users that feedback may be used for research or analysis.

- Remove or anonymize any names, emails, or sensitive identifiers like gender or race before coding.

- If quoting users in presentations or reports, ensure consent and contextual clarity.

In regulated industries (healthcare, education), qualitative data must be treated with the same privacy standards as structured user data. When in doubt, consult your organization's legal or compliance team to be sure you understand where the lines are drawn for your industry and your organization.

---

[1] Brian Tarran, "What Can We Learn from the Facebook–Cambridge Analytica Scandal?" *Significance* 15, no. 3 (June 2018): 4–5, `https://doi.org/10.1111/j.1740-9713.2018.01139.x`

Finally, it's worth noting that quantitative data often obscures the experience of marginalized users because they're represented in smaller numbers. Qualitative feedback lets you hear directly from voices that may otherwise be underrepresented, ensuring your content serves all your audiences.

Ethical considerations are covered in more detail in Chapter 12.

Techniques for Analyzing Qualitative Content Data

Once you've gathered qualitative feedback, the next step is to analyze it in a systematic and rigorous way. This doesn't require a PhD in qualitative methods, but it does require a framework for identifying patterns, extracting meaning, and making decisions based on what you find.

Thematic Analysis

Thematic analysis is one of the most accessible and widely used methods of analyzing qualitative data. It involves coding the data—tagging portions of text with labels that capture their meaning—and then grouping those codes into themes. Unlike the kind of tagging that you do when you're grouping content by the intentions you have for it as a content creator, thematic coding is a structured process in which labels are applied consistently across a dataset to allow for comparison and synthesis of how your audiences are responding to it.

Here's a step-by-step approach to the process:

1. **Familiarize yourself** with the dataset (read through all responses once).

2. **Generate initial codes** for recurring ideas (e.g., "confusing layout," "helpful video," "too much jargon").

3. **Group codes** into broader themes (e.g., "usability issues," "content clarity," "tone mismatch").

4. **Summarize** each theme with representative quotes and their implications for content strategy.

For example, after analyzing 75 open-ended survey responses about a tutorial page, a content team found two dominant themes:

- "Too technical" (used in 47% of responses)

- "Lacked real examples" (noted by 35%)

As a result, they simplified the language on their tutorial page and added three annotated examples to help users get more out of the content.

Sentiment Analysis

Imagine discovering a sudden spike in negative sentiment in video feedback. Usually, emotional responses precede rational ones, so sentiment analysis focuses on interpreting the tone and emotional content of that feedback first—which could suggest a need for a deeper review of your video content. Often this is done manually (using human judgment to tag positive, negative, or neutral feedback), but it can sometimes be done automatically using text analysis tools (like MonkeyLearn, Lexalytics, or basic NLP (natural language processing) in Python). However, while machine sentiment analysis is fast, it often struggles with sarcasm, ambiguity, or context. Human review is still essential—especially for content involving sensitive topics.

Discourse and Narrative Analysis (Advanced)

For more advanced needs, discourse analysis examines the language people use to frame their problems, reveal deeper beliefs, or express their identity. Narrative analysis looks at the structure of how people tell stories—what they emphasize, omit, or build toward—which can inform how content creators structure testimonials or case studies.

While these methods are more interpretive and often used in academia or UX research, their insights can be invaluable, especially when analyzing content tied to trust, health, or identity.

For example, a narrative analysis of discussion around a redesign project for a university admissions site might reveal that prospective students are framing college not just as a financial decision but as a "rite of passage." This insight could lead to new homepage content focused on personal transformation, not just the economic benefits of a college degree.

Combining Qualitative and Quantitative Insights

Qualitative and quantitative data aren't competing sources of truth; they're complementary. Together, they create a fuller, more strategic view of how content performs and why users behave the way they do. Quantitative data gives you patterns; qualitative data gives you meaning.

Advanced teams often use triangulation—looking for evidence to support a conclusion that seems consistent across multiple data collection methods (e.g., survey comments, chat logs, and A/B tests)—to strengthen their insights and justify major changes.[2]

---

[2] Creswell, J. W., and J. David Creswell. *Research Design: Qualitative, Quantitative, and Mixed Methods Approaches*, 5th ed. Thousand Oaks: SAGE Publications, 2018.

For example, quantitative analytics show that the bounce rate on a "Research Highlights" page is unusually high—72%, compared with the site average of 45%. Additionally, qualitative insights from open-ended responses from a recent user survey reveal comments like

- "I couldn't find what I was looking for."

- "Too much jargon—hard to understand."

An A/B test comparing the original page with a simplified version (featuring clearer headings and lay-friendly summaries) also shows a 30% increase in time on page and a 25% decrease in bounce rate.

Ultimately, all three data sources suggest that the page's content is too complex and not user-friendly, which should point you toward the need for a strategic redesign of the page to improve its clarity and accessibility.

A mixed-methods approach is especially powerful when

- A quantitative signal is ambiguous or surprising (e.g., drop in conversion despite high engagement).

- You're trying to understand the *why* behind a trend (e.g., a particular blog post has exceptional time on page but poor conversions).

- You're preparing for a redesign or major campaign shift and want to uncover unmet needs or emotional cues.

- You want to test hypotheses that come to the surface through user feedback.

By considering both quantitative and qualitative insights as you plan content tests, you'll find it easier to produce more meaningful answers to your research questions.

Using Qualitative Data to Form Hypotheses

Qualitative feedback is often the spark that fuels new content tests. For example:

- Commenters repeatedly say, "This page feels too salesy."

  Hypothesis: A less promotional tone might increase conversions.

  Test: Run an A/B experiment with revised copy that emphasizes user outcomes.

This illustrates a natural handoff:

1. **Qualitative analysis** identifies friction.

2. **Quantitative testing** validates potential solutions.

This approach can also help you refine the research questions you developed in Chapter 2 by giving you the opportunity to ask questions that involve emotional impact, frustrations, aspirations, etc. The five types of research questions can all address issues that involve qualitative aspects.

- **Descriptive**: What themes are emerging in user feedback?

- **Comparative**: How do comments vary by channel or segment?

- **Correlational**: Is negative sentiment linked to low time on page?

- **Causal**: Does changing tone (based on qualitative input) increase engagement?

- **Predictive**: Can user feedback help us anticipate where future users may drop off?

Finally, in analytics, opinion and behavior are two very different things. Don't make the mistake of assuming that someone's opinion or intent to do or not do something has any bearing on what they actually do. It's important to understand what your audiences are thinking, but it's equally important to follow up on those insights with quantitative efforts that measure how they actually behave. For example, a potential buyer may love the idea of your product but never actually buy it. That disconnect can provide you with a goldmine of new research questions and testing ideas.

DISTINGUISHING CONSUMER OPINION FROM CONSUMER BEHAVIOR

Consumer opinion refers to what people say they think or feel about a product, service, or brand. This includes reviews, ratings, and survey responses, reflecting their attitudes and perceptions.

Consumer behavior, on the other hand, involves the actions consumers take, such as purchasing decisions, usage patterns, and engagement with content. It reveals how consumers actually interact with products and services in real-world scenarios.

It's not uncommon for a consumer's opinion to *not* reflect how they behave. Understanding both opinion and behavior and how they differ is crucial for content analysts to develop strategies that align with consumer preferences and drive effective engagement.

Visualizing Qualitative Insights

Presenting unstructured feedback can be challenging—especially to stakeholders used to bar charts, line graphs, and financial statements. However, qualitative data visualizations can also be especially powerful for the very reason that they offer stakeholders refreshing new insights into consumer thinking. Consider these techniques:

- **Theme Tables**: List themes, representative quotes, and suggested actions.

- **Word Clouds**: Show common terms from feedback (but beware: these show frequency, not importance).

- **Heatmaps with Callouts**: Combine scroll depth or click data with user quotes at different screen positions.

- **Meaning Maps**: Show how concepts or ideas are connected in terms of their meaning, helping to illustrate relationships, hierarchies, and associations within a subject or topic.

- **Annotated Screenshots**: Pair screenshots with user reactions, such as "confusing navigation" or "unclear CTA."

Mixed-methods analysis gives you both the "what" and the "why," which is a powerful combination for refining content and making more user-centered decisions.

If you're presenting to nontechnical stakeholders, pairing quotes with annotated screenshots can make your findings more tangible. For example, overlay "Confusing layout" on a screenshot where users stalled or dropped off.

To get the most out of data visualization, you'll find it helpful to have someone on your team—ideally a graphic designer—who can develop the expertise with data visualization tools like Tableau or Looker Studio to create the kind of graphics you'll need on a regular basis.

Measuring Reputation and Perception

For some organizations, the challenge of content analytics isn't about tracking sales, subscriptions, or applications; it's about understanding how your audience feels about your work, your mission, or your brand and how your content shapes those opinions.

For those organizations, reputation isn't about the number of clicks a piece of content receives; it's about the trust or the engagement that it creates. In content analytics, those are some of the hardest things to measure well, but the task isn't impossible.

Reputation analytics is the practice of tracking and interpreting how your organization is perceived, often by combining qualitative signals with quantitative frameworks. It spans both brand sentiment and stakeholder trust, and it's especially important for

- Nonprofits and advocacy organizations

- Higher education institutions

- Public agencies and mission-driven brands

- Organizations facing reputational risk (e.g., during a crisis or controversial campaign)

What Counts as Reputation Data?

Most reputation signals come from public-facing and feedback-driven sources, such as

- Open-ended survey responses

- Social media mentions and replies

- Comments on owned content (e.g., blogs, YouTube)

- Reviews and third-party platforms (e.g., Glassdoor, Reddit, Rate My Professors)

- News coverage or earned media summaries

- Email replies, chat transcripts, and help desk logs

These are not just sentiment signals; they often include framing language that reflects how people categorize or narrate their experiences with your organization:

- *"They're not very transparent."*

- *"I trust them to get the science right."*

- *"They always speak down to their audience."*

This kind of language helps you understand the intangibles that shape your organization's reputation. When analyzed alongside quantitative metrics, these insights become powerful tools for developing strategy, messaging, and engagement.

Tools and Methods for Reputation Analytics

While the matter of capturing data points in reputation analytics may seem more problematic than simply tallying up clicks in GA4, Table 6-2 lists a variety of the tools available to help quantify sentiments and opinions.

Table 6-2. Reputational data approaches and related tools

Approach	How It Helps	Tools
Sentiment analysis (manual or AI)	Measures tone—positive, negative, or neutral	Sprout Social, HubSpot, Awario
Thematic coding	Identifies repeated descriptors, values, or concerns	ATLAS.ti, MAXQDA, NVivo

(continued)

Table 6-2. (*continued*)

Approach	How It Helps	Tools
Media coverage mapping	Tracks how often your organization is mentioned and in what context	Talkwalker Alerts, Google Alerts, CoverageBook
Word clouds and frequency maps	Surface the most common terms associated with your name or mission	Free Word Cloud Generator, Mentimeter, Wordclouds.com
Social listening tools	Monitor reputation in real time across public platforms	Hootsuite, Brand24, BuzzSumo

Before you choose a tool, however, it's essential that the metric or metrics you choose to observe are ones that your organization's leaders find meaningful. Once you have that consensus, your job is to demonstrate how those metrics are impacted by the content your team creates. The task isn't impossible, but it does pose some unique challenges.

1. **Data Fragmentation:**

   - **Challenge**: Reputation data is often scattered across multiple platforms (social media, news sites, review platforms), making it difficult to consolidate and analyze comprehensively.

   - **Solution**: Using integrated tools like Hootsuite or Brandwatch can help aggregate data from various sources into a single dashboard for easier analysis.

2. **Sentiment Analysis Accuracy:**

   - **Challenge**: Automated sentiment analysis tools can misinterpret context, sarcasm, or nuanced language, leading to inaccurate sentiment scores.

- **Solution**: Combining automated tools with manual reviews can improve accuracy. Tools like Sprout Social offer both automated and manual sentiment analysis options.

3. **Real-Time Monitoring:**

   - **Challenge**: Public opinion can change rapidly, especially during a crisis, making it challenging to keep up with real-time shifts.

   - **Solution**: Implementing real-time monitoring tools like Awario or Mention can help track changes as they happen and allow for quick responses.

4. **Attribution Complexity:**

   - **Challenge**: Determining which specific content pieces are driving changes in opinion can be complex due to the multitude of factors influencing public perception.

   - **Solution**: Using advanced analytics and attribution models can help identify the impact of individual content pieces. Tools like Google Analytics and HubSpot can assist in this analysis.

5. **Volume of Data:**

   - **Challenge**: The sheer volume of data generated can be overwhelming, making it difficult to extract meaningful insights.

   - **Solution**: Employing AI and machine learning algorithms can help sift through large datasets to identify trends and patterns. Tools like IBM Watson Analytics can be particularly useful.

6. **Bias in Data:**

- **Challenge**: Data collected may be biased, either due to the platforms used, the demographics of the respondents, or, most commonly, flaws in the design of a survey, all of which will lead to skewed insights.

- **Solution**: Ensuring a diverse range of data sources and using tools that account for bias can help mitigate this issue. Tools like Talkwalker and Brand24 offer comprehensive data collection from diverse sources. Using an experienced survey designer is also essential to producing useful results and minimizing the negative impacts of survey research like frustration, loss of trust, and survey fatigue.

Addressing these challenges requires a combination of the right tools, strategic planning, and continuous adaptation to the evolving digital landscape. But even with the most powerful tools available, human review of these metrics is still essential. Even good sentiment models can make significant mistakes and see things that aren't really there.

Reputation As a Strategic Signal

Reputation metrics rarely stand alone. But they can serve as a powerful early-warning system:

- A spike in negative sentiment can flag a misunderstanding or values conflict.

- A pattern of passive or disengaged feedback might signal eroding trust.

- A consistent mismatch between your messaging and how users describe you may require a strategy reset.

MINI CASE: HOW TONE IMPACTS ENGAGEMENT

A healthcare nonprofit tracked sentiment across open survey responses and discovered that many users felt the tone of its educational content was "too technical" and "clinical." The organization revised its content voice, leading to improved engagement and perception.

Reputation analytics asks us to measure what's often felt more than said. It's messy and elusive, but it's an essential part of understanding how your content is shaping behavior in ways that aren't always obvious or easy to articulate. The more effective you are at reading the signals, the faster you're able to respond to problems that could change the perception of your brand on a grand scale.

Integrating Reputation Analytics into the Content Analytics Process

Despite the additional challenges, the process of analyzing the impact of your content on your organization's reputation is much the same as it is for an organization that's simply focused on converting leads to sales.

1. **Align Analytics with Business Goals**

   Just like traffic or conversion data, it's essential to have a clear and specific purpose in mind when you're attempting to read reputation signals. You might ask:

- Are we trying to build trust with a skeptical audience?

- Are we tracking brand perception after a major campaign or crisis?

- Are we testing whether our values and tone are landing as intended?

These become strategic anchors for your reputation analysis efforts.

2. **Formulate Research Questions**

Reputation challenges lend themselves to descriptive, comparative, and even correlational questions.

Examples:

- *What themes are most common in open-ended survey responses over time?* (Descriptive)

- *How do faculty and alumni differ in their perceptions of our brand voice?* (Comparative)

- *Do changes in sentiment correlate with changes in donation behavior?* (Correlational)

This allows you to structure fuzzy concepts into answerable, actionable questions.

3. **Map the Content Journey**

Reputation isn't shaped by a single moment; it accumulates across touchpoints.

Ask:

- Where do users first form impressions of us?

- What experiences shape how we're talked about later—on social media, in surveys, or on review sites?

- What feedback signals are we collecting at each stage?

Mapping feedback opportunities alongside user touchpoints helps ensure that reputation insights are grounded in real content experiences.

4. **Collect and Prepare Data**

    Reputation data is messy and may come to you from a variety of different sources, but it can be collected and prepared just like any other content dataset:

    - Use consistent tags (e.g., by audience, campaign, channel).

    - Apply text analysis or thematic coding tools.

    - Maintain a shared archive of feedback, media mentions, and reviews.

    This is where your tagging, archiving, and metadata practices from Chapter 4 pay off. Consistency in how you collect and prepare the data is essential. Your procedures for doing the work should be clearly codified and reviewed by your team on a regular basis to make sure questions are addressed and boundary lines between categories of data are clearly drawn and correctly applied.

5. **Analyze Content Performance (Qualitatively)**

    Instead of clicks, you're looking for language patterns, emotional tone, or recurring concerns. The following analytical techniques can help you interpret qualitative content more deeply:

- **Word frequencies** help identify which terms or topics dominate the conversation.

- **Sentiment scoring** reveals emotional tone, showing whether content trends positive, negative, or neutral.

- **Theme clustering** groups related ideas to uncover underlying patterns or concerns.

- **Comparative breakdowns across segments** allow you to contrast how different audiences or time periods engage with the content.

These tools help you move beyond surface metrics and uncover meaningful insights that inform strategy and messaging. There are online courses and tutorials available to learn these techniques, but there are also plenty of experts who can do the work for you.

6. **Communicate Insights and Take Action**

Reputation analytics should have clear impact on how you make decisions, especially about

- Content tone and voice

- Community engagement strategy

- Message testing

- Crisis response

- Thought leadership positioning

We'll explore effective reporting principles in Chapter 10, but the important ingredients are clarity, audience-centered storytelling, and framing for business impact.

7.   **Build a Sustainable Reputation Insight Loop**

Reputation analytics isn't a one-time project. It's ongoing work that requires

- Regular listening

- Repeatable tracking methods

- Human interpretation supported by cross-functional collaboration (e.g., involving communications, leadership, customer experience, and data teams to ensure insights are contextualized, actionable, and aligned with broader organizational goals)

Incorporate reputation into the regular rhythms of your larger analytics process—from monthly or quarterly reviews to cross-department updates and so on.

Case Study: Elevating UX Through Qualitative Content Feedback

A regional community college system launched a new "Transfer Guide" microsite to help students navigate the process of transferring to four-year universities. Initial quantitative reports from GA4 showed high traffic to the site but also high exit rates and low interaction with links to transfer advisors or application forms.

The Challenge

Stakeholders were puzzled. The content was thorough and well-structured, but users weren't converting. The analytics manager flagged the drop-off but needed help explaining *why* users were leaving.

The Approach

A qualitative research sprint was launched:

- A one-question pop-up survey was added to key pages: *"What else would you like to see on this page?"*

- Ten brief Zoom interviews were conducted with current students who had recently visited the microsite, and responses were transcribed and analyzed using Otter.ai to identify recurring themes and emotional tone.

- Comments from social media and Reddit were also collected and thematically analyzed using NVivo, which supports qualitative coding and sentiment analysis across unstructured text data.

Findings

Thematic coding of 80+ responses revealed

- **Emotional Friction**: Many users reported feeling "intimidated" or "uncertain" about whether their credits would transfer.

- **Information Gaps**: Students wanted real examples— "What did it look like for someone from my school who transferred to State U?"

- **Language Mismatch**: Terms like "articulation agreements" were unfamiliar and confusing.

Actions Taken

- The team added short video testimonials from successful transfer students.

- Created a visual, step-by-step "Transfer Journey" timeline.

- Replaced bureaucratic terms with plain language (e.g., "Will your classes count?" instead of "credit articulation").

Results

- Time on page increased by 34%.

- Exit rate on the transfer homepage dropped by 18%.

- Click-through to contact a transfer advisor rose by 46%.

Takeaway

Quantitative signals raised the flag, but qualitative analysis provided the diagnosis and the path forward. By listening carefully to users, the community college system created a more human-centered experience that empowered students at a critical decision point.

Workbook Exercise: Analyze a Qualitative Dataset

This short exercise will walk you through basic qualitative analysis using open-ended feedback. It's designed to help you practice coding responses, identifying patterns, and drawing actionable conclusions.

Step 1: Read the responses

Here are five (sample) user comments left on a nonprofit's donation landing page:

1. "I wasn't sure where my money would actually go."

2. "It looks like a great cause, but the form was too long."

3. "I started to donate, but I didn't have time to finish."

4. "There were too many steps—why do you need my mailing address?"

5. "I wasn't sure if I'd get a confirmation email."

Step 2: Generate codes

For each comment, write down a brief code or label that captures the main issue.

Examples:

- Unclear impact

- Long form

- Time constraint

- Friction

- Confirmation concern

Step 3: Group into themes

Now organize your codes into broader themes.

Theme 1: User uncertainty

- Unclear impact

- Confirmation concern

Theme 2: Form friction

- Long form

- Too many steps

- Time constraint

Step 4: Draft recommendations

Based on your themes, what content or UX changes would you recommend?

Examples:

- Add a short "Where your donation goes" section at the top of the form.

- Simplify the form (remove optional fields; reduce the number of screens).

- Include confirmation messaging during and after submission.

By practicing even a small-scale analysis like this, you build your ability to listen for patterns, summarize findings, and generate clear next steps—all skills you can apply immediately to your own content analytics work.

And keep in mind that according to Steve Portigal, author of *Interviewing Users: How to Uncover Compelling Insights*, "Even a small sample of user comments can reveal patterns that preempt expensive design failures."[3]

Integrating the Team

As with every aspect of content analytics, qualitative insight gains power when it's embedded across teams, not siloed within UX or research. To build a culture of listening and responsiveness, content and marketing teams should treat qualitative data collection and interpretation as an ongoing, collaborative practice. Use Table 6-3 to help identify how to make the best use of the expertise of each member of your team.

---

[3] Portigal, S. *Interviewing Users: How to Uncover Compelling Insights*. Brooklyn, NY: Rosenfeld Media, 2013.

Table 6-3. *Key team roles in qualitative analytics*

Team Member	Role in Qualitative Analytics
Content strategist	Translates feedback into editorial guidance; leads thematic analysis for content decision-making
UX researcher	Designs and conducts user interviews, usability testing, and survey instruments
Content designer	Uses qualitative insights to improve clarity, tone, and user comprehension
Data analyst	Supports mixed-methods integration, validates patterns, and visualizes findings
Customer support lead	Surfaces recurring user issues from tickets or chat transcripts
Social media manager	Gathers and summarizes trends from replies, shares, and audience sentiment
Graphic designer	Develops expertise in using data visualization tools like Tableau and Looker Studio

Collaboration Tips

Formalizing your collaboration efforts ensures that your team understands that it's an essential part of the team culture and creates opportunities for them to contribute and to succeed.

- **Create a Shared Feedback Repository:** Use tools like Airtable, Google Sheets, or Notion to log feedback across teams. Include source, timestamp, theme, and follow-up actions.

- **Schedule Feedback Reviews:** Hold monthly or biweekly "listening sessions" to review qualitative feedback as a team and identify emerging trends.

- **Tag Team Commentary in Real Time:** Encourage social and support teams to tag content strategists when they spot feedback patterns worth investigating.

- **Pair Qualitative and Quantitative Leads:** When reporting on performance, assign one person to represent metrics and another to surface quotes or user themes. Together, they tell a more complete story.

When multiple roles treat user input as a core data source—not as an afterthought—qualitative analytics becomes not just a technique but a mindset: one grounded in empathy, shared responsibility, and continuous improvement.

Budget-Friendly Approaches to Qualitative Analytics

Collecting and analyzing qualitative data doesn't require enterprise research software or a team of UX researchers. With a thoughtful, lightweight approach, even small teams can surface powerful insights that shape better content experiences.

Low-Cost Data Collection Methods

- **Add an Open-Ended Survey Question:** Use free tools like Google Forms, Microsoft Forms, or SurveyMonkey's basic tier to ask one key question: "What was helpful or confusing about this content?"

- **Use Built-In Feedback Features:** Enable comment sections, "thumbs up/down," or "Was this helpful?" widgets to gather input passively.

- **Monitor Support Channels:** Review email replies, chat logs, and common ticket tags to surface issues and language patterns.

- **Watch Screen Recordings:** Free or low-cost tools like Microsoft Clarity allow you to see where users hesitate, scroll, or abandon.

Simple Analysis Techniques

- **Code with a Spreadsheet:** Copy responses into a spreadsheet and create columns for codes, themes, and potential actions.

- **Sample Strategically:** If you can't review every comment, select a representative sample (e.g., 50 responses from a high-traffic campaign).

- **Ask Internally:** Customer-facing staff often have qualitative insights already; they just need to be asked and included.

Time-Saving Tools

A variety of useful tools have free versions that may do just enough to save you an expensive subscription. Table 6-4 lists just a few.

Table 6-4. *Free qualitative analytics tools*

Tool	Use	Free Version?
Claude AI	Qualitative coding	Yes
MonkeyLearn	Basic text classification	Yes (limited)
Jotform	Survey collection	Yes
Microsoft Clarity	Session recording and heatmaps	Yes

No matter what tools you use to do the job, keep in mind that qualitative analytics doesn't require perfection; it requires *curiosity*, a willingness to listen, and a simple system for turning words into action. Start with what you have and build from there.

Final Thoughts

Qualitative analytics is about more than gathering quotes or interpreting open-ended survey fields. It's about listening for the human signals behind the numbers—the emotions, obstacles, values, and needs that shape how users engage with your content.

In a world awash with dashboards and KPIs, qualitative data reconnects us to what matters most: how people feel, what they're trying to do, and where content helps or hinders their progress. When we pair that understanding with the rigor of structured data, we gain not just information but insight.

Here's what to take forward:

- Use qualitative methods to uncover the *why* behind your metrics.

- Build mixed-methods feedback loops that turn user comments into hypotheses and improvements.

- Treat qualitative data as a first-class input, not a soft supplement.

In Chapter 8, we'll look at how to validate those qualitative insights through testing and experimentation—turning user observations into evidence-based improvements. But as you move forward, remember: Meaningful analytics begin with listening. The answers you need may already be in your users' own words.

Before we explore testing and experimentation, though, we'll take a look at predictive analytics and how to transform your analytics into a simple but highly effective instrument of change for your organization.

CHAPTER 7

Forecasting Content Performance

When people hear the word *forecast*, they often picture complex mathematical models or machine learning algorithms trained on massive datasets. And while those tools exist, they're not where most content teams need to start or even where they need to finish.

In the context of content analytics, forecasting simply means using past performance to make smarter, evidence-informed guesses about the future. The process involves looking at what's worked, spotting emerging patterns, and asking, *"If this trend continues, what might we expect next quarter? Next campaign?"*

Forecasting helps content teams

- **Plan** more confidently.

- **Advocate** for budget and resources.

- **Prioritize** formats, channels, or topics with greater expected returns.

- **Spot risk** or fatigue before performance drops.

The goal isn't necessarily to guarantee what's going to happen tomorrow; it's to identify trends and probabilities and to use them to make better decisions today.

© Russ Bahorsky 2026
R. Bahorsky, *The Fundamentals of Content Analytics*,
https://doi.org/10.1007/979-8-8688-2601-6_7

This chapter introduces practical, low-barrier approaches to forecasting that any marketing or communications team can begin using—regardless of budget, platform, or statistical fluency. We'll start with a simple but powerful idea: lift.

Starting Simple: Lift As a Predictive Tool

Before you dive into the complexities of developing trendlines and linear regressions, you may find that lift—a forecasting tool that's easy to calculate and highly persuasive—is all you really need to make a huge difference in the impact your team has on your organization.

Basically, lift is a way to describe the expected improvement of one version of content (or strategy) over another. It's also a building block for creating meaningful growth.

Why Lift Matters

Let's say you recently ran an A/B test on a landing page CTA (we'll explore A/B tests in more detail in the next chapter). Version A converts at 2.5%, while version B converts at 3%. That's a 0.5 percentage point improvement, but what does that mean in business terms?

If your landing page gets 40,000 visits per month, a 0.5-point lift means

- 200 *more* conversions per month

- 2,400 more conversions per year

Simply put, identifying the lift you get from the changes and improvements you make to your content gives you a way to assign a clear, quantifiable value to your content and the improvements you make to it. You could even say it's the key to turning the art of content development into a science.

Two Types of Lift

Strictly speaking, there are two types of lift: absolute and relative. Table 7-1 explains how to understand both.

Table 7-1. *Absolute vs. relative lift*

Type	Formula	Example
Absolute lift	New Version − Old Version	5% − 8% = **3%**
Relative lift	(New Version − Old Version) ÷ Old Version	(5% − 8%) ÷ 8% = **60%**

Absolute lift measures the direct, numeric increase in a metric—for example, an increase in conversion rate from 5% to 8% due to a change you made to the content or its formatting represents a 3% improvement. In other words, you can expect the new version of your content to continue to generate a conversion rate of 8% in the future—a number you can build into your revenue projections for the next reporting period. You'll need to continue to observe and validate this conversion rate going forward, but we'll take a closer look at that in the next chapter.

In contrast, relative lift expresses the change in your conversion rate as a percentage relative to the baseline (in this case, a 60% improvement over the original 5%). Of course, the number sounds more impressive, but remember that it's just referring to the amount of improvement your change created. In other words, if you're reporting to the C-suite about expected revenue next quarter, you can either tell them you expect an 8% conversion rate or a 60% increase in last quarter's rate of 5%. The second option is the one you use to justify raises for you and your team, and the first option is the number you'll need to plug into your projected revenue forecast.

However, when reporting on your results, it's best to share both the percentage *and* the projected real-world outcome: "This version delivered a 20% lift, which could mean 2,400 additional conversions annually."

Forecasting with Lift

While it seems like a relatively simple concept, lift can be a highly effective forecasting tool even in the most complex marketing or communications environment. Whether you are using it to quantify the results of A/B testing; comparing the effectiveness of campaigns, channels, or content formats; or pitching or prioritizing new content initiatives, it is the only tool you need to transform your content development efforts into an engine for continuous and intentional improvement. It's also an effective tool for assessing whether or not user opinions (such as those you uncover in the kinds of qualitative methods we discussed in Chapter 6) actually align with their behavior.

The concept of lift is even additive, which allows you to move from simple A/B tests to highly sophisticated and layered conversion models.[1]

For example, let's say you find that shorter headlines give your blogs a 3% lift, while bigger photos give them a 2% lift. Assuming that your blogs already generate a conversion rate of 10%, you can combine the two features to give your blogs a 5% lift. Factor in the 5% lift you get when you push the blogs to your most responsive audience segment and the -2% drop in lift you get when you publish blogs in the off-season, and you begin to see how precise your projections can become and how effective they can be at quantifying the complexities of your market.

---

[1] Lift is often treated as additive across independent changes—for example, headline length and photo size—but caution is warranted when changes interact (e.g., when personalization affects the layout of the page). When in doubt, validate combinations with additional testing.

It's also important to remember that forecasts using lift assume that you have accounted for all the variables: same audience, promotion strategy, time frame, etc. Strictly speaking, they're not definitive (because controlling for all of the variables that could impact a user isn't realistic), but they can be highly useful indicators of future performance, especially over the short term, and they can become even more so if you continue to validate your results with additional observation and testing.

Other Low-Complexity Predictive Techniques

While you can build your entire content analytics program on the work of assessing and applying lift, there are certainly a number of other tools that you may want to consider. Fortunately, not every one of these tools requires expensive consultants, specialized platforms, or machine learning technology. Many useful forecasts can be generated with tools like Excel, Google Sheets, or free resources like Looker Studio that you may already know or have available to you. These approaches are accessible, interpretable, and often robust enough to support short-term planning or inform solid editorial decision-making.

Moving Averages

A moving average smooths out fluctuations by averaging performance over a sliding time window of time—say, the last 7 or 30 days. The tool is particularly useful for forecasting content engagement that follows a stable pattern like weekly newsletter opens or monthly blog traffic. For example, you might take the 30-day moving average of daily blog views to project expected traffic next month—assuming no major campaign changes.

Let's look at an example of a spreadsheet that you could recreate in Excel or Sheets.

The results of the averages in the last three cells in column C give you a rolling view of users' baseline engagement with your content on a seven-day basis (beginning with day 7). Once you have identified a series of moving averages, you can also project it forward by assuming the trend continues (e.g., using =TREND() in Excel). The function uses a statistical tool known as the least squares method to create a predictive linear model of what the next sequence of values is likely to be.

The formula for the Table 7-2 would be =TREND(C7:C9, A7:A9, A10), where C7:C9 represents the three 7-day moving averages, A7:A10 represents the corresponding days, and A10 is the day you'd like to predict.

Table 7-2. *Moving average example*

A (Days)	B (Daily Page Views)	C (7-Day Average)
1	100	
2	120	
3	110	
4	130	
5	140	
6	150	
7	160	=AVERAGE(B1:B7)
8	170	=AVERAGE(B2:B8)
9	180	=AVERAGE(B3:B9)

Compared with a simple average, a moving average offers a few advantages:

1. **Trend Identification**: It helps identify trends by smoothing out short-term fluctuations and highlighting longer-term patterns.

2. **Noise Reduction**: Reduces the impact of random, short-term variations, making the data easier to analyze.

3. **Dynamic Adjustment**: Continuously updates as new data points are added, providing a more current view of trends.

Determining Content Cadence Using Moving Averages

One way to use a moving average is when you're planning content cadence—for example, if your four-week moving average shows that Thursdays outperform Tuesdays by 20%, you may want to shift more content to that day.

For example, create a table in Excel that collects the number of page views you're seeing on each day of the week (Table 7-3).

Table 7-3. *Weekly moving average example*

Week	Monday	Tuesday	Wednesday	Thursday	Friday
1	120	130	110	150	140
2	125	135	115	160	145
3	130	140	120	170	150
4	135	145	125	180	155
5	140	150	130	190	160

In a new row calculate your moving averages:

=AVERAGE(B2:B5) → for Monday

=AVERAGE(C2:C5) → for Tuesday

...and so on. This gives you a smoothed performance view, reducing noise from weekly fluctuations.

You can also apply the concept of lift with this approach by creating an additional row that calculates the relative lift that you're seeing for each day:

$$=(D6 - C6)/C6 \rightarrow \text{Tuesday vs. Wednesday}$$

Format the result as a percentage to see relative gains.

If you want to get even more specific, you can track moving averages on a different time scale (hourly vs. weekly), for different types of content, or for different types of audiences—depending on the kind of questions you need to answer.

You can also use moving averages to evaluate the impact of how often you publish new content.

1. **Track your publishing volume** by recording how many pieces of content you publish per week or month.

2. **Measure performance per unit** by dividing total engagement (e.g., page views, conversions) by the number of posts to determine your engagement per post.

3. **Look for diminishing returns.** If engagement per post drops as frequency increases, you may be over-publishing or saturating your audience.

Simple Linear Regression

Linear regression helps model the relationship between two variables—like how word count (a feature) or publish date (also a feature) correlates with conversions (a target variable). Most spreadsheet tools include a basic regression function or allow you to create a trendline on a chart.

For example, if you plot word count (x-axis) against engagement rate (y-axis) and the slope of the line is positive, you might conclude that longer articles drive more engagement—up to a point.

You can use any "learnings" that you derive from this relationship to

- Predict how a new article *might* perform based on known characteristics.

- Identify thresholds (e.g., content length or CTA placement) that impact performance.

Let's look at another example that you can create yourself. Using Excel's linear regression tools, you can easily analyze the relationship between the number of blog posts published and the number of website visitors.

Here's our data (Table 7-4).

Table 7-4. *Sample input data for a simple linear regression*

A (Blog Posts Published)	B (Website Visitors)
5	1,000
10	1,500
15	2,000
20	2,500
25	3,000
30	3,500
35	4,000

To create the linear regression using this data, here are the steps to follow:

1. **Install Analysis ToolPak** (if it isn't already installed):

   - Go to File ➤ Options.

   - Select Add-ins.

   - In the Manage box, choose Excel Add-ins and click Go.

   - Check the box for Analysis ToolPak and click OK.

2. **Perform Linear Regression:**

   - Go to the Data tab and click Data Analysis.

   - Select Regression and click OK.

   - In the Regression dialog box

     - **Input Y Range**: Select the range for website visitors (e.g., B1:B7).

     - **Input X Range**: Select the range for blog posts published (e.g., A1:A7).

     - Check the box for Labels if you included headers.

     - Choose an Output Range where you want the regression results to appear.

   - Click OK.

3. **Interpret the Output Created by Excel:**

Table 7-5 is an example of the kind of output Excel creates.

Table 7-5. *Sample output data for a simple regression*

Regression Statistics	Values
Multiple R	0.99
R Square	0.98
Adjusted R Square	0.97
Standard Error	100
Observations	7
Coefficients	**Values**
Intercept	500
Blog Posts	100

1. **Multiple R (0.99)**: This is the correlation coefficient, indicating a very strong positive relationship between the target or dependent variable (number of website visitors) and the feature or independent variable (the number of blog posts). A value close to 1 suggests that the model's predictions are highly correlated with the actual data.

2. **R Square (0.98)**: This represents the proportion of the variance in the dependent variable that is predictable from the independent variable. An R Square of 0.98 means that 98% of the variability in y can be explained by the number of blog posts.

3. **Adjusted R Square (0.97)**: This metric refines the R Square value by accounting for the number of predictors in the model. It's slightly lower than

R Square because it corrects for overfitting—a situation where the model becomes too complex and starts capturing noise instead of meaningful patterns. An Adjusted R Square of 0.97 still indicates a very strong model fit.

4. **Standard Error (100)**: (100) indicates the average distance that the observed number of website visitors falls from the predicted number of visitors. In this context, a Standard Error of 100 suggests that the actual number of visitors can vary by about 100 from the predicted value for each blog post published. While the model shows a strong relationship, this variability should be considered when making predictions. In other words, and in this case, a prediction using this model will be accurate give or take 100 visitors.

5. **Observations (7)**: This is the number of data points used in the regression analysis.

6. **Blog Posts (100)**: This coefficient indicates the change in the dependent variable (y) for each one-unit change in the independent variable (Blog Posts). In this case, for each additional blog post, the dependent variable increases by 100 units.

Depending on how you, your team, or your consultants build your regression models, Table 7-6 lists a few additional terms to know.

Table 7-6. *Other regression terms you may encounter*

Term	What It Tells You
Dependent variable	The outcome you're trying to explain (e.g., conversions).
Independent variable	A factor or feature of your content that might influence the outcome (e.g., format, channel).
Coefficient	The size/direction of the relationship (+ or − impact). The closer the number is to 1, the bigger the impact a variable has on your outcome or dependent variable (i.e., coefficients can be useful for ranking the importance of variables in creating the outcomes you want).
P-value	Whether the result is statistically significant (rule of thumb: your P-value should be < 0.05).

You don't need to memorize these, but knowing how to read them helps you work with analysts, consultants, or tools more effectively.

In our example, then, the regression analysis shows a strong positive relationship between the number of blog posts published and the number of website visitors. For each additional blog post published, the number of website visitors increases by approximately 100.

And here are a few of the learnings you might take away from the model:

1. **Positive Impact:** Publishing more blog posts significantly increases website visitors.

2. **Predictive Power:** The model can reliably forecast visitor numbers based on blog post frequency.

3. **Variability Awareness:** Expect some fluctuation in visitor numbers around the predicted values.

4. **Content Strategy:** Focus on increasing blog post frequency to drive more traffic.

5. **Resource Allocation:** Invest in content creation to boost website engagement.

Obviously, the learnings are going to be useful to the manager of a web content team interested in quantifying the relationship between content publishing and website traffic, making it easier to predict outcomes and optimize strategies and resources. They'll help with

1. **Trend Identification:** Understanding how content publishing frequency impacts website traffic

2. **Decision-Making:** Providing data-driven insights to optimize content strategy, such as determining the ideal number of posts to publish for maximum visitor engagement

3. **Performance Measurement:** Allowing analysts to measure the effectiveness of their content efforts and make adjustments based on the results

One way to think of using a regression is to focus on how it helps you generate smarter questions, not final answers. If images seem linked to higher engagement, test that insight in your next A/B experiment.

Using Linear Regression to Optimize Cadence

The example above explains how a linear regression could help you understand how frequently you should publish content, but another way to understand how to optimize your cadence is by using data visualization to identify your linear model's inflection point.

While linear regression shows a consistent relationship between blog posts and website visitors in this example, real-world data often reveals nonlinear behavior—especially when performance gains begin to flatten or decline as frequency increases. An inflection point is where the rate of change shifts—typically from increasing returns to diminishing returns.

To recognize an inflection point

1. Plot your data using a scatter plot with a trendline (Insert → Chart → Scatter).

2. Look for the point where the curve starts to bend— that is, where each additional blog post yields less incremental traffic than before.

3. If the trendline is linear, no inflection point is present. But if it curves (e.g., upward and then flattens), the inflection point is near the bend.

For more complex patterns, you may need to consider developing regression models for each of your audience segments, or you can call in an expert to do a change-point analysis to statistically detect shifts in the slope of your model.

Ultimately, these methods help you identify when "more" stops meaning "better"—a critical insight for optimizing both your content cadence and your team's resources and capacity.

Deriving and Applying Your Predictive Equations from a Simple Regression

Building on the regression you ran in the previous section, you can also use the regression output into a concrete forecasting tool. Let's take a look at how this is done using the blog-posts-vs.-visitors example.

1. **Extract the Key Coefficients**

    From Excel's regression table, note

    - Intercept (a) = 500

    - Blog Posts coefficient (b) = 100

These give you the predictive equation: Predicted Visitors = 500 + 100 × (Number of Blog Posts)

2. **Run a Quick Forecast**

   Plug in any planned post volume to estimate traffic:

   - **For 15 Posts:** 500 + 100 × 15 = 2,000 visitors

   - **For 25 Posts:** 500 + 100 × 25 = 3,000 visitors

3. **Account for Uncertainty**

   Your model's Standard Error (~100 visitors) reminds you that actual traffic will vary around the point estimate. Frame each forecast as a range: "With 15 posts, we expect ~2,000 visitors ±100."

4. **Apply These to Your Planning Efforts**

   - **Set Content Targets:** Aim for 20 posts if you need ~2,500 visitors.

   - **Run What-If Scenarios:** "What if we boost to 30 posts? We'd forecast ~3,500 visitors."

   - **Align with OKRs:** Translate these forecasts into quarterly objectives (e.g., "Publish 18–22 posts to hit 2,300–2,700 visitors").

Testing Your Regression with Hold-Out Data

Before we leave the subject of regressions, let's look at one more tactic you'll need to make sure your regressions are working.

As you can imagine, even a perfectly clean formula can mislead if it only works on the data you used to create it. Hold-out testing shows whether your model truly generalizes—that is, makes good predictions on new, unseen data. If statistics isn't your strong suit, it may be best to enlist the help of a consultant to do this work, but if you and your team are ready to take this on, here are the steps you'll need to take to test your regression.

1. **Split Your Data to Create a Training Set and a Hold-Out Set**

    - **Training Set**: ~80 % of your records, used to build the model

    - **Hold-Out (Test) Set**: ~20% set aside, used only for evaluation

    By never touching the hold-out set during model fitting, you simulate how the model performs in the real world.

2. **Make Predictions on the Hold-Out Set**

    - Run your formula (for each x) on the hold-out data to get a list of predicted y values.

    - Compare these to the actual y values you collected.

    This comparison reveals how close your forecasts are to reality.

3. **Measure Error with RMSE**

    - RMSE (Root Mean Squared Error) is the square root of the average squared differences between predicted and actual values.

    - **Formula**:

        1. For each record, subtract predicted y from actual y and square the result.

        2. Average all squared differences.

3. Take the square root of that average.

- A lower RMSE means your predictions are, on average, closer to real outcomes.

- See Appendix C to learn how to create an Excel spreadsheet to calculate RMSE.

4. **Watch for Overfitting**

- Overfitting happens when a model captures random noise in the training set instead of the true underlying pattern.

- A sign you've overfit is the RMSE on your hold-out set is much larger than on your training set.

- If overfitting appears, simplify the model (fewer predictors) or gather more data.

By validating on hold-out data, you can truthfully say, "Our regression predicts visitor counts or lead volume with an average error of ±x." That transparency builds trust with stakeholders and prevents surprises when you roll out forecasts in your content strategy.

REGRESSION RED FLAGS

If your regression isn't producing good predictions, there are a few diagnostics tests an expert can use to uncover the problem.

Red Flag: Autocorrelation

Your model's errors—the differences between predicted and actual values—should appear random. If you notice a pattern where one inaccurate prediction is followed by another, that's a sign of autocorrelation. In other words, it's a condition that means your model may appear to be more accurate than it really is.

How to Spot It: Plot your errors in order (by time or record) and look for run patterns or waves, rather than a scatter of points.

Red Flag: Uneven Error Spread

Your prediction mistakes should stay about the same size across all your data. If errors are tiny for some values and huge for others, that's a problem known as heteroskedasticity, which can give you misleading confidence in your results.

How to Spot It: Plot errors against your predicted values—if you see a funnel or fan shape, your error spread isn't consistent.

Time-Series Visualizations

Apps like Looker Studio and GA4's Explorations allow you to create another simple predictive tool: time-series graphs, a type of chart that displays data points across a meaningful span of time. Use a time-series graph if you need to

- Highlight seasonal trends.

- Show correlations between content releases and audience behavior.

- Provide stakeholders with visual cues for future planning.

These tools often allow trendlines or forecast overlays, which can help nontechnical stakeholders grasp future patterns more easily.

When presenting trend-based forecasts, always note your assumptions (e.g., "Assumes consistent publishing schedule and no major platform changes").

Now let's jump right into an example. Say you want to visualize the number of daily active users on your website over the past month. Here's how you might approach that using a time-series visualization tool.

Steps to Create a Time-Series Visualization in GA4 Explorations

Step 1: Open Explorations

1. Go to your GA4 property.

2. In the left-hand menu, click Explore.

3. Click Blank to start a new exploration.

Step 2: Set up the variables

1. In the Variables panel on the left

   - **Dimensions:**

     - Click the "+" next to *Dimensions*.

     - Search for and add

       - Date

       - Device category

   - **Metrics:**

     - Click the "+" next to *Metrics*.

     - Search for and add

       - Active users

Step 3: Build the tab configuration

In the Tab Settings (middle panel)

1. **Technique**: Choose Line chart.

2. **Rows (X-Axis):**

   - Drag Date to the Rows field.

3. **Columns (Segments)** *(Optional)*:

   - You can leave this blank or use it for advanced comparisons.

4. **Values (Y-Axis)**:

   - Drag Active users to the Values field.

5. **Breakdowns (for Lines)**:

   - Drag Device category into the Breakdowns field.

This will create a separate line for each device category: Desktop, Mobile, and Tablet (if applicable).

Step 4: Filter the data (optional)

To focus only on Desktop and Mobile

1. Under the Filters section, click Add filter.

2. Set the filter to Device category → matches regex → desktop|mobile.

3. Click Apply.

Step 5: Adjust the date range

1. At the top right of the exploration, click the date range picker.

2. Choose a range like Last 30 days, or set a custom one (e.g., March 24 to April 21, 2025).

3. Click Apply.

Step 6: Customize and export

- Hover over points to see exact values.

- Use the gear icon to change chart styles or sort order.

- Click the Download icon (top right) to export the chart as a CSV or PNG if needed.

The chart should look something like Figure 7-1.

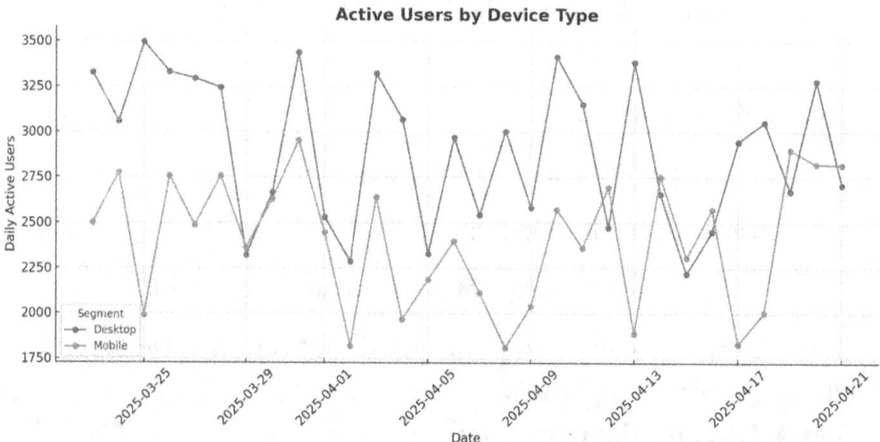

Figure 7-1. *Example visualization*

Your line chart will be a simple graph displaying the number of daily active users on your website over the past month, with the x-axis representing the dates and the y-axis representing the number of active users.

Benefits of Time-Series Visualization

As with any time-series graph, you'll be able to easily spot trends and patterns in user activity over time or see any unusual spikes or drops in user activity that may require further investigation. You'll also be able to see the impact of marketing campaigns, content updates, or other changes in user engagement over time at a glance, making it a useful addition to a dashboard or report.

Forecasting with Segments: A Strategic Shortcut

One of the simplest ways to predict future performance is to look at how different audience segments behave and extrapolate from there. The strategy is a long-established practice in consumer behavior modeling.[2]

Think of segments as user subgroups defined by shared traits:

- Device (mobile vs. desktop)

- Source (organic vs. paid)

- Behavior (repeat visitor vs. first-time)

- Audience type (customers, alumni, prospective students, donors, partners)

When you examine performance by segment, you uncover patterns that are often far more stable and actionable than broad averages.

Why Segment-Based Forecasting Is Important

Let's say your average landing page conversion rate is 3%. But when you break it down

- Desktop users convert at 3.8%.

- Mobile users convert at 2.2%.

If you're planning a campaign that will be promoted heavily via Instagram Stories (a mobile-first channel), your realistic expected conversion rate may be closer to 2.2%. Depending on the size of your campaign, a 27% drop in relative lift could be disastrous if your forecast

---

[2] Sharp, B. *How Brands Grow: What Marketers Don't Know*. Oxford: Oxford University Press, 2010.

is based on an unrealistic forecast of how your audience will respond. Table 7-7 suggests ways to think about how segmenting your audience could lead to more effective research questions.

Table 7-7. *Common segment-based forecasting questions*

Segment	What to Look At	Forecasting Insight
Device type	Time on page, form completions	Mobile users often bounce faster—optimize early content load.
Traffic source	Conversion rate by source	Paid traffic may convert faster but drop off sooner.
Audience status	Returning vs. new users	Returning visitors often require different CTAs.
Geography	Email engagement, event sign-ups	Regional differences may affect seasonality and tone.

An especially effective use of segment-based forecasting is to segment performance first and then use lift or moving averages *within* those segments to forecast more accurately. Almost any audience can be segmented in some meaningful way.

A Quick Forecast Scenario

Your last three email newsletters had the following open rates by segment (Table 7-8).

Table 7-8. *Basic segmentation forecasting scenario*

Segment	Week 1	Week 2	Week 3	3-Week Avg.
New subscribers	41%	43%	42%	42.0%
Existing list	27%	26%	25%	26.0%

If you're launching a new content series aimed at new subscribers, you can confidently project an average open rate of 40–42% and use that as a benchmark for success.

FORECASTING RE-ENGAGEMENT—LESSONS FROM FUNDRAISING

When planning for future engagement, most teams focus on how to grow their audience or expand their reach. But often, the best forecast opportunities lie with users who already engaged once but haven't returned.

Fundraising professionals have a name for these audiences. Two well-known segments—LYBUNT (Last Year But Unfortunately Not This) and SYBUNT (Some Year But Unfortunately Not This)—help nonprofit teams identify lapsed donors with a history of giving. These segments don't represent new audiences; they represent audiences at risk. And that makes them excellent candidates for re-engagement forecasting.

If you've tracked past behavior through a CRM or donor database (i.e., a closed system), you can forecast

- Expected response rates to reactivation campaigns

- Projected lift from personalized outreach to LYBUNT or SYBUNT users

- Likely conversion gaps if these audiences aren't addressed

This logic applies across sectors:

- In higher education, a "LYBUNT" student might be someone who applied last year but didn't this year. Forecasting their reapplication likelihood can guide follow-up messaging and incentives.

- In ecommerce, customers who bought last year but haven't returned can be modeled for repurchase probability and used to project loyalty revenue.

- In SaaS, churned users with strong historical usage patterns are forecasted for win-back potential using previous session frequency and recency.

- In healthcare, patients overdue for routine care can be prioritized by last-visit date and communication responsiveness.

The key to using audience segmentation in forecasting is using past interaction data to estimate the probability of re-engagement. Whether you're projecting open rates for a win-back campaign or estimating lift from a retargeting sequence, LYBUNT/SYBUNT-style segments give you a reliable behavioral baseline to work from.

Tip   LYBUNT and SYBUNT segments are most useful in closed-audience environments where you can tie behavior to individuals over time (e.g., donor CRMs, student databases, or customer email lists). For open audiences (like web traffic), use segment proxies such as "visited last quarter but not this quarter" to apply similar re-engagement logic.

Limitations of DIY Forecasting

Forecasting is a valuable decision-making tool, but it's not a crystal ball. Even simple projections come with caveats, and recognizing those limits is part of being a responsible, credible analyst.

1. **Performance Isn't Always Predictable:** External variables—algorithm changes, news events, platform bugs—can derail even the most reasonable projection. Content success is also contextual, not just mathematical.

   Example: A nonprofit sees a 30% spike in engagement after an influencer reposts their story. That doesn't mean they should forecast future growth at +30%.

2. **Trendlines Hide Volatility:** Moving averages and linear trends work well for smoothing out noise. But they can mask

   - Sudden drops (e.g., unsubscribes after a campaign)

   - Saturation points (e.g., diminishing returns on ad creative)

   - Cyclical behavior (e.g., summer traffic slumps in higher education)

3. **Correlation Is Not Causation:** Just because a variable (like word count or social shares) is associated with performance, it doesn't mean it *causes* the change.

   A longer post might rank better in search—not because it's long, but because it covers the topic more thoroughly.

   Regression helps spot associations, not truths. Treat these insights as hypothesis generators, not absolute rules.

4. **DIY Tools Can Mislead Without Oversight:** Many marketers use Google Sheets, Looker Studio, or built-in platform reports to make projections, and that's fine. But keep in mind

   - Default settings (e.g., rolling averages, filters) can obscure problems.

   - Outliers can skew small datasets.

   - Poor data hygiene (e.g., inconsistent tagging) makes trend analysis unreliable.

The bottom line is that you'll need to know your data well enough to ask good questions about it, especially if you're presenting it to others. Understanding the shortcomings of predictive techniques can help steer you toward finding the answers you need if your predictions don't match your outcomes.

Case Study: Forecasting Campaign Outcomes in a Digital Publishing Team

A mid-sized digital publishing organization specializes in professional development content for educators. Their editorial team produces weekly articles, downloadable toolkits, and video explainers. In preparation for a new fiscal year, leadership asked the content team to estimate which formats and topics would drive the most engagement and email sign-ups in Q3 and Q4.

The Challenge

In past years, content strategy relied mostly on intuition, driven by internal brainstorms and basic web metrics. But the team wanted to improve planning accuracy, justify investments in video production, and identify seasonal patterns. They turned to predictive analytics.

The Approach

The team started by exporting 18 months of data from their CMS and Google Analytics, including

- Publication date

- Format (article, guide, video)

- Topic tags

- Word count

- Engagement metrics (views, time on page, scroll depth)

- Conversion data (email sign-ups per content piece)

With support from a data analyst, they

1. Cleaned and labeled the data

2. Used linear regression to test which variables correlated with higher email sign-up rates

3. Created a moving average model to estimate future sign-ups by content type

4. Built a more sophisticated prediction model that factored in topic, source, and seasonal timing

Key Findings

- "How-to" articles published in August and January had the highest sign-up rates.

- Guides that included a downloadable PDF had an average 1.7x lift in conversions.

- Video content drove high time on page but only modest lift in email conversions—unless paired with a text summary and CTA.

Strategic Use of Lift

The team calculated predicted lift from proposed content investments:

- Upgrading five popular articles with embedded CTAs and downloadable checklists was expected to lift conversions by 22% (absolute lift of 0.8 percentage points).

- Publishing four new video–text hybrids in back-to-school season was projected to yield a 16% lift over baseline sign-ups.

These findings helped leadership approve a modest budget increase for interactive guide development while delaying broader video expansion.

Outcome

By Q4, email subscriptions increased 19% year over year. Equally important, the team had built a predictive framework that could guide future planning, test hypotheses, and communicate value to stakeholders with greater precision.

Workbook Exercise: Building a Simple Forecast and Estimating Lift

Use this exercise to create a basic forecast using historical content data and estimate the lift from a potential change.

Step 1: Choose a metric to forecast

Pick one goal-related metric (e.g., email sign-ups, average time on page, downloads).

Example: Email sign-ups per article

Your Metric: ________________________________

Step 2: Gather 6–12 months of historical data

You can use Google Analytics, GA4, or CMS export data. For each content asset, capture

- Publish date

- Format or topic

- The metric you chose in Step 1

Input this into a spreadsheet with one row per content item.

Step 3: Calculate a moving average

If you have dates and a goal metric

- Sort by date.

- Calculate a four-week or six-week moving average of your goal metric using =AVERAGE() formulas.

This gives you a baseline forecast.

Your Baseline Forecast (Moving Average): ___________ per week/month

Step 4: Model a hypothetical change

Now assume a proposed content change—like adding a new CTA, simplifying a page layout, or testing a new format.

- Estimate the expected change using past test results or similar content.

- If unsure, start with a conservative hypothetical (e.g., 10–20% lift).

Expected Lift: _____%

New Forecasted Metric: Baseline × (1 + Lift %) = ___________

Example:

Baseline = 40 sign-ups/week

Expected lift from new CTA = 25%

New forecast = 40 × 1.25 = 50 sign-ups/week

Step 5: Reflect

- What assumptions did you make in your estimate?

- What data would you need to improve confidence in your forecast?

- How might this prediction inform a strategic content decision?

This simple exercise shows how forecasting and lift estimation can turn past data into future planning without requiring complex tools.

Integrating the Team

Forecasting works best when it's not siloed within analytics. Content forecasting draws on historical data, contextual judgment, and strategic planning, which means it benefits from the insights of everyone involved in content creation, promotion, and evaluation.

Table 7-9 offers some insight into how to bring your team into the forecasting process.

Table 7-9. *Team roles in the content forecasting process*

Role	How They Contribute
Content strategist	Frames the questions and identifies content areas where forecasting will guide planning
Data analyst	Pulls and prepares datasets, runs lift calculations, creates trend visualizations
Writer/editor	Provides insight into content themes, tones, or formats that affect performance
UX or web designer	Flags technical friction points (load times, mobile layout) that influence user behavior
SEO or marketing lead	Adds context around traffic drivers and search intent over time
Manager or exec sponsor	Uses forecasts to make resource and budgeting decisions

Ways to Collaborate

- **Content Planning Meetings**: Use lift and trend data to inform your quarterly roadmap.

- **Forecasting Workshops**: Host a working session to identify what performance trends are emerging and what they might mean.

- **Cross-Team Debriefs**: When campaigns underperform or overperform, use the postmortem to ask: *Was this a deviation from the forecast? Why?*

Forecasting isn't just a technical skill; it's a tool for building shared expectations, setting goals, and improving decision-making across the organization.

It can also be an essential ingredient in your editorial planning. Don't just ask "What should we publish?" Ask: "Based on past patterns, what do we *expect* to happen if we do?"

Budget-Friendly Forecasting

You don't need predictive algorithms or machine learning to make smart forecasts. Even teams without a dedicated data analyst can use lift, trendlines, and segmentation to project future outcomes.

Here's how to do it cost-effectively.

1. **Use Free Tools First**

   You don't need expensive tools; you just need clarity. One well-labeled spreadsheet can often beat a dashboard. See Table 7-10 to identify a few tools you can start using right away.

Table 7-10. *Free forecasting tools*

Tool	Use Case
Google Sheets	Calculate lift, moving averages.
GA4 Explorations	Segment traffic and engagement trends.
Looker Studio	Create dashboards with filters and trendlines.
Microsoft Excel*	Run basic linear regression.
Free forecasting templates	Use built-in spreadsheet models (monthly, quarterly).

**Excel isn't free, but if you already have access, you may also have access to its Analytics ToolPak add-in. To add it, go to File ➤ Options ➤ Add-ins (on a PC) or Tools ➤ Excel Add-ins (on a Mac), select Excel Add-ins in the Manage box and click Go, then check the box for Analysis ToolPak, and click OK. Restart Excel and the ToolPak will appear under the Data tab.*

2. **Forecast with Aggregated Past Data**

Even without technical analysis, you can

- Calculate average open rates by month.

- Plot traffic by channel across the last three quarters.

- Measure conversion trends from your last five content campaigns.

Use simple averages and lift estimates to project what a similar campaign might deliver.

3. **Collaborate with Generalists**

If you don't have a data analyst, find your most spreadsheet-fluent marketer or content strategist and start there. Forecasting is often about asking the right question, not building a perfect model.

4. **Tie Forecasts to Action**

Don't forecast for forecasting's sake. Use them to

- Justify resourcing decisions.

- Set stakeholder expectations.

- Prioritize what gets tested or promoted.

Even a directional forecast is more persuasive than no projection at all. And don't overlook the value of content that has *failed* as a reference. Knowing what missed the mark can be just as useful as projecting what might just work.

Final Thoughts

You might think of forecasting as a window into the future, but it's really about making it possible to make better decisions today.

When you forecast lift based on a successful A/B test or use trendlines to anticipate a seasonal dip or apply regression to see which content types drive deeper engagement, you're moving your team toward evidence-informed strategy.

And you're shifting the conversation.

Instead of "We hope this will work," you're saying, "Here's what we expect and why." You're preparing stakeholders for possible outcomes. You're making smarter bets with your content budget. You're giving your team confidence to test, invest, or adapt based on actual patterns, not just preferences.

You also don't need to master statistical modeling or invest in pre-packaged digital solutions to develop effective forecasts. You just need the curiosity and the commitment to see and act on patterns that are relevant to your business model.

In the end, forecasting is more than just collecting data or chasing clicks; it's about using content to understand your market and create change. It's about using the past to take your next steps more deliberately, more efficiently, and with greater impact.

In the next chapter, we'll take a closer look at testing: what that means, what it doesn't, and how to incorporate it into your analytics program.

CHAPTER 8

Testing Content Effectiveness

In a content-saturated world, success in content development isn't always a by-product of talent or creativity; it's something you earn through trial and error. It's a process that leads you to the content that creates a solid connection to your audience, especially when what you *think* they want isn't what they want at all. That's where testing makes a difference.

Content testing is how we move from opinion to observation, from guessing to knowing what will work, for whom, and under what conditions.

> **Forecasting** asks: "Based on past patterns, what do we expect to happen?"

> **Testing** asks: "If we change something, how does user behavior change?"

Done well, content testing helps teams

- Make smarter decisions faster.

- Avoid investing in changes that don't produce meaningful results.

- Identify opportunities to scale what *does* work.

- Create a shared language of evidence across teams.

© Russ Bahorsky 2026
R. Bahorsky, *The Fundamentals of Content Analytics*,
https://doi.org/10.1007/979-8-8688-2601-6_8

Testing is also not something you do once, or once in a while, and move on; it's fundamental to an effective and ongoing analytics program. Once you establish a process for testing your content and its features, it becomes the basis for continuous improvement. You'll find an endless number of features, enhancements, and modifications to test and retest once you have the tools at your disposal, and each test will continue to add value to your content and increase its impact. And let's face it: people change, so the subjects, the media, and the digital platforms that grab their attention this year may not have the same appeal next year. That means testing keeps you from becoming yesterday's news.

This chapter focuses on accessible testing practices that don't necessarily require large budgets, paid platforms, or complex statistics, and they are practices that will work whether you manage marketing or communications for a leading brand or whether you're an entrepreneur with your own business. We'll look at the best practices in

- Choosing the right type of test

- Setting up a well-structured experiment

- Avoiding misleading metrics

- Learning from the results, even when they're inconclusive

Most importantly, you'll walk away with practical strategies for embedding testing into your content strategy one clear question at a time.

Choosing the Right Test for Your Question

Before running a test or an experiment, it's important to match the type of test to the type of question you're trying to answer. Not all tests are built for the same purpose, and choosing the wrong one can lead to misleading results or wasted effort.

Here's a guide to four of the most commonly used testing methods in content analytics.

A/B Testing: Simple and Reliable

An A/B test, easily the most reliable tool for optimizing content,[1] compares two versions of a piece of content—version A (the control) and version B (the variant or the test)—by splitting your audience randomly. The goal is to see which version performs better on a specific metric, such as click-through rate or conversion rate. It's a straightforward way to test one change against the current standard.

- **Use When**: You want to compare one version of content against another.

- **Example**: "Will changing the CTA from 'Sign Up' to 'Start Now' increase conversions?"

- **Strengths**: Easy to understand, fast to set up, statistically sound.

- **Limitations**: Only tests *one change* at a time; however, you can run multiple tests at the same time.

- **How to Run Them:** To conduct these types of tests, you need to integrate third-party experimentation tools into your data collection system, like GA4 (or use custom implementations). Or tools like Optimizely, VWO, or AB Tasty can manage experimental traffic distribution for you, and then you can use GA4 to analyze the outcomes.

---

[1] Kohavi, R., Diane Tang, and Ya Xu. *Trustworthy Online Controlled Experiments: A Practical Guide to A/B Testing*. Cambridge: Cambridge University Press, 2020.

HOW TO ESTABLISH A TESTING BASELINE

Establishing a baseline to use as a control (or what you might call an internal benchmark) in your testing efforts is a critical step in web content analytics, because it gives you a reference point for measuring performance and identifying trends, anomalies, or the impact of content changes.

The most meaningful approach is to use historical averages (e.g., three months, six months, or one year) to calculate an average. Be cautious about seasonality—some periods of time may naturally perform better or worse than others if you're a university, for example.

It will also be useful to calculate a standard deviation (SD) too, so you'll know how much that baseline rate is likely to fluctuate. See Appendix D to learn how to calculate a standard deviation.

Using baselines established by others in your industry, otherwise known as peer benchmarking, can be useful if you have no data of your own, but those benchmarks can be misleading and are likely to be very different from a baseline drawn from your own data.

Also see the section on single-rate sample sizes later in this chapter to understand the role sample size plays on determining a baseline.

Multivariable Testing: For More Complex Pages

Unlike A/B tests that change just one element, multivariable testing (usually in the form of a multiple regression) explains how many elements (like headlines, images, and calls to action) affect the outcome you're trying to achieve. It tests all possible combinations of these changes to determine not only which individual elements work best but also which combination of elements produces the most effective overall result.

- **Use When:** You want to test multiple elements simultaneously (e.g., headline + CTA + image)

- **Example:** "Which combination of hero image, headline, and button color gets the best engagement?"

- **Strengths:** Shows interaction effects.

- **Limitations:** Requires a large amount of traffic; complexity increases exponentially.

- **How to Run Them:** While you could develop your own platform for running these tests, it's easiest to integrate third-party experimentation tools into your data collection system. Optimizely, VWO, or AB Tasty has this functionality as well. However, if you aren't a trained statistician and you don't have one on your team, it may be a good idea to hire someone to help with this kind of testing.

Time-Split Testing: For Low-Traffic or Tool-Limited Teams

A time-split test (or temporal split test) involves running different versions of content during distinctly different time periods, rather than splitting the audience and running tests simultaneously. For example, you might show one version in the morning and another in the afternoon. This method is useful when you need to account for time-dependent factors, such as varying audience behavior throughout the day or week.

- **Use When:** You can't split users simultaneously but still want to compare performance.

- **Example:** "Let's try version A for one week, version B for the next, and compare results."

- **Strengths**: No special tools required.

- **Limitations**: Risk of external interference (e.g., variables like news cycles or your competitors' activities that could alter the way your audience responds or their demand for what you're offering).

- **How to Use Them:** Because a time-split test is about comparing performance across different time periods (e.g., running version A during one period and version B during another), GA4 can effectively analyze this by segmenting data by date or time. You manually control when different versions are live, and GA4's built-in reporting will let you compare the performance metrics (like conversion, engagement, etc.) across those time periods. A best practice is to aim for one to two weeks of normal traffic before evaluating your results.

Multi-armed Bandit (MAB) Testing: Adaptive Optimization

A multi-armed bandit approach is an adaptive testing method that continuously allocates more traffic to the better-performing versions as data comes in—balancing between exploring different options (exploration) and exploiting the best option (exploitation). This means that as the test proceeds, the system automatically adjusts to favor the content that's showing higher performance, potentially leading to quicker optimization and less lost opportunity compared with evenly split tests.

- **Use When**: You want your test to *optimize in real time*, sending more users to the better performer.

- **Example:** "Let's test two donation page designs. If one starts outperforming, shift more traffic to it."

- **Strengths**: Maximizes value during testing.

- **Limitations**: Less statistical clarity and transparency, assumes user behavior won't change over time, and often requires a testing platform.

- **How to Run Them:** Here again, the easiest option is to rely on tools like Optimizely, VWO, or AB Tasty to handle these tests for you.

Choosing a Test Based on Your Research Question Type

Your research question can also suggest what kind of test to run (Table 8-1).

Table 8-1. *Matching research questions with test types*

Question Type	Example	Best Test Type
Descriptive	"What's our average open rate?"	No test needed; just track performance.
Comparative	"Which CTA performs better?"	A/B or time-split.
Correlational	"Is engagement related to scroll depth?"	Exploratory (have your UX expert focus on this in user testing, i.e., answer this using quantitative methods).
Causal	"Does changing the CTA increase conversions?"	A/B, multivariable.
Predictive	"What kind of CTA might perform better next time?"	Start with forecast, and then test to validate.

Tip   If you want to *explain* why something performs better, you need a test. If you want to *understand* what's happening, use descriptive or exploratory methods like user testing instead.

A/B TEST IDEAS FOR WEB CONTENT, BY MEDIA TYPE

By organizing your tests around each content medium, you can identify which element to optimize for better engagement and conversion. Here are some ideas to get you started:

Landing Pages

- Headline wording and length

- Hero image or video choice

- Call-to-action (CTA) copy, color, and placement

- Above-the-fold layout vs. long-scroll format

- Social proof elements (test testimonials vs. trust badges)

- Form fields (number, order, inline)

- Offer type and framing (e.g., free trial vs. discount, urgency vs. exclusivity)

Blog Posts and Articles

- Title formats (question, listicle, how-to)

- Featured image style or size

- Intro paragraph length and hook style

- In-body CTAs (text link vs. button)

- Content length (short vs. long-form)

- Frequency of new posts

- Author byline prominence

Email Newsletters

- Subject line phrasing and emoji use

- Sender name (brand vs. person)

- Preview text length

- Email layout (single-column vs. multi-column)

- Button vs. text link CTAs

- Send day and time

- Offer positioning (e.g., top vs. bottom, bold vs. subtle)

Display and Social Ads

- Ad copy variants (problem–solution, benefits, urgency)

- Creative formats (static image vs. carousel vs. video)

- Primary image or thumbnail choice

- Call-to-action button text

- Audience targeting segments

- Offer messaging (e.g., "Save 20%" vs. "Get 2 Free")

Video Content

- Thumbnail image vs. autoplay muted preview

- Video length (15s vs. 30s vs. 60s)

- Intro hook (question vs. bold statement)

- Video player controls (autoplay on/off)

- End-screen CTAs (overlay vs. end-card)

Mobile and In-App Content

- Push notification copy and timing

- In-app banner design vs. native message

- Swipe-up vs. tap-to-open CTAs

- Onboarding sequence step order

- Dark mode vs. light mode layouts

A/B Testing in Practice

The success of a content test depends less on the tool you use and more on how well you design it. Even with free platforms or time-based comparisons, a thoughtfully structured experiment can yield actionable insights, while a sloppy one will leave you chasing noise.

Use the following steps to set up a reliable, low-friction content test.

Step 1: Write a clear, testable hypothesis

After reading Chapter 2, you should have a strong research question or set of questions. A research question is typically an open inquiry into a relationship or effect, and at this stage, you'll need to convert that question into a clear, concise, and testable prediction about that relationship. Here's how to convert one into the other:

1. **Identify the Variables:** Break down your research question into key variables. Determine which one is the independent variable (the cause or input) and which is the dependent variable (the effect or outcome). For example, if you're studying how the timing of donation appeals affects donor response rates, "appeal timing" is the independent variable, and "response rate" is the dependent variable.

2. **Clarify the Relationship:** Decide what you expect to happen based on theory, prior studies, or intuition. Are you predicting that an increase in one variable will lead to an increase (or decrease) in the other? This helps you form a directional hypothesis. For instance, if your research question is "Does increasing the number of blogs you publish each month affect conversions?", you need to decide whether you think that may be the case or not and by how much (there will always be some guesswork involved).

3. **Formulate a Testable Statement:** Turn your expectation into a statement that can be measured, typically in an "if–then" format. For the blogging example, you might hypothesize, "If a company adds a blog each month, then conversions will increase by at least 10% over the next quarter."

4. **Be Specific and Measurable:** Ensure that the hypothesis includes specific details, so you can measure the outcome. This means defining what "increase" means in quantitative terms and setting a clear time frame or context for the test.

If you're new to testing, start with a subject line or button color. Pick a platform you already use (like Mailchimp or GA4), choose one variable, and run the test for one week. The key is not to be perfect but to practice and learn.

Caution   When testing donation or conversion CTAs, sensitive topics, or emotionally charged content, it's essential to prioritize user trust. Don't mislead or pressure users just to generate lift—even if it's just a test. Ethical testing builds sustainable strategies and protects your brand, while deceptive or high-pressure tactics will do lasting damage.

Here's an example of how you might convert a research question into a testable hypothesis:

- **Research Question:** "Does incorporating video content on a website increase user engagement?"
- **Identify Variables:**

    - **Independent Variable**: Presence of video content

    - **Dependent Variable**: User engagement (e.g., time spent on site, click-throughs)

- **Clarify the Relationship:** You might believe that video content will boost engagement because it can attract and hold visitors' attention better than text alone.

- **Hypothesis:** "If a website includes video content, then user engagement, measured by average time on site, will increase by at least 15% compared with websites without video content."

By translating a broad inquiry into a clear, testable prediction like this, you set the stage for designing experiments or studies to empirically verify, or quantify, the relationship.

Step 2: Choose a primary success metric

Not all metrics are equally important. Decide up front what you're optimizing for, and keep it simple. Table 8-2 offers a simple way to connect your goal with your primary metric.

Table 8-2. *Choosing a primary success metric*

If You're Testing ...	Your Primary Metric Might Be ...
CTA language or placement	Click-through rate (CTR)
Page layout or visual treatment	Time on page or scroll depth
Email subject line	Open rate or click-to-open rate
Sign-up page format	Conversion rate

Secondary metrics can provide helpful context, but don't let them dilute your decision-making.

Step 3: Define the audience and timeline

Make sure you know

- **Who's included** in the test (e.g., new visitors, mobile users, returning donors)

- **How long** the test will run (ideally long enough to smooth out day-of-week effects)

- **How much traffic** or how many impressions you'll need for results to be meaningful (we'll look at sample size later in this chapter)

Step 4: Isolate the variable

Change one thing at a time. If you alter the headline *and* the CTA *and* the image, and performance improves, you won't know which change caused it. The best practice is to use an A/B test to test the impact of a change in one variable. You can use a multivariable regression to test multiple variables in combination, but it's also advisable to follow up that test with A/B tests on the individual variables that your regression suggests are the most impactful.

If you can't isolate a variable, test in stages, but also remember that there will always be variables—like what's going on in the news or the economy—that will always be outside of your control. Again, it's important to retest and validate to make sure that your lift remains consistent as those outside variables change over time.

Step 5: Set up and deploy the test

If you're sending your content out to your audience via a newsletter or some other channel that allows you to randomly select who receives version A and who receives version B, deploying your test should be relatively easy, provided you've tagged each version to allow you to distinguish between the two different levels of response or engagement. If you don't, there are a number of tools you might consider.

1. **Optimizely:** A comprehensive platform for running A/B tests on websites, mobile apps, and other digital products. It offers robust analytics and easy integration with other marketing tools.

2. **VWO (Visual Website Optimizer):** Provides a suite of tools for A/B testing, multivariable testing, and split URL testing. It also includes heatmaps and visitor recordings to understand user behavior.

3. **Google Optimize:** A free tool that integrates seamlessly with Google Analytics. It allows you to run A/B tests and multivariable tests and to redirect tests to optimize user experiences.

4. **Adobe Target:** Part of the Adobe Experience Cloud, this tool offers A/B testing, personalization, and automated decision-making to enhance user engagement and conversions.

5. **AB Tasty:** Focuses on experimentation, personalization, and feature management. It helps businesses optimize their digital experiences across websites, mobile apps, and other channels.

These tools provide the necessary features to design, implement, and analyze A/B tests, but there are a few additional things to set up.

First, you'll need to establish a control group—a subset of the total mailing list that does not receive the experimental treatment. This group will serve as a baseline to compare against the experimental group. Make sure the control group is similar to the experimental group in all aspects except for the variable being tested. If possible, make sure you're not making your A/B test a 50/50 split unless

1. You have absolutely no idea what your baseline response should be or which version will produce it. Any time you test an alternate version of your content that has the potential to be less effective than your control, you risk missing out on the kinds of responses you need your content to produce. Before choosing a 50/50 split, ask yourself, "How costly will it be if the test group underperforms?"

2. You are unlikely to get enough responses to produce statistically valid datasets from both groups. We'll take a closer look at sample size later in this chapter, but keep in mind that your test version should only go to enough people to produce a statistically significant sample.

3. The impact of the test group underperforming is minimal, you have high traffic, and you need to make a quick decision based on the results.

Tip   If you have the traffic to do it, you can certainly test how a particular feature of your content affects a particular *segment* of your audience. This is an especially valuable tool to use when you're optimizing your audience journey. Always remember, though, to be sure that both your control group and your test group represent the same subset of your audience.

Your test should also have a clear timeline. This should include the start and end date, as well as any intermediate checkpoints. Ensure the time frame is long enough to gather sufficient data and account for variations (e.g., day-of-week effects).

When choosing what percentage of your prospective audience should receive the test version, the goal is to choose the lowest split that still lets you hit the required sample size within a reasonable time frame. You may not get this right the first time, but it should get easier with each test you roll out.

You can also make real-time adjustments on the fly if necessary:

- Monitor live traffic and conversion rates daily or hourly.

- If traffic exceeds expectations, reallocate more to the variant.

- If your variant shows signs of overperforming or underperforming early, you can pause the test or ramp it up.

Table 8-3 offers some guidelines for making adjustments to your test once it's live.

Table 8-3. *Guidelines for real-time test adjustments*

Scenario	Action Taken	Why It's Done
Variant is underperforming.	Pause or reduce traffic.	Minimize risk or user impact
Variant is outperforming.	Ramp up traffic allocation.	Accelerate learning and gains
Results are ambiguous.	Let the test continue to run.	Wait for more data before deciding

Step 6: Plan for what happens after the test

Before you launch, ask:

- What will count as a "win"?

- What's the minimum detectable effect (MDE) that would justify a change?

- What will you do if the result is inconclusive?

Plan your action in advance, not just your measurement. If you're faced with the question, "Now what?" after the test concludes, you've wasted your time. If you're faced with that question before your test, it's likely that you're dealing with a vanity metric.

While an A/B test compares two versions of something to see which performs better, analysts also turn to basic statistical tools to determine whether a difference you've observed is just random fluctuation or a real signal. Concepts like standard deviation, t-tests, z-tests, and p-values provide the math behind deciding whether your results are trustworthy. You don't need to master these calculations to run useful tests, but it's important to know they exist.

Unless you're asked for this level of validation from your stakeholders, it's more practical to take an iterative approach to determining significance, which allows you to simply assume that your results are valid in order to roll out an additional test to a new audience, a larger sample, etc. This approach can be a risky one if it turns out that your findings are wrong, but each iteration will provide additional validation of your findings or give you the means to dial in a lift value that produces consistent results over time.

If you need a guide to understanding and using statistical tools for determining significance and reliability, see Appendix D.

PUSH VS. PULL: TAILOR YOUR TESTING TO HOW CONTENT
REACHES YOUR AUDIENCE

Not all content gets delivered the same way, and that changes how you test it. If your content is pushed to an audience (like through email, SMS, or in-app notifications), you control

- Who sees it

- When they see it

- How they're split into test groups

That makes A/B testing clean and highly reliable. But if your content is pulled by the audience (via search, social media, or blog traffic), you're working with

- Unpredictable timing

- Uneven exposure

- Algorithm-driven delivery

That means your tests must adapt—using time-based comparisons, segmented content variants, or engagement proxies like scroll depth and bounce rate.

Consider the characteristics of each approach (Table 8-4).

Table 8-4. *Push vs. pull*

Push (e.g., Email)	Pull (e.g., Blog or Search)
Controlled delivery timing.	Audience behavior drives exposure.
Easy to assign test groups.	Harder to isolate test groups.
Short test windows.	Longer test durations needed.
Strong attribution.	Attribution is fuzzier.
Use tools like Mailchimp, HubSpot.	Use tools like GA4, Clarity, Optimize.

Tip   Push tests are ideal for clean A/B splits. Pull tests often require longer windows, time-split setups, or engagement metrics instead of conversion alone.

If you're using both models (as many marketers do), treat your results as though they only make sense in the same context, that is, what works for your email subscribers might produce different results in search or social.

Understanding Sample Size

One of the most common questions teams ask when testing content is: *"How many users do we need for the results to be meaningful?"*

The short answer? It depends on what you're testing and how confident you want to be. But here are some useful rules of thumb, especially if you want to assess the impact of a video, for example, or if you're running an A/B test.

Before we look at how to select a sample size for a particular test, we need to make a distinction between "users," or the number of people that are exposed to a piece of content (e.g., a control, a test, a video, or a newsletter), and "conversions," or the actions you want those users to take (e.g., sign-ups, purchases, click-throughs). The term "sample size" can sometimes be used to mean either, so it's important to make sure you understand how much of each of these samples or subsets of a larger group, or population, represents a statistically meaningful amount.

SAMPLE SIZE CONVERSION

There are several free sample size calculators available on the internet, and it's also fairly easy to build one using Excel or Google Sheets, but make sure you understand whether the number those calculators generate is the number of users you need to *test* or the number of conversions you need to *observe*.

If the calculator you're using produces one and not the other, converting the number is easy. If you know, for example, that 10% of users click your CTA (i.e., your baseline conversion rate), and your calculator tells you that you need to test 1,000 users, just multiply the two numbers to get 100, the number of conversions you need to observe. And vice versa, if you know the number of conversions you need to observe, just divide that number by your conversion rate ($100 \div .10 = 1,000$).

Let's look at how to determine sample sizes for a variety of tests, including for the purpose of taking meaningful baseline readings.

Single-Rate Sample Sizes

If you want to estimate what percentage of visitors to your website do something (e.g., what percentage view a video or click a button) with a reasonable level of precision, a good rule of thumb is that you'll need to observe about 385 unique conversions, at a 95% confidence level with a ±5 percentage point margin of error (more on this later) when the audience is very large (e.g., everyone with an internet connection).

This is also known as a single-proportion sample size and assumes your sample represents a typical subset of the audience you're trying to reach.

If your audience or population is a closed one—a mailing list with fewer than 385 people on it, for example—the picture, as Table 8-5 suggests, is a little different.

Table 8-5. *Sample sizes for small audiences (same parameters: 95%/±5%/p=0.5)*

Audience Size	Adjusted Sample Size
100	80
200	132
500	218
1,000	278
5,000	357
10,000	372
100,000+	≈385

Estimating a single rate (the single-proportion case above) tells you how precisely you can measure one percentage. This can be useful for

- **Baseline setting and benchmarking.** Knowing where you start so you can judge future changes ("Right now, 12% of pages autoplay video.").

- **KPI tracking and reporting.** Many dashboards are about single metrics (open rate, bounce rate, video completion rate) that stakeholders expect to see.

- **Quality assurance and auditing.** Measure prevalence of problems: for example, percentage of pages with broken links or accessibility errors.

- **Sizing and resource planning.** Estimate how many conversions, incidents, or errors you'll see, which can be helpful for staffing and capacity planning.

- **Segmentation and prioritization.** See which segments are underperforming (e.g., mobile vs. desktop view rate) to prioritize fixes.

- **Trend monitoring.** Track trends and detect changes in seasonality or lift over time.

Quantitative A/B Tests

A/B tests are different: they compare two rates or proportions (control vs. test), so you need a sample for each variant. In practice, A/B tests typically require larger samples to reach statistical significance, and of course, you can use a sample size calculator, but you can also use some rules of thumb to determine how many users or conversions you need to determine how good your test will be at predicting future performance of your findings.

As with determining single-rate sample sizes, you'll need to start by determining whether or not your audience numbers in the millions, or is virtually unlimited, or if it's a more select group.

Understanding Sample Size If Your Audience Is Very Large

When you're creating content for the open web—like a blog, landing page, or search-optimized resource—your potential audience size is theoretically unlimited. That doesn't mean you need a massive audience to run a good test, but it does mean that you control how much traffic to include, rather than being limited by a fixed user list. This flexibility makes it easier to reach your required sample size—as long as you're willing to keep the test running long enough, or distribute the content widely enough, to collect sufficient data.

The key trade-off here is between speed and statistical confidence. If you have high traffic volume, you can hit your sample size target in days or even hours. If your volume is lower, you'll need to let the test run longer—possibly a week or two—to get a clear result.

When your audience is effectively unlimited or even if it's a proprietary database that numbers in the millions

- **You can afford to be more selective.** Instead of testing every visitor, test a random subset until you have enough data to be confident in the results.

- **You can retest frequently.** Unlike closed-audience tests (like emails or internal messages), open-audience tests can be repeated without overexposing your list.

- **You still need to control for external factors.** Seasonality, algorithm changes, or traffic spikes can distort results, so always monitor for changes in the context in which your content is being received.

There are several factors you'll need to keep in mind when evaluating how much of a sample you'll need, such as

- Your baseline conversion rate and how much of a lift you're observing

- The minimum lift you want to be able to detect, like a 1% or a 10% lift (the smaller the expected lift, the bigger the sample you'll need)—typically known as a minimum detectable effect, or MDE

- Your desired confidence level (e.g., 95%)

However, rather than determining a precise number for your sample size, using some rules of thumb will often be enough.

You should already know your baseline conversion rate, since an A/B test aims to find an alternative to improve that rate, and we can assume that you're comfortable working with a conventional confidence level of 95%. However, if you're not sure what your MDE should be, Table 8-6 offers some typical examples.

Table 8-6. *MDE rules of thumb*

Context	Typical MDE Range (Relative Change)	Why This Range Is Common
Email campaigns (open/ click rate)	15–25%	Low baseline rates; large changes needed to be meaningful.
Landing page conversion	10–20%	Moderate traffic; conversions are key business metrics.
Headline or CTA testing	10–20%	Small changes can drive noticeable engagement shifts.
Blog or article engagement	15–30%	Engagement metrics (scroll depth, time on page) are variable.
Navigation or UX changes	5–10%	Even small improvements can enhance user flow.
Video or multimedia content engagement	10–25%	Completion rates and interactions vary widely.
Search or filter functionality	5–15%	Functional changes often have subtle but important effects.

With an approximate MDE range in mind, use Table 8-7 to determine what your sample size should be based on your approximate baseline conversion rate.

Table 8-7. *A/B test sample size guide by response rate and detectable change*

Baseline Response Rate	5% MDE	10% MDE	15% MDE	20% MDE	25% MDE	30% MDE
1–2%	~600,000+	~150,000+	~90,000+	~62,000	~48,000	~39,000
2–3%	~400,000+	~100,000+	~60,000+	~39,000	~30,000	~25,000
3–4%	~300,000+	~75,000+	~45,000+	~25,000	~20,000	~18,000
4–5%	~240,000+	~60,000+	~36,000+	~18,000	~14,000	~12,000
5–10%	~100,000–240,000	~25,000–60,000	~15,000–36,000	~6,000–14,000	~5,000–11,000	~4,000–9,000
10–20%	~40,000–100,000	~10,000–25,000	~6,000–15,000	~2,500–6,000	~2,000–5,000	~1,500–4,000
20%+	~16,000–40,000	~4,000–10,000	~2,500–6,000	~1,000–2,500	~800–2,000	~600–1,500

Here's an example of how to use the two charts to run a test to decide whether a new headline improves conversion rate on a landing page.

Step 1: Identify your baseline response rate

Let's say your current conversion rate is 4%.

From the Sample Size Chart, look at the row for 4–5% baseline response rate.

Step 2: Choose a realistic MDE based on context

From the MDE Context Chart, for headline or CTA testing, the typical MDE range is 10–20%. Let's say you want to detect a 15% relative improvement (i.e., from 4% to 4.6%).

Step 3: Find your sample size

From the Sample Size Chart, under the 4–5% baseline row and the 20% change column, the recommended sample size per variant is ~14,000–18,000 (i.e., the number of users you need to test).

Since you're aiming for a 15% change, your sample size will be slightly higher—around 20,000 per variant is a safe estimate.

Table 8-8 offers an overview of the key test details.

Table 8-8. *Test plan summary*

Component	Value
Baseline conversion rate	4%
Desired improvement (MDE)	15% (i.e., 4% → 4.6%)
Sample size per variant	~20,000
Conversions needed per variant (based on 4% conversion rate)	~800
Total sample size	~40,000 (A + B groups combined)

If the sample size you need doesn't match what you have, there are still some things you can do. The problem is a common one, and it's one of the most delicate balancing acts in experimentation: squeezing statistical insight out of limited data without compromising validity. Here's how a resourceful content analyst might approach it:

- **Use More Sensitive Metrics:** Swap coarse metrics like conversion rates for more frequent signals.

  - **Microconversions** (clicks, scroll depth, form engagement).

  - **Engagement proxies** (indirect metrics like scroll depth or time on page that signal user interest or interaction, especially helpful when conversion events are rare or take time to happen).

- **Pool Traffic Across Variants or Time:** If your current traffic is too low

  - Lengthen your testing period.

  - Expand your test across similar pages (like multiple blog posts or product categories).

  - Settle for the possibility that your findings are less certain and validate your findings through additional iterations of the test.

- **Accept and Quantify the Limitations:** Settle for a test that produces a lower level of confidence (90% over 95%, which is still pretty good), and communicate the additional risk to stakeholders clearly. Even if your test results aren't a strong predictor of future impact, they may still be a strong indicator that you're on a clear path to growth, improvement, or even just greater clarity in your decision-making.

- **Use Another Testing Method:** If your audience is small or time is limited, consider using time-split testing instead of full A/B.

- **Call in an Expert:** There are other methods that a statistician might use, like Bayesian A/B testing or bootstrap resampling. Those techniques are outside of the scope of this book but should be well within the capabilities of an analytics firm.

It's easy to get paralyzed by sample size math, but remember: testing is a process. Even if your first test isn't conclusive, it can point you in the right direction. Many teams run "directional" tests with 200–300 conversions just to see if one version appears to outperform and then validate it in a broader follow-up test.

In fact, this is the advantage you have if you're developing a content research program for your organization rather than just using the tools for one-time or occasional testing. By building a program, your testing should become iterative, so if your sample sizes aren't large enough or the results you're getting don't give you the confidence you need, you can simply repeat the test until a clear pattern develops, provided you take a more conservative approach with your predictions for the next test and your additional investment in the effort is incremental and not exponential.

Of course, if you absolutely need to pinpoint your sample size, whether to satisfy your own curiosity or the requirements of a stakeholder, there are plenty of resources available, from online calculators to consultants, available to help you.

Sample Size If Your Audience Is Limited

Finally, if you aren't creating content for the world to see, just a small subset like the users in your company database or on your mailing list, the rules for sample size are a little different. Smaller audiences require bigger changes to be detectable, so your options may be more limited depending on the size of your database or mailing list.

Use Table 8-9 to decide whether your test is feasible and what kind of change you can realistically detect.

Table 8-9. *Rules of thumb for small audiences*

Audience Size per Variant	Baseline Conversion Rate	Run the Test If You Expect …	What You Can Detect
<1,000	Any	A big change (30%+ relative lift)	Only large effects will be statistically visible.
1,000–5,000	3–10%	A moderate change (15–30%)	Good for testing bold messaging or layout shifts.
5,000–10,000	5–10%	A small-to-moderate change (10–20%)	Suitable for refining headlines, CTAs, or offers.
10,000–50,000	5–20%	A small change (5–10%)	Ideal for optimizing well-performing content.
50,000+	10%+	A very small change (2–5%)	Great for precision testing and micro-optimizations.

For example, let's say you have a mailing list of 2,000 people and your current click-through rate is 5%. That gives you about 100 clicks per variant. Based on Table 8-9, you should only run the test if you expect a 15–30% improvement—for example, from 5% to 6.5%. If you're hoping for a tiny lift (like 5%), your audience is probably too small to detect it reliably.

Multivariable Testing

Multivariable tests like multiple regressions evaluate the interaction effects between multiple elements (e.g., headline × image × CTA). This increases the number of combinations exponentially along with the sample size required. For example, your test of two headlines and three CTAs means 2 × 3 = 6 versions to test. To detect meaningful differences, you'll need 1,000+ users per combination, which means 6,000+ users total. If your traffic doesn't result in that kind of volume, you're better off sticking to A/B tests that allow you to test one element at a time.

Here are a few rules of thumb if you're considering a multivariable test:

- Only run a multivariable test if you expect high traffic (more than 10,000 users) within the test window.

- Limit the number of tested elements or variants to avoid underpowered results.

- Use multivariable testing to fine-tune landing pages or high-volume content, where small optimizations can lead to big results.

However, before you dismiss multivariable testing because the sample size is out of your organization's reach, there is a method you can use if you're launching a campaign that might have the potential to fulfill your sample size needs over time.

By using data from prior campaigns or a small pilot launch that generates a few hundred responses, you can build a multiple regression model that will help you understand the impact of predictors like

- Source channel

- Audience segment

- Time of day

- Pre-click behavior

- Creative attributes

If the model appears to be strong, you can validate your results using the data you collect from your campaign as you roll it out. If you roll out your campaign in successive phases, each phase should generate data that can be used to validate or improve the model you've developed, and your content can be modified to reflect those results.

Finally, if you suspect different types of users may respond differently to your content, multivariable testing can reveal valuable patterns—like which CTAs perform better for donors vs. prospects.

However, because segmented tests require much larger sample sizes, consider running A/B tests within a single segment or analyzing segment performance after an A/B test concludes. If traffic is limited, start with your most valuable or active segment and then scale up from there.

Multi-armed Bandit Testing

Multi-armed bandit tests automatically shift more traffic to better-performing variants as the test progresses. This means

- Users are exposed to higher-performing versions sooner, increasing total conversions during testing.

- The system adapts in real time, but you may sacrifice statistical rigor for faster wins.

If this kind of testing looks like a promising opportunity, keep in mind that MAB tests will require an even larger total sample size to identify a clear winner (e.g., 10,000+ users), but if you want to optimize performance in real time and not just compare outcomes after the fact, this kind of testing could be worth a try, especially when

- You're running a long campaign (e.g., a month or more).

- Your goal is to maximize conversions during the test, not just evaluate variants.

- You don't need deep statistical significance, just fast, directional learning.

Qualitative User Testing

It's also worth mentioning that when running user interviews, content comprehension tests, or usability sessions with your UX expert, you're not looking for statistical confidence; you're looking for insight.

UX guru Jakob Nielsen's rule of thumb is that testing with five users will uncover about 80% of the major usability problems in a design or experience.[2]

For content-specific testing

- Test with five to eight users per segment (e.g., donors, prospective students).

- Make sure your test includes diverse perspectives, especially if content is highly targeted, and make sure you test your content on a variety of devices.

- Prioritize patterns, not outliers. If three out of five people hesitate on a CTA, that's a signal.

---

[2] Jakob Nielsen. "Why You Only Need to Test with 5 Users." Nielsen Norman Group. March 19, 2000. https://www.nngroup.com/articles/why-you-only-need-to-test-with-5-users/

Interpreting Results Responsibly

Finally, as the test ends and the results roll in, it's tempting to go straight to declaring a winner. But if you want your test to drive real learning—and real change—interpretation matters as much as measurement.

Understanding Confidence

Statistical tools will often produce a confidence level with each test you run, which is a way of saying, "We're 95% sure this difference isn't due to chance." Some tools will also let you set the level of confidence you're willing to accept (rule of thumb: stick with 95%).

If you want to be reasonably confident that the lift you're seeing has a reasonable chance of predicting future performance, there are a couple of steps you'll want to take.

1. Calculate the mean or average (if the tool you're using hasn't already done this for you).

2. Calculate the standard deviation (Appendix D includes Excel formulas that will make this a snap).

3. If your sample size is under 30, run a t-test, and if it's over 30, run a z-test (again, see Appendix D).

The results should tell you if the difference you're seeing between the control group and the test group is statistically significant or is likely to hold up over repeat testing.

If your test turns out to be statistically insignificant, that doesn't mean there's no effect; it just means the data didn't give you a clear answer *yet*. When in doubt, extend the test (if feasible), or run it again with a larger sample.

If you find yourself in a situation where your test fails to produce meaningful results, that can produce meaningful takeaways:

- Maybe both versions perform equally well.

- Maybe the change was too subtle to matter.

- Maybe your users just didn't care about that variable.

Each of these outcomes tells you something useful about your audience or priorities.

Understanding Validity

In addition to your confidence level, you'll also want to address whether or not your test has validity or whether what you're measuring actually reflects the underlying behavior you care about.

There are a number of kinds of validity, but in a business environment there are only three that have practical value:

1. **Face Validity:**

   - **What It Is:** A straightforward, almost "gut-feel" check to see if a metric appears to measure what it's supposed to.

   - **Practical Determination:** It's the easiest to assess because if a click-through rate or time-on-site measure "looks right" to those familiar with the campaign, you already have a preliminary indication of validity.

   - **Usage:** You can rely on face validity as a first pass to decide if a metric makes sense before diving into deeper analysis.

2. **Construct Validity:**

   - **What It Is:** An evaluation of whether the measure truly captures the concept it intends to (e.g., using engagement metrics like time on page, social shares, and comments to represent "user engagement").

- **Practical Determination:** While it requires comparing several related metrics to ensure they align with the intended concept, it's still relatively straightforward. You can often validate a metric by checking its consistency with other indicators that measure the same idea.

- **Usage:** It's often used to tweak and refine dashboards or reports so that the data truly reflects the underlying notion—such as engagement, satisfaction, or conversion intent.

3. **Predictive Validity:**

- **What It Is:** The extent to which a metric or test result forecasts future outcomes that matter (e.g., how well early engagement predicts eventual conversion, revenue, or customer retention).

- **Practical Determination:** With historical data, marketers can run analyses (like simple regressions or correlation studies) to see if improvements in a given metric reliably lead to better future performance.

- **Usage:** This is highly actionable because if you know that a 10% increase in click-through rate today predicts a 5% boost in sales later, you can directly justify optimizations. While it may require some statistical work, its clear business relevance often makes it one of the more valued and "practically determinable" forms of validity.

Obviously, the easiest form of validity to determine from a practical, day-to-day marketing standpoint is face validity—which is akin to intuition or the kind of business sense you develop when you've been doing this kind of thing for a while. Predictive validity is also highly practical. Your audience isn't like to stop looking at your content after your test concludes, and if you continue to see the kind of lift your test produced, it's safe to assume your results were sound by this definition of validity.

Determining construct validity is also manageable, but it requires some cross-referencing among related measures. User testing can provide you with either a first step or a second step in determining construct validity (e.g., an A/B test could validate what you observed in user testing or vice versa), but you can also compare tests across broader categories of content or with similar segments of your audience to be sure that any changes you make as a result of your testing appear to generate lift in other contexts. Ultimately, the level of validity you'll need will depend on the amount of certainty you need and the resources you have to achieve that certainty.

DIFFERING PERSPECTIVES ON VALIDITY: BUSINESS VS. ACADEMIA

While analytics in a business environment may not appear to have the same degree of rigor that you might find in a research lab, that's because differences in data access between business and academic analytics directly shape how each domain approaches the idea of validity.

In business, analysts often work with abundant, real-time data that allows for iterative testing and rapid feedback loops, so validity tends to be pragmatic—focused on whether insights are good enough to drive action and rapid adaptation right now. They're also working under the assumption that consumer behavior may change from week to week, month to month, or even year to year, but that it's ultimately a moving target.

In academia, social scientists work with more limited, intentionally gathered datasets, so validity is treated with greater methodological discipline. Analysts use the peer review process and statistical controls to ensure findings are theoretically sound and verifiable, and they are typically working toward the goal of uncovering findings about human behavior that are more durable.

Document and Learn

Finally, once the testing is done and evaluated, it's a good idea to keep a record of what you've done that you can refer to when you're exploring opportunities for new tests or revisiting results over time. Make it a standard practice to record

- The hypothesis

- What was tested

- The outcome

- What decision was made

- What questions the result raised

And remember, you're building a testing culture, not just checking boxes. Even if the result is unclear, the process of testing sharpens the questions and the judgment that you and your team bring to the process over time.

Case Study: Optimizing a Nonprofit's CTA Strategy

An environmental nonprofit traditionally used urgency-based CTAs in its fundraising emails and landing pages: "Donate Now—Every Dollar Helps Today!"

While effective in bursts, their communications team wondered if a story-driven approach might resonate more deeply and lead to more donations during their spring giving campaign, especially for first-time supporters.

Hypothesis

The content team developed the following hypothesis: *"A more emotionally specific CTA ('You can give a student clean water. Start with $10.') will outperform our urgency-based CTA in both conversion rate and average donation."* They tested it using the test plan in Table 8-10.

Table 8-10. *Test design plan*

Element	Version A (Control)	Version B (Test)
CTA message	"Donate Now—Every Dollar Helps Today!"	"You can give a student clean water. Start with $10."
Landing page	Standard layout and form	Same
Traffic source	Split evenly between email list and paid social ads	Same
Duration	10 days	Same
Primary metric	Donation conversion rate	Same
Secondary metrics	Click-through rate, average donation size	Same

The test results are shown in Table 8-11.

Table 8-11. *Test results*

Metric	Version A	Version B
CTR from email	3.7%	3.4%
Donation conversion rate	1.8%	2.5%
Average donation	$25.40	$30.80

While version B had a slightly lower click-through rate, it significantly outperformed in conversion rate and donation amount—the metrics that mattered most.

What They Learned

- The storytelling concept improved both the emotional resonance and clarity of the CTA.

- Higher conversions and gift amounts more than offset the slightly reduced traffic.

- Emotionally grounded messages can *lift performance* without requiring layout changes.

Takeaway

Don't just test formats; test message framing. Small changes in language can tap more meaningful user engagement.

What They Did Next

- Rolled out story-driven CTAs across campaign channels

- Tested impact framing on social ads and SMS

- Created a test log to document findings and track future experiments

Workbook Exercise: Plan and Document a Test

Use this structured exercise to plan your next content test. This can be adapted for team brainstorming, editorial planning, or individual work.

Step 1: Identify your hypothesis

What do you expect will happen, and why?

Example: *"If we switch our blog CTA from 'Read More' to 'Get the Full Guide,' we'll increase resource downloads by 15%."*

Your Hypothesis:

____

____

____

Step 2: Select your metrics

What are you measuring to determine success?

Primary Metric   _______________________________________

Secondary Metric(s)   _______________________________________

Step 3: Define the audience and timeline

Who will be part of the test and for how long?

Audience Segment   _______________________________________

Channels   _______________________________________

Start Date   _______________________________________

End Date   _______________________________________

Step 4: Describe the versions

**Variable Being
Tested**   _______________________________________

Version A (Control)   _______________________________________

Version B (Variant) ______________________________

Step 5: Record results

After the test, fill in the actual performance data.

Metric	Version A	Version B	Winner?
Primary metric			
Secondary metric(s)			

Step 6: Interpretation

- Did the test validate or challenge your hypothesis?

- Were the results significant or inconclusive?

- What surprised you?

Notes:

Step 7: Next steps

Ask the questions:

- Will you roll out the winning version?

- Will you run a follow-up test?

- What new question does this test raise?

Action Plan:

Integrating the Team

Testing is most powerful when it's not owned by one person or siloed in analytics, and it works best when it reflects creative curiosity, technical coordination, and shared strategic goals.

Use Table 8-12 to explore how you might engage your full content team in the process.

Table 8-12. Team roles in a testing workflow

Team Member	How They Contribute
Content strategist	Frames the test's purpose and aligns it with business objectives
Writer/editor	Crafts clear, distinct content variants (e.g., headlines, body text, CTAs)
Designer/UX lead	Adjusts layout or visual treatments for multivariable tests
Developer or platform owner	Implements test in CMS or testing tool, ensures tracking is functional
Marketing manager	Integrates the test into campaign workflows, monitors channel consistency
Data analyst	Reviews performance, calculates lift, evaluates significance
Project manager	Tracks timelines, ensures documentation, manages follow-ups

Collaboration Tactics

Engaging the whole team in the testing process can be a powerful way to build a sense of shared ownership in the work and its outcomes. A few simple changes to your process are all you need.

- **Hypothesis Brainstorming**: Schedule 30 minutes for your team to pitch quick test ideas—no data required, just instincts and creative exploration.

- **Test Calendar**: Keep a shared calendar or dashboard of live and planned tests.

252

- **Monthly Debrief**: Discuss test results (wins *and* losses) with the broader team to build a shared evidence base.

Tip   Document *why* you tested something, not just *what* you tested. These insights can inform future projects.

Testing isn't just about metrics; it's about building a culture of thoughtful experimentation. The more cross-functional your testing efforts are, the faster your team learns and adapts.

Budget-Friendly Ideas for Testing Content Effectiveness

Testing doesn't require enterprise platforms or advanced analytics support. You can launch effective tests with some of the tools you may already have available.

- **Email platforms** like Mailchimp and Constant Contact offer A/B tools for subject lines, content blocks, and send times.

- **CMSs** like WordPress and HubSpot often support plugin-based or native A/B testing modules.

- **Analytics tools** like Google Analytics 4 and Microsoft Clarity allow for time-split comparisons by date range, channel, or page.

And there's no need to complicate things at first. It's okay to keep things simple, especially if you're trying to reshape your organization's culture. You just need to start with a few proof points.

- Test one variable at a time (headline, CTA, image).

- Use time-based testing when you can't split audiences.

- Use engagement metrics that are easy to interpret (click-through, scroll depth, form fills).

Make Testing Part of Content Creation

Instead of asking your team to "test something," build testing into the flow:

- "Which subject line variant should we try this week?"

- "Let's write two CTA versions and split the email list."

- "Let's launch the new landing page with a fallback and compare results by week."

Share Results, Even When They're Inconclusive

One of the cheapest, most effective ways to build value from testing is to document what you learn, especially when the results are ambiguous. This helps avoid retesting the same ideas later and creates a baseline for future improvements.

Even a "no clear winner" test builds useful institutional knowledge.

Final Thoughts

Testing is more than a tactic. Done well, it becomes a mindset.

It's a way of approaching content creation not as a finished product but as an evolving interaction with your audience. It shifts the team from saying, *"This feels right"* to asking, *"How does this perform, and how can we improve it?"*

You don't need to test everything. But when you treat each content decision as a small opportunity to learn, you build

- Sharper instincts

- Faster iteration cycles

- More resilient, data-informed strategies

- A clear sense of purpose for your team's work

The most successful teams aren't always the ones with the best ideas from the start. They're the ones who test thoughtfully, learn continuously, and act deliberately.

If forecasting is how you look forward, testing is how you shape what comes next.

In the next chapter we'll look at some advanced methods in content testing and both how to recognize when you need additional help and how to get the most out of it.

CHAPTER 9

Advanced Methods and Partnering with Experts

If the last few chapters helped you get your bearings in content analytics—asking sharper questions, making informed predictions, and validating ideas through testing—this chapter is an invitation to look further ahead.

Once you have established a working content analytics program, you'll begin to see more of the possibilities. Adding more sophistication to your efforts can help

- Attribute value across complex user journeys.

- Create highly targeted predictions at the individual or group level.

- Prioritize content in large archives or libraries.

- Segment audiences for more relevant personalization.

- Extract patterns from open-ended or unstructured feedback.

At this point, you may also begin to see that these capabilities also bring greater complexity and require considerably more resources. The good news is that most content analytics managers don't do this work

© Russ Bahorsky 2026

R. Bahorsky, *The Fundamentals of Content Analytics,*

https://doi.org/10.1007/979-8-8688-2601-6_9

themselves, and they don't always have in-house expertise to help them. However, they do know when deeper analysis is warranted, what kinds of questions it can answer, and how to work with analysts or consultants who can help them do it right.

This chapter is for when your content program outgrows simple dashboards or lift calculations—when forecasting and A/B testing still leave you asking, *But why did that work? Or for whom? Or how can we replicate it across a hundred other assets?*

The next step in the analytics journey is about understanding what options are out there, asking more sophisticated questions, and translating results into strategy without drowning in technical detail.

In this chapter, you'll learn

- What kinds of advanced techniques you may encounter (and what they can do)

- How to know when it's worth exploring them

- How to scope your needs, frame requests, and avoid common pitfalls

- What it looks like to collaborate effectively with internal analysts or external consultants

At the end of the day, you should have a solid understanding of when and how a strategic investment in advanced analytics will take your organization to the next level.

Recognizing When Advanced Methods Are Warranted

The tools we've explored so far can serve as the backbone of a highly effective content analytics program, but some challenges are just too big— or too complex—for simple tools to solve. Considering advanced analytics is the step to take when those tools stop giving you answers or when the stakes are high enough to justify deeper analysis.

Here are a few signs you may have reached that point:

- **You're Working with Large or Growing Content Libraries**

    "We have over 300 articles. Which ones are still pulling their weight? Which should we retire, revise, or promote?"

    Advanced methods like content clustering or engagement scoring can help you prioritize at scale.

- **Your Audience Interacts with You Across Many Channels**

    "Did that donation come from an email, a social post, or the webinar?"

    Attribution modeling can help assign value to multiple touchpoints, not just last click.

- **You Want to Personalize Based on Behavior, Not Just Demographics**

    "Can we group our audience by how they interact with content, not just who they are?"

    Behavioral segmentation or clustering can uncover hidden user patterns.

- **Your Performance Is Stagnant, and You're Not Sure Why**

    "Engagement is flat, but we're publishing more. What's driving the plateau?"

    Regression analysis, clustering, or even text classification may point to overlooked variables.

- **Your Testing Results Are Inconclusive or Too Slow**

  "We can't get enough traffic to validate this A/B test."

  Advanced methods like propensity modeling may help you find directional insights without waiting for statistical significance.

Asking Practical Questions

Use the following framework (Table 9-1) to determine whether the kind of questions you're asking suggest that you need to incorporate an advanced method into your program.

Table 9-1. *Questions that signal a need for advanced techniques*

If You're Asking ...	You Might Need ...
"Which of these 300 assets should we invest in updating?"	Content scoring, regression
"Which user groups respond best to educational content?"	Behavioral clustering
"How much credit should each channel get for a conversion?"	Attribution modeling
"What's the likelihood that this visitor will subscribe?"	Propensity modeling
"What are the common themes in 500+ survey responses?"	NLP or text classification
"What topics drive long-term engagement?"	Topic modeling/trend analysis

You and your team don't need to know how to do these things, but you do need to recognize the shape of the problem and whether it might be worth getting expert help to solve it.

Ultimately, the trigger for using advanced analytics isn't technical; it's strategic. Ask yourself: *Will this analysis help us make a better or faster decision or one that gives us more confidence?*

Techniques You Might Encounter (and What They Can Do)

If you partner with an analyst or data science team, you may hear terms like "logistic regression" or "clustering" thrown around. Don't be intimidated. You don't need to understand the math or the mechanics; you just need to know what these tools are *for*.

Here's a plain-English guide (Table 9-2) to some of the most common methods used in advanced content analytics. Each one can be used to support better decisions or meet more complex challenges.

Table 9-2. *Advanced methods, explained simply*

Technique	What It's For	Typical Research Question
Clustering (e.g., k-means)	• Groups users or content into clusters based on similar behavior, such as identifying "scanners" who quickly browse content and "deep readers" who engage more thoroughly • Helps tailor content strategies to different user segments	*"What distinct groups of users interact with our site, and how do their behaviors differ?"*

(*continued*)

Table 9-2. *(continued)*

Technique	What It's For	Typical Research Question
Multiple regression	• Shows how more than one variable influences an outcome (e.g., it can determine if word count affects conversions and quantify how much more or less influential it is compared with other factors like subject matter or headline length)	*"Which factors (e.g., headline length, word count, topic) most strongly predict conversions?"*
Logistic regression	• Predicts a yes/no outcome (like "will they convert?") by turning inputs into probabilities between 0 and 1 • More realistic for consumer behavior, but harder to build and interpret	*"What is the probability that a visitor will subscribe to our newsletter based on their behavior?"*
Content scoring	• Used with regression modeling to rank or prioritize content assets by assigning each a score based on multiple performance indicators (e.g., traffic, engagement, conversions, cost to update) • Helps allocate limited resources to the most impactful updates	*"Which of our 300 content assets should we prioritize for updates to maximize impact?"*

(continued)

Table 9-2. *(continued)*

Technique	What It's For	Typical Research Question
Attribution modeling	• Assigns value to multiple content touchpoints along a user journey, not just the last click • Gives a fuller view of how content contributes to conversions	*"Which pieces of content contributed most to driving conversions across the full journey?"*
Propensity modeling	• Predicts the likelihood of a user taking a specific action, such as downloading a guide or unsubscribing from a newsletter • Useful for targeting with personalized content	*"Which users are most likely to download our whitepaper if we show it to them?"*
AutoML (automated machine learning) platforms (e.g., BigQuery ML, DataRobot, MonkeyLearn)	• Automates forecasting, classification, or scoring, making advanced analytics more accessible to non-coders • Speeds up building and deploying machine learning models	*"Can we automatically predict next month's content engagement without building a model from scratch?"*

(continued)

Table 9-2. (*continued*)

Technique	What It's For	Typical Research Question
Natural language processing (NLP)	• Structures and analyzes large volumes of text (surveys, comments, chat logs) • Extracts themes, identifies sentiment, and categorizes feedback	*"What are the most common themes in user feedback, and how do people feel about our brand?"*
Reputation analytics	• Integrates data from news, social, and public platforms to assess brand perception and how it changes • Useful for higher ed, nonprofit, and policy spaces	*"How is our organization being talked about in the press and on social media, and is sentiment improving or declining?"*
Lift modeling	• Compares predicted outcomes with and without an intervention (e.g., an email campaign) to assess impact and improve future strategy	*"How much additional engagement did our campaign generate compared with doing nothing?"*

(continued)

Table 9-2. *(continued)*

Technique	What It's For	Typical Research Question
Behavioral targeting and intent-based segmentation	• Uses behavioral cues (e.g., what users click, how long they stay, their navigation paths) to infer intent or even demographics • Enables more precise audience segmentation than static categories like age or gender	*"Which users are showing buying intent based on their browsing patterns?"*
Predictive personalization	• Forecasts which content will perform best for specific segments based on historical engagement and real-time behavior	*"What type of article should we show this user right now to maximize engagement?"*
Microsegmentation	• Breaks down audiences into very small, behaviorally defined groups to deliver highly tailored content • Powerful, but risks complexity, intrusiveness, and inefficiency if overdone	*"Can we identify and target niche subgroups, like repeat visitors who only engage with long-form content?"*

(continued)

Table 9-2. *(continued)*

Technique	What It's For	Typical Research Question
Reputation and authority analytics	• Goes beyond sentiment to measure trust, credibility, and thought leadership (e.g., how often your content is cited, linked, or referenced)	*"Is our content being recognized as authoritative by peers, journalists, or influencers?"*
Topic modeling/trend analysis	• Identifies recurring themes in large collections of content and tracks how they evolve over time • Useful for monitoring shifts in audience interest, industry trends, or academic topics	*"What topics are emerging or declining in our content, and which ones drive sustained engagement?"*

As with all of the analytical tools we've examined, these are most effective when paired with a clearly defined business goal, strong research questions, and strong cross-functional collaboration.

AUTOML VS. AI

AutoML (automated machine learning) is a subset of AI that focuses specifically on automating the process of selecting, training, and optimizing machine learning models. It reduces the need for deep expertise in model development, making AI more accessible to those who may not be data scientists. This book generally uses the terms AI and AutoML interchangeably.

Automated machine learning (AutoML) platforms offer powerful tools to run predictive models with less technical skill required. These tools are improving rapidly and may ultimately provide an easier way to incorporate modeling into your analytics program. However, AutoML still requires

- Good problem framing

- Clean, well-structured data

- Careful interpretation and proofing of results

Think of AutoML as a smart assistant for the work you are already capable of doing, not a replacement for a qualified and insightful data modeler. And note that not every challenge needs machine learning. If you can answer the question with a GA4 comparison or a simple funnel report, do that first.

Mistakes to Avoid with Advanced Analytics

Advanced methods can unlock powerful insights, but they can also lead you astray if applied without the right guardrails. Below you'll find some of the most common pitfalls content teams encounter when diving into more complex analytics and how to avoid them.

Mistake 1: Chasing complexity for its own sake

Sophisticated analysis doesn't always equal better insight. If a question can be answered with a pivot table, you don't need a machine learning model.

Instead: Start with the simplest tool that gives you a clear answer. Upgrade when the decision demands it.

Mistake 2: Overfitting the model

When a model is too tightly tuned to historical data, it may perform well on past observations but fail to predict future behavior (e.g., it's like memorizing the answers to last year's test ...it won't help if the questions change).

Instead: Ask for a validation plan. A good analyst will test the model's performance on new or hold-out data and suggest ways to move ahead.

Mistake 3: Interpreting correlation as causation

Just because two variables seem to be related doesn't mean one causes the other. A regression might show that longer blog posts are associated with more conversions, but that doesn't mean longer posts cause conversions. For example, say your model finds that longer posts lead to more sign-ups, but what if those longer posts were also promoted more heavily? Without controlling for promotion, your results might reflect distribution strategy, not content length."

Instead: Treat correlations as hypotheses, not conclusions. Test insights before scaling them.

Mistake 4: Using small or dirty datasets

Advanced methods require clean, consistent data. Incomplete tagging, unstructured identifiers, or low traffic volumes can produce misleading results or no result at all.

Instead: Focus first on improving data hygiene and event tagging. Ask your analyst to assess data readiness before modeling begins.

Mistake 5: Asking for "the number" instead of framing a decision

Analysts are often asked for a single magic metric—"What's our best-performing content?"—without any context. This can lead to narrow or irrelevant answers.

Instead: Focus on the decision: "Which of our evergreen articles should we promote during our year-end campaign?" The right question unlocks the right method.

Working with Data Experts

Many content teams can perform excellent basic analysis on their own. But some questions—or opportunities—require deeper technical expertise, the kind of skills that come with advanced degrees in statistics and experience in research methodologies. Working with a data analyst, statistician, or consultant isn't like handing off a design request. Successful collaboration requires knowing when to bring in help, how to find the right partner, and how to work productively together once the engagement begins.

When to Bring in a Data Expert

Here are some signs that you should consider working with a data expert, consultant, or agency:

- You want to build predictive models (e.g., forecasting which content leads to conversions).

- You're dealing with very large datasets (e.g., multiple years of multichannel content engagement data).

- You need statistical significance testing (e.g., A/B testing variations of a landing page).

- You're considering segmentation beyond basic demographics (e.g., behavior-based cohorts).

If hiring a social scientist isn't in your budget, you're in luck. There are a number of companies that offer these services at prices that make them considerably more affordable. Ultimately, developing some of these competencies may be within the reach of your team in time, but working with experts to get you started will save you trial and error and will enhance the validity of your results.

How to Partner with Data Experts

Successful collaboration starts with a shared understanding of

- What decision you need to make

- What data is available

- What assumptions or limitations exist

Step 1: Define the business decision

Start with the question behind the question:

- Should we retire or revise these 100 blog posts?

- Should we invest in more long-form content?

- Which audience segments are underperforming, and why?

Avoid asking for a technique ("Can you run a regression?") before you've defined the purpose.

Step 2: Frame a clear analytics question

Once the decision is clear, work together to shape a useful question:

- Which characteristics of our top-performing content predict high engagement?

- What are the shared traits of users who bounce in under ten seconds?

A well-scoped question is narrow, measurable, and decision-driven.

Step 3: Share what you know (and what you don't)

Bring context to the table:

- What business problems you're trying to solve

- What decisions you're trying to make

- What problems you've encountered

- What past tests or reports have shown

- Any limitations in your dataset or tagging practices

Analysts don't need you to know the math, but they do need you to frame the environment in which your content lives and the challenges you face.

Step 4: Discuss data sources and constraints

Some questions will require structured data (metrics, identifiers); others may pull from surveys, transcripts, or CRM exports. Be ready to answer

- Where is the data coming from?

- How clean and complete is it?

- Can it be joined across platforms?

If you're unsure, a good data partner will help audit what's available.

Step 5: Agree on deliverables and format

Before analysis begins, align on what you'll get back and how it will be shared:

- A short report? A dashboard? A ranked list?

- Will there be visualizations, explanations, or just raw outputs?

- Who will interpret the findings for nontechnical audiences?

The best analytics partnerships include a feedback loop, not just a file drop. Analysts are most helpful when treated as partners, not service providers. Bring them in early, ask what they need, and share what you know. Good collaboration always outperforms a perfect model.

Finding the Right Data Modeling Partner

Finding a service to help with data modeling and other aspects of your content analytics program depends on your budget and your specific needs, whether you're looking for consulting expertise, software solutions, or a combination of both. Here are some effective ways to identify the best provider:

1. **Define Your Requirements**

   - Do you need consulting for enterprise data architecture?

   - Are you looking for software tools to manage data models internally?

   - Do you require industry-specific expertise (e.g., healthcare, finance, retail)?

2. **Research Top Providers**

   - **Consulting Firms**: Deloitte, Accenture, Capgemini, and Cognizant offer full-service data modeling and analytics consulting. Smaller firms may also be capable of the same services, often with more personalized approaches.

   - **Software Vendors**: Informatica, IDERA (ER/Studio), and Oracle provide specialized data modeling tools.

   - **Industry-Specific Experts**: Some firms focus on niche markets, such as Experian for financial data modeling.

3. **Compare Tools and Services**

   - Check comparison guides for overviews of top data modeling tools.

   - Review case studies to see how providers have helped businesses similar to yours.

4. **Network and Ask for Recommendations**

   - Join data analytics forums or LinkedIn groups for firsthand recommendations.

   - Attend industry conferences where vendors showcase their solutions.

5. **Request Demos and Consultations**

   - Many providers offer free trials or consultations.

   - Ask about integration capabilities with your existing systems.

Partnering Smartly

As with bringing any outside organization into your business processes, the better prepared you are and the better you can define your needs, the more you'll get out of the experience. Before your first meeting with a data expert

- Bring a clear business question, not just "Can you find something interesting?"

- Involve them early in project planning—they can often suggest better ways to structure data from the start.

- Focus on actionable insights, not just "interesting" statistics.

- Make sure you understand your team's qualifications and capacity to support the work.

It's also important to have a candid conversation with your team both before and after meeting with the expert to surface obstacles and ensure your team members have the tools they need. Ask about relevant, underused skills or about new skills they may want to acquire. For example, perhaps a colleague has their own YouTube channel and already dabbles in analytics, or maybe someone minored in statistics in college. Developing your in-house capabilities can sometimes be more cost-effective and faster than hiring a consultant.

A SAMPLE DATA REQUEST BRIEF

Project: Help us identify the top 25 pieces of content in our resource library that are most strongly associated with email sign-ups.

Goal: Prioritize updates and promotion for the most effective evergreen content.

Available Data: Page-level engagement from GA4, CRM email acquisition timestamps, metadata on content format and topic.

Desired Output: A ranked list with notes on which features (topic, format, length) correlate with conversions.

Budgeting for Outside Expertise

Consulting arrangements can range from a few thousand dollars for a narrowly scoped project to six-figure annual retainers for ongoing support. Start by scoping the decision you need to make and the likely level of effort required. Ask potential partners for transparent pricing models—hourly, project-based, or retainer—and weigh these against your own team's capacity. Build in extra budget for follow-up work, as initial findings often raise new questions. When possible, pilot a smaller project first to confirm value before committing to larger engagements.

Aligning Vendor Selection with Collaboration Style

Selecting a provider is not just about technical skills; it's also about how well they work with your team. When reviewing proposals, pay attention to communication styles: Do they explain concepts clearly? Are they responsive to questions? Do they encourage collaboration, or do they seem to prefer working in isolation? A technically strong partner who cannot engage with your business context will provide less value than a slightly less advanced firm that communicates effectively.

RED FLAGS IN A PREDICTIVE ANALYTICS CONVERSATION

If you hear any of the following without follow-up explanation, pause and ask clarifying questions:

- "We're 100% confident in this prediction." (No model should claim certainty.)

- "Just trust the algorithm." (Transparency matters. Ask for assumptions.)

- "We trained the model on last year's data." (Is it still relevant?)

- "The results say X, so we should do X." (Do they account for context or business constraints?)

Remember: A model is a tool, not a mandate. Data informs decisions; it doesn't make them for you.

Managing Long-Term Relationships

Analytics partnerships often extend beyond a single project. To maintain momentum

- Set regular check-ins (monthly or quarterly) to revisit goals and track progress.

- Evaluate the impact of recommendations—did the consultant's work lead to measurable improvements?

- Document workflows and decisions so that knowledge remains with your team, not just the outside partner.

- Periodically reassess whether you still need the same level of external support or whether more of the work can transition in-house.

Clear performance metrics and ongoing communication will help you sustain a relationship that evolves with your needs.

Keywords for Finding Analytics Partners

When searching for outside help, it helps to know the right terms. Table 9-3 lists keywords you can use and what to expect from the experts who advertise under them.

Table 9-3. *Keywords to use in searching for analytics partners*

If You Need Help With ...	Search For ...	What to Expect from These Experts
Designing or interpreting A/B tests	"freelance A/B testing consultant" "experiment design analyst"	Help setting up valid, statistically sound experiments

(continued)

Table 9-3. *(continued)*

If You Need Help With …	Search For …	What to Expect from These Experts
Building dashboards or automated reports	"Google Data Studio expert" "Looker/Tableau freelancer"	Visualization and BI professionals who connect multiple data sources
Forecasting user behavior or content performance	"predictive analytics consultant" "content demand modeler"	Analysts who forecast trends and identify likely outcomes
Combining data across platforms	"data integration specialist" "ETL developer"	Engineers who unify data from multiple sources
Cleaning messy data or validating tracking	"data hygiene audit consultant" "GA4 implementation specialist"	Experts who fix broken tags and validate tracking
Analyzing unstructured data	"natural language processing analyst" "content metadata tagging service"	Help extracting meaning from text, audio, or images
Optimizing website structure or user flow	"UX researcher content strategy" "user journey analyst"	Analysts who connect analytics to user behavior

(continued)

Table 9-3. (*continued*)

If You Need Help With ...	Search For ...	What to Expect from These Experts
Running adaptive or complex experiments	"multi-armed bandit testing expert" "Bayesian experimentation consultant"	Advanced experiment designers
Structuring your analytics team or workflow	"analytics operations consultant" "marketing data strategy advisor"	Advisors who align analytics with business goals
Doing advanced segmentation or modeling	"data scientist content analytics" "machine learning marketing freelancer"	Experts who segment audiences and build predictive models

Case Study: Working with an External Analyst

An educational media company had over 250 evergreen articles aimed at K–12 educators and administrators. Their content library was rich, but increasingly difficult to manage. They had

- No clear sense of which content was still helping them acquire new subscribers

- No process for retiring or refreshing older posts

- Limited insight into which features (length, format, topic) were most effective

The Ask

The marketing director wanted to

"Identify our top-performing evergreen content by conversion value and understand what makes it successful."

With no in-house data science capacity, the company hired a freelance data analyst to conduct a two-phase project:

1. Audit and score all evergreen articles based on their contribution to form fills and trial sign-ups.

2. Analyze which attributes predicted higher content performance.

The Analysis

The analyst used

- Page-level engagement data from GA4

- Metadata on topic, author, format, and publish date

- Lead data from the CRM (e.g., email sign-up, trial request)

Using a mix of linear regression and decision tree analysis, the analyst produced

- A ranked list of top- and bottom-performing content

- A feature importance summary showing which factors most strongly predicted conversions (i.e., how much each content trait contributed to conversions)

Key Findings

- Articles between 800 and 1,200 words had the highest conversion rates.

- "How-to" and "Template" headlines outperformed narrative features.

- Content published in the last 18 months converted 1.4× better than older content.

- Author-specific engagement patterns were minimal (i.e., topic mattered more than writer).

The Outcome

The company used the analysis to

- Retire or redirect 64 low-performing articles.

- Refresh 40 high-potential posts with updated examples.

- Shift future production toward short-form, instructional content.

They also shared the findings with their content writers, not to evaluate individual performance but to sharpen strategy and shape upcoming editorial calendars.

Lessons Learned

- A clear business question led to a focused, efficient analysis.

- The freelance analyst didn't just provide numbers— they helped translate them into content strategy.

- Trust grew on both sides because expectations were clear from the start.

Takeaway

You don't need in-house data science to get smart answers; you need good scoping, clean data, and clear communication.

Workbook Exercise: Scoping an Advanced Analytics Question

You don't need to know Python or R to get value from an advanced analysis. But you do need to be able to describe the decision you're trying to make, the data you have, and the insight you're hoping to gain.

This exercise will help you prepare to

- Collaborate with an analyst or consultant.

- Make a strong internal case for support.

- Avoid scope creep and miscommunication.

You can use this template alone, as a team, or during discovery conversations with a vendor.

Step 1: Define the business goal

What strategic decision are you trying to make?

Example: "We want to identify and prioritize the top 30 pieces of content in our archive that contribute to newsletter subscriptions."

Your Goal:

____

____

Step 2: Frame the analytics question

What do you want to learn from the analysis?

Example: "Which article features—topic, format, author, publish date—correlate most strongly with user sign-ups?"

Your Question:

____

____

Step 3: List available data sources

What data do you currently have access to?

Data Type	Source (e.g., GA4, CMS, CRM, Survey)
Page-level engagement metrics	
Conversion events or outcomes	
Metadata (topics, tags, authors)	
Qualitative inputs (optional)	

Step 4: Note any known data limitations

Are there gaps, inconsistencies, or tracking issues?

Examples: *"Some content lacks unique IDs." "Older posts don't have scroll depth tracking."*

Notes:

Step 5: Define the deliverable

What would a successful output look like?

Example: *"A ranked list of pages by predictive value + summary of top three predictive traits."*

Your Ideal Output:

Step 6: List key stakeholders

Who will use this analysis to make decisions?

-
-
-

Tip Bring this worksheet to your kickoff meeting with a data partner. It shows you've done the thinking needed to get the project off to a clear, focused start.

Integrating the Team

Advanced analytics work is often cross-functional by necessity: it draws from content, data, web, UX, and business strategy. If it lives in just one department, it's likely to fail or be neglected, and it certainly won't stand a chance of becoming part of your organizational culture.

Here's how to keep your team aligned and informed.

Who Needs to Be Involved

Make sure each team member understands how they contribute to the work, and don't just assume they understand what you need from them.

Use Table 9-4 to frame those discussions.

Table 9-4. *Team member contributions to advanced analytics projects*

Role	Contribution
Content strategist	Frames the problem, defines the business goal
Data analyst or partner	Chooses method, executes analysis, explains limitations
Marketing manager	Connects insights to channel and campaign planning
Writer/editor	Applies insights to new content, refreshes legacy assets
Web or UX lead	Flags structural issues or interface patterns in content
Executive sponsor	Uses insights to prioritize and fund decisions

How to Collaborate Effectively

Analysts want context. Writers want clarity. Managers want outcomes. Integrating the team and making the objectives and the responsibilities clear to everyone ensures everyone brings the right skill set to the project and that everyone gets what they need from the results.

- **Kick Off with Clarity**: Make sure everyone agrees on the question, not just the method.

- **Check in Midstream**: A quick review after the first round of analysis can catch misalignments.

- **Translate the Output**: Make space for both data interpretation and content/creative input.

- **Debrief as a Team**: Use the findings to ask, "What now?"—not just "What did we learn?"

Budget-Friendly Approaches to Advanced Analytics

Not every organization can afford a full-time data scientist, and not every project requires one. But budget shouldn't be a barrier to using advanced analytics thoughtfully. You have more options than you might think.

Start Small with the Right Project

If you can't fund a full-service analytics partnership, look for a single, high-impact use case:

- Prioritize legacy content for pruning.

- Understand bounce drivers on your top ten pages.

- Identify themes in open-text survey responses.

Choose a problem where better insight could justify the expense by saving your team significant time or money.

Hire a Freelancer or Consultant for a Targeted Sprint

Instead of contracting a full analytics agency, try

- Freelancers with experience in marketing or UX analytics

- Local data science graduate students (often affordable and motivated)

- Short-term audits with scoped deliverables (e.g., "score 200 articles by engagement")

Tip   Use the worksheet from this chapter to scope the project clearly before hiring.

Use Free or Freemium Tools to Simulate Advanced Methods

Sometimes, advanced tools just make analytics more convenient. A number of free resources can help you achieve the same ends with a little more work (Table 9-5).

Table 9-5. *Free advanced analytics tools and their uses*

Tool	Use Case	Notes
MonkeyLearn	Text classification, sentiment analysis.	Free tier supports small-scale projects.
BigQuery (Google)	Run SQL queries on content data.	Free up to 1TB/month.
GA4 + Looker Studio	Filter, segment, and trend content data.	Combine dimensions to approximate clustering.
ChatGPT (with code interpreter)	Quick exploration, regression, mock clustering.	Useful for concept testing or pilot planning.

Even if these tools don't replace expert analysis, they can help you form better questions, spot opportunities, or prepare data for a future partner.

Partner Strategically

If you can't fund external help, look for collaborators in your organization:

- A UX or product team that shares performance concerns

- A central analytics group that owns dashboards or CRM data

- A data-minded team member who can help wrangle a few spreadsheets or one who's ready to expand their skill set by taking a course, attending a workshop, or earning a new certification

If you don't work for a large organization, there are still options worth exploring.

For starters, you can reach out to local universities or colleges: many academic programs—especially in data science, business analytics, or marketing—offer

1. Capstone projects or internships where students work on real-world problems

2. Opportunities to collaborate with faculty or research centers

3. Access to tools and expertise at little or no cost

This can be a win–win in which students gain valuable experience and you gain valuable insights.

Small business networks like local chambers of commerce, startup incubators or accelerators, and online communities (e.g., LinkedIn groups, Reddit, Indie Hackers) can be a gold mine of data-savvy professionals or freelancers looking for collaboration opportunities. You might find someone willing to work at a reduced rate or in exchange for equity, referrals, or portfolio-building.

Rember that analytics is a team sport. You don't need to own the playbook; you just need to know when and how to call in support. And "advanced" doesn't have to mean expensive. Thoughtful framing, clean data, and strategic partnerships often matter more than tools or budget.

Final Thoughts

You don't need a predictive model to be data-driven. And you don't need to know Python to participate in advanced analytics work. You just need to understand what these tools are good for—what kinds of questions they help answer—and how to engage the right people when you need deeper insight.

Advanced methods are not a badge of technical sophistication. They provide specific answers to specific challenges, like the need for more fine-grained prioritization or to track more nuanced user reactions and behaviors.

At the same time, learning advanced skills isn't always the best use of your time or your team's. Even if you never run a regression or build a scoring model, you can still lead a team that can meet those challenges with confidence. You can scope powerful collaborations with partners inside and outside of your organization, you can champion responsible data use, and you can turn complex analysis into creative, human-centered action.

Ultimately, you can't buy success with a new tool or by hiring a consultant without understanding what they can do for you and the part they play in helping your organization reach its goals.

In practice, that means

- Focusing on the decision, not the data

- Framing questions clearly, so your partners know what you need

- Knowing enough to recognize when the answers don't make sense

- Asking for explanation, not just output

- Building relationships, not just reports

Next ...just having data is never enough. In Chapter 10, we'll look at some of the tools and techniques you'll need to make your numbers inform and persuade.

PART III

Leadership in Analytics

Reporting and Communicating Insights

Effective reporting is the final link in the chain connecting raw data and real-world decisions. Without clear, compelling communication, even the most robust analyses risk gathering dust. In content analytics, this means transforming dashboards and spreadsheets into narratives that answer stakeholders' specific questions—whether that's "What happened to our engagement last month?" or "Which campaign will drive the next wave of subscriptions?"

Reporting adds power and credibility to your efforts to create meaningful content when it

- **Connects to precise research questions.** You can align your reporting with the types of questions you created in Chapter 2: descriptive ("What happened?"), comparative ("Which version performed better?"), correlational ("What relationships exist?"), causal ("What drove that change?"), or predictive ("What does the future hold?").

© Russ Bahorsky 2026

R. Bahorsky, *The Fundamentals of Content Analytics,*
https://doi.org/10.1007/979-8-8688-2601-6_10

- **Matches audience needs.** Executives want high-level takeaways and forecasts, editors may prefer deep dives into correlational patterns, and analysts need access to drilldown dashboards.

- **Drives action.** Every insight should point toward a next step—whether that's launching an A/B test, reallocating budget, or revising content strategy.

By establishing a regular cadence (weekly dashboards, monthly deep dives, quarterly strategic reviews) and choosing formats that resonate—slides for presentations, one-pagers for quick reads, interactive dashboards for exploration—you ensure that your analytics work fuels decisions rather than sitting unused on someone's desktop.

Principles of Effective Reporting

High-impact reports share three essential qualities:

1. **Clarity:** Reports should address the "So what?" question immediately. Avoid cluttered visuals and jargon. Use simple charts with clear labels and highlight key figures in call-outs or bold text.

2. **Relevance:** Every metric (click-through rate, bounce rate, conversion, etc.) and every comparison must tie back to a business objective or research question. For example, if leadership cares about subscriber growth, emphasize comparative and predictive insights like "Which newsletter themes drove the highest projected subscriptions?"

3. **Actionability:** Insights without recommendations leave readers unsure how to proceed. Pair each finding with a concise, practical next step, such as

   - "Test new CTAs on high-traffic articles."

   - "Shift 20% of Q3 ad spend to social video based on performance trends."

It's also important to choose the format for your reporting that is most likely to have the biggest impact on the stakeholders in your program or that best suits the culture of your organization. See Table 10-1 for examples of the most common reporting media and their uses.

Table 10-1. *Optimum reporting media based on use case*

Medium	Best Use Case	Tips for Success
Interactive dashboard	Ongoing monitoring by analysts	Use filters and drilldowns; keep navigation intuitive.
Slide deck	Executive presentations and reviews	Lead with headlines; annotate key visuals.
One-page brief	Busy managers needing quick updates	Summarize context, findings, and recommendations.
Written report	Detailed archival or compliance needs	Include methodology appendix; use clear subheadings.

By balancing narrative, visuals, and clear calls to action—tailored to the format and audience—you create reports that not only inform but also inspire confidence in your team's efforts and prompt decisive action.

Designing Action-Oriented Dashboards

Ultimately, dashboards should do more than display numbers; they have to do the job of guiding users toward insights and actions. Often, they'll also need to translate the complexity of the content analytics process into something easily digestible—for those who need context or background information. The key is to start with clear goals and design every element to support those objectives.

Successful dashboards typically follow these principles:

- **Offer a limited scope**. Include no more than three primary views per dashboard to preserve visual clarity and improve performance.

- **Define a focused purpose**. Begin with a question like "Which content categories drove the most sign-ups last quarter?" and display only the charts and filters needed to answer it.

- **Use logical layout and hierarchy**. Adopt an "inverted pyramid" structure: place the most important metric top left, secondary details beneath, and filters to the side for deeper dives.

- **Provide context**. When possible, include benchmarks—internal (past periods or peer departments) or external (industry standards)—to add meaning to your metrics.

Table 10-2 offers a brief look at some of the best practices for developing dashboards.

Table 10-2. *Best practices in dashboard design according to reporting objectives*

Objective	Best Practice
Limit views	Two to three key charts per dashboard.
Goal alignment	Tie each metric to a core business question.
Minimalism	Remove non-essential visuals; use whitespace to focus attention.
Visual hierarchy	Employ size and position to signal importance—top left for highest priority.
Visual clarity	Use color, shape, and orientation sparingly to highlight outliers or trends.
Clear context	Provide clear titles, units, and benchmarks (e.g., "vs. target") to help viewers interpret values.

Interactive features—such as dropdown filters for date ranges or content segments—allow analysts to explore "what-if" scenarios without cluttering the primary view. However, it's crucial to maintain simplicity: each interactive control should serve a single purpose, like toggling between desktop and mobile performance or filtering by lead source. Best practice research suggests that dashboards become hard to use when they offer more than five filters, leading to user fatigue and misinterpretation.[1,2]

Finally, dashboards should link directly to action steps. Embed call-outs or buttons that connect users to the next phase of work: scheduling an A/B test, exporting the data, or assigning a task. This

---

[1] Yanna Lin, Haotian Li, Aoyu Wu, Yong Wang, and Huamin Qu. "DMiner: Dashboard Design Mining and Recommendation." Accessed May 22, 2025. arXiv.

[2] Sisense. "4 Design Principles for Creating Better Dashboards." Accessed May 22, 2025.

"cooperative dashboard" approach reframes dashboards as active participants in analytical workflows, fostering faster, more confident decision-making.[3]

Designing Slide Decks That Drive Conversations

Slide decks are one of the most common vehicles for communicating analytics to decision-makers. They're also one of the most misused. Too often, they're overloaded with charts and jargon or reduced to dense blocks of bullet points. But when done well, slides become a powerful tool for storytelling, consensus-building, and sparking strategic discussion.

The Goal: Deliver Just Enough Insight to Start a Dialogue

Unlike dashboards (which invite exploration) or written reports (which document findings), decks are performative. They're meant to support a conversation, not stand alone. That means they should

- Be visually clear.

- Stay focused on each slide's key message.

- Include interpretation, not just data.

---

[3] Vidya Setlur, Michael Correll, Arvind Satyanarayan, and Melanie Tory. "Heuristics for Supporting Cooperative Dashboard Design." Accessed May 22, 2025. arXiv.

What to Include in Your Slide Decks

When building a slide deck, it's always best to use fewer slides with more whitespace. The deck should guide discussion, not deliver a monologue. And keep in mind that cognitive load theory suggests that too much information can be a barrier to decision-making.[4]

Here are a few guidelines for building the various slides you're likely to need in your deck (Table 10-3).

Table 10-3. *Slide types and their uses*

Slide Type	Purpose
Title slide	Clear title, time frame, and contact person.
Executive summary	Two to three bullets on what happened and why it matters.
Key insights	Each insight gets one slide—include a chart, an interpretation, and an action.
Comparative slides	Show lift, drop, or trend (before/after visuals are powerful here).
Recommendations	Translate data into next steps or questions for discussion.

Visual and Verbal Cues

The worst thing you can do when you bring a slide deck to a meeting is read it verbatim. Don't try to make the slide deck do your job for you; use it to illustrate or emphasize what you have to say.

- Highlight key takeaways (e.g., "+18% CTR since CTA change").

---

[4] Mayer, R. E. *Multimedia Learning,* 2nd ed. Cambridge: Cambridge University Press, 2009.

- Keep charts and tables simple and descriptive.

- Rehearse your transitions between slides (this is where most speakers lose their audience).

Common Pitfalls

If you find yourself losing your audience every time you present a slide deck, here are the first things to look at as you rethink how your decks are designed:

- Too many metrics per slide

- Slides that require reading instead of listening

- "Chart dumps" with no interpretation

- Too much animation (your audience isn't there to admire your PowerPoint skills)

A good slide deck is like a storyboard for strategy. Each slide moves the narrative forward, builds trust in the data, and makes the next decision easier to make.

Creating One-Page Insight Briefs

Not every stakeholder wants a 12-slide deck or a dashboard walkthrough. Some want a single, well-structured document they can review in five minutes between meetings. That's the purpose of the one-pager. They distill essential insights into a concise format that supports decision-making without overwhelming the reader.

The Goal: Synthesize, Prioritize, and Recommend

A good one-pager delivers

- A focused summary of key findings

- One or two visuals that highlight the most important trends

- A clear recommendation or question to act on

Think of it as a briefing note—something an executive or busy colleague can read over a cup of coffee and immediately grasp the implications.

And before you finalize any insight brief, ask yourself: "If my reader only remembers one thing, what should it be?" That takeaway should be in your headline, chart, and summary sentence.

Here's how a typical one-pager is structured (Table 10-4).

Table 10-4. *Suggested structure for one-pagers*

Section	Content
Headline or title	"October Email Performance: Strong Open Rate, Weak Conversions"
Summary bullet points	Two to four key findings or changes ("Open rate up 15% MoM; click-to-convert ratio down 20%")
One key visual	A simple bar chart, trendline, or table highlighting a meaningful change
Interpretation	What it means ("New subject lines worked, but CTA needs testing")
Next steps or questions	"Test CTA placement; segment conversions by device"

With a one-pager, you want your readers to be able to skim to get right to the information they want. To make that easier, use bold headers, call-out boxes, and consistent formatting.

Tip   The format of your one-pager can be an obstacle to readers who are seeing it for the first time. If you stick to a formula that you can use from one document to the next, your readers will spend more time focused on what you're saying and less time on how you're saying it.

When to Use a One-Pager

One-pagers can be a powerful tool for getting your point across or getting approval quickly. Use them if you need to

- Brief executives before a decision meeting.

- Summarize a single campaign or test.

- Update cross-functional teams on recent trends.

- Share pilot findings or A/B test results.

It's also a good idea to prepare additional documentation for a more in-depth discussion. One-pagers are often filed away in the to-be-read-later file, but if they strike an immediate chord with a stakeholder, you don't want to get caught unprepared.

And if you have a graphic designer on your team, bring them into the process of developing a format for your one-pagers that's visually effective.

As a rule, however, avoid trying to cram in too many metrics. Get to the point quickly and don't assume your reader understands the context of your findings without adequate explanation, that they'll remember your team's technical terms or acronyms, or that they'll understand your visuals without interpretation. Finding the right balance is a matter of trial and error. When you find a format that's effective at getting the kind of response you want, turn it into a template and keep using it.

The one-pager is also a test of your own understanding of the results your team has produced. If you can explain what happened, what it means, and what should happen next in one page, you're likely to understand the insight better yourself.

Writing Insightful Reports

A well-crafted report transforms analysis into a compelling story that stakeholders can understand and act upon, and reports that use a narrative arc typically have more impact, especially with nontechnical stakeholders.[5] Follow a three-part narrative arc—context, findings, recommendations—to lead readers through the data with clarity and purpose:

1. **Context**

   - **Objective and Question**: Briefly restate the business goal and the specific research question (e.g., "Which blog topics produce the highest CTR?") to anchor the report in purpose.

   - **Methodology**: Summarize data sources and methods in one or two sentences (e.g., "Based on GA4 page view data and email campaign tracking from Q1").

---

[5] Dykes, B. *Effective Data Storytelling: How to Drive Change with Data, Narrative and Visuals*. Hoboken, NJ: Wiley, 2020.

2. **Findings**

- **Visual Highlights**: Present two to three key charts—each with a clear takeaway headline (e.g., "Listicles generate 25% higher CTR than interviews")—and annotate anomalies or trends directly on the visuals.

- **Link to Question Types**: Frame each insight according to your research question framework: descriptive ("Page views are up 15% month over month"), comparative ("Variant B outperformed A by 8% CTR"), correlational ("Scroll depth correlates at 0.6 with conversions"), causal ("A/B test showed a 5% lift in donations"), or predictive ("Model forecasts a 12% increase in leads next quarter").

3. **Recommendations**

- **Action Steps**: For each finding, provide a concise, prioritized next step (e.g., "Run follow-up test on CTA placement").

- **Ownership and Timeline**: Assign responsibility ("Content strategist to update article template by May 1") and a deadline to ensure accountability.

Clear, concise language is essential. Replace technical jargon with everyday terms even if you think they *should be* common knowledge: instead of "bounce rate," use "percentage of visitors who left without engaging." Reports that score high in readability (Flesch–Kincaid Grade

Level $\leq$10) see 30% higher adoption among nontechnical stakeholders, according to communication design research.[6]

In longer reports, use appendices for detailed tables or methodology deep dives. This keeps the main narrative focused while preserving transparency for those who need it. Conclude your report with a brief "What's Next" section that previews upcoming analyses or experiments, reinforcing the continuous cycle of insight, action, and learning.

Finally, note that research shows that reports designed to be scanned visually (i.e., using headers, bullets, and call-outs liberally) are 40% more likely to be read all the way through.[7]

Case Study: Turning Metrics into a Boardroom Brief

When a mid-sized nonprofit struggled to convert growing website traffic into meaningful donations, their analytics team realized that their monthly spreadsheet wasn't telling a compelling story. They decided to revamp their reporting approach to align with executive needs.

Challenge

Despite a 40% year-over-year increase in page views, the development director couldn't see which content was driving gift form submissions, and leadership grew skeptical of the analytics team's value.

New Approach

The analytics team decided on a new reporting strategy tied to a specific research question.

---

[6] Pencil & Paper. "Dashboard Design UX Patterns Best Practices." Accessed May 22, 2025.

[7] Malamed, C. *Visual Language for Designers: Principles for Creating Graphics That People Understand.* Beverly, MA: Rockport Publishers, 2009.

- **Focused Question:** The team applied the research question, "Which three article series on donor impact generate the highest net new donation rate?"

- **Dashboard Design:** They built a two-panel dashboard showing, side by side, article series performance (CTR to donation page) and actual gift conversions—placing the decision metric (gifts) immediately next to the engagement metric (clicks).

- **Narrative Slide Deck:** Then they created a five-slide executive brief structured as Problem ➤ Key Finding (series A outperformed B and C by 25%) ➤ Implication (redirect content budget to series A) ➤ Next Steps (launch A/B test on series A headlines) ➤ Timeline and Owners.

Outcome

At the next board meeting, the C-suite praised the clarity of insights. They approved a 15% shift in editorial resources toward high-performing topics and greenlit an A/B test on series A headline formats. Within three months, donations attributable to that series rose 18%, validating the power of targeted, action-oriented reporting.

Key Takeaway

A case study report that ties a specific research question to clear visuals and recommendations can transform skepticism into a growth opportunity.

Workbook Exercise: Crafting Your Insight Brief

Use this exercise to practice converting analysis into a concise, decision-ready deliverable. Pick a recent dataset or dashboard and work through the steps below:

1. **Define Your Question**

   - Identify one salient research question from your analytics work (e.g., "Did our spring newsletter redesign increase click-to-donation rates?").

2. **Summarize Context in One Sentence**

   - Frame the objective and scope (e.g., "Comparing open and click rates between newsletters V1 and V2 among new subscribers from March–April").

3. **Select Two Visuals**

   - Choose one chart that addresses the engagement metric (opens or clicks) and one that shows the outcome (donations or sign-ups).

   - Annotate each with a five-word headline that captures the key insight.

4. **Write Down Your Findings**

   - In three bullet points, state

     - **What Happened**: "Click-to-donation rate rose from 2.1% to 2.8%."

     - **Which Variation Performed Better**: "Variant B's redesigned header drove a 33% lift."

- **What Correlation or Causal Insight Emerged**: "Higher click rates on mobile correlated with 18% more donations."

5. **Recommend Next Actions**

    - For each finding, propose one clear step:

        - "Deploy variant B header to all newsletters."

        - "Schedule A/B test on CTA placement in variant B for June send."

        - "Review mobile rendering to ensure consistency across devices."

6. **Tailor to Your Audience**

    - Write a one-sentence summary for each stakeholder type:

        - **Executive:** "Our newsletter update generated a 33% lift in donation clicks. We recommend full rollout and mobile optimization."

        - **Editor:** "Variant B's header outperformed. Let's adopt that style and test CTA placement next."

        - **Analyst:** "Data shows a significant comparative uplift; next, segment by region to refine targeting."

Once complete, assemble your one-page insight brief and share it with a colleague or manager. Solicit feedback on clarity, relevance, and actionability. Use their input to refine future reports and build a habit of data-driven storytelling.

Integrating the Team

Effective reporting isn't a one-person task; it's a cross-functional process that brings together data producers, interpreters, and decision-makers. A good report isn't just a data artifact; it's a conversation starter. The most impactful insights emerge when people from different roles bring their questions, context, and judgment to the table (Table 10-5).

Table 10-5. *Team roles in analytics reporting*

Team Member	Reporting Contribution
Content strategist	Frames the report around content decisions and maps insights to business objectives
Data analyst	Ensures metrics are accurate, interprets trends, and builds or maintains dashboards
UX designer	Highlights friction or usability insights from behavioral data or user feedback
Social media manager	Brings audience sentiment, reach metrics, and social listening context
SEO specialist	Interprets organic traffic shifts, rankings, and content visibility changes
Marketing manager	Aligns reporting with campaign goals and revenue-driving metrics
Executive stakeholder	Uses reporting to track strategic progress and allocate resources accordingly

Reporting As a Shared Ritual

Consider structuring reporting as a regular, collaborative exercise, not something that's assembled piecemeal:

- **Monthly Insight Roundups**: Share highlights across teams in a short meeting or Slack thread. Each member contributes one observation.

- **Quarterly Strategy Syncs**: Bring together content, UX, and analytics to reflect on trends, surface questions, and reset KPIs.

- **Post-campaign Retrospectives**: Use reports to spark a discussion on what worked and what didn't, not just to prove impact but to improve it.

Finally, make sure everyone gets the credit they deserve. List the team members involved in the analysis or interpretation in your reports. This reinforces shared ownership and visibility.

Build a Feedback Loop

Reports should be actionable, but you should also think of them as performances that can be improved with each iteration. After presenting a report, ask your team to note

- Which insights led to decisions?

- Which metrics felt unclear or misleading?

- Where were there gaps or obstacles?

When team members see reporting not as a deliverable but as a tool for better thinking, they engage more deeply with both the data and the process. Over time, that engagement sharpens questions, improves metrics literacy, and embeds content analytics into the culture of decision-making.

Budget-Friendly Reporting and Communicating Solutions

You don't need enterprise dashboarding tools or full-time analysts to communicate insights effectively. In fact, a well-organized spreadsheet or a single-slide summary—framed in the language of your stakeholders—can be more valuable than a dozen auto-generated charts.

Here are some cost-effective strategies for insight reporting that still pack a punch.

Prioritize Clarity Over Complexity

The work of content analytics is often complicated, but the real challenge is translating that complexity into a simple recipe for action.

- **Use Built-In Tools**: Excel, Google Sheets, and Looker Studio all allow for basic charting, conditional formatting, and even interactive filters at no cost.

- **Choose the Right Visualization**: A simple bar chart showing before/after engagement or conversion rates can often do more than a complex scatter plot.

- **Stick to One Message per Chart**: Avoid clutter. Each visual should answer one clear question.

- **Focus on What's Next**: Tie your results to a clear decision or a brief list of action items (Where do we go from here? What do we need to do that?)

It's always useful to think of analytics reporting as a two-step process. Report your findings simply and clearly using the tools that your organization uses and understands but be prepared to explain your findings in detail if the question arises.

Emphasize the Most Strategic Metrics

Don't try to report everything. Instead, identify three to five KPIs that matter most to each stakeholder group:

- **Executives:** Performance vs. goal, budget impact, trend direction

- **Creators:** Format-level engagement, scroll depth, top traffic sources

- **Marketers:** Conversion funnel, referral channels, segment performance

Consider adopting a "Core + Custom" reporting model, where each report includes a core set of standardized, top-level metrics that are shared across all teams to ensure consistency and alignment. In addition, include one or two insights that are customized to the unique goals, strategies, or needs of each team or campaign. This makes your reporting both universally informative and locally relevant.

Use Free Templates and Shortcuts

- Pre-built dashboard templates (from Looker Studio, HubSpot, or Canva) can give you a fast, professional starting point.

- Many free tools now support visual exports you can copy into slides (e.g., GA4 Explorations, Microsoft Clarity).

Empower Generalists

Even if you don't have a dedicated analyst, your content strategist, project manager, or marketing lead can often build basic dashboards with light training. Host a knowledge-sharing session or assign one team member to build and maintain a "starter" dashboard that evolves over time.

Insight communication doesn't require expensive tech. It requires structure, intention, and a user-first mindset—just like good content.

Final Thoughts

Reporting is where the rubber meets the road. All the research, tagging, modeling, and testing in the world means little if your stakeholders don't understand the results or if your team can't act on them.

Great reporting isn't about dazzling people with charts or overwhelming them with information. It's about framing your findings clearly and in the language of action:

- *What happened?*

- *Why does it matter?*

- *What should we do next?*

Insight is never obvious; it needs translation. When you connect the dots between data and decision-making, you elevate analytics from a reporting function to a leadership tool.

As your organization matures, your reporting should evolve too. Early-stage teams may rely on simple spreadsheets and campaign debriefs. More advanced teams might build interactive dashboards or quarterly insight briefings. Whatever the format, the goal is the same: make your insights understandable, memorable, and actionable.

We've already seen how important it can be to think of your content analytics as a team effort, but in the next chapter, we'll take a closer look at how to build your team, how to grow it, and how to lead it to success.

CHAPTER 11

Building and Sustaining a Content Analytics Program

Most organizations begin the formal practice of content analytics with isolated reports or one-off dashboards, but only a few build enduring analytics programs that drive strategic decision-making. Whether your analytics team is just getting started or you're ready to take things to the next level, an analytics maturity model is the ideal roadmap.

Models like the one developed by the analytics platform company Alteryx suggest that the journey to a full-fledged analytics program happens in five stages:

1. **Analytics Beginner**: Organizations at this stage have limited data accessibility and poor data quality. Decision-making is based on intuition rather than analytics, and data is often siloed or disorganized.

2. **Localized Analytics**: Analytics is used for basic business intelligence, such as dashboards and reporting. Data is still siloed within departments, and predictive analytics is limited, often relying on spreadsheets.

© Russ Bahorsky 2026
R. Bahorsky, *The Fundamentals of Content Analytics*,
https://doi.org/10.1007/979-8-8688-2601-6_11

3. **Analytical Aspirations**: Organizations begin centralizing data sources and workflows, adopting tools to democratize analytics. Predictive models may be developed, but adoption across departments is inconsistent.

4. **Analytical Companies**: Data and analytics are widely used for decision-making, with automation and benchmarking integrated into business processes. Machine learning and AI are increasingly leveraged.

5. **Analytical Competitors**: Organizations at this stage fully integrate analytics into their strategy, using data science, machine learning, and AI to drive competitive advantage. Analytics is transparent, accessible, and central to all decision-makers.[1]

While a number of different models exist, most suggest that sustainable impact is a by-product of progressing through each successive level of capability. According to the business intelligence and data analytics company TDWI, at the nascent stage, teams ask simple descriptive questions ("What happened?") and rely on basic KPIs. Once they reach established maturity, they're routinely conducting comparative and correlational analyses to optimize performance. At the advanced/visionary levels, organizations are leveraging causal experiments and predictive modeling to anticipate outcomes and prescribe actions.[2]

Research by TDWI indicates that only 8% of firms reach the final stages of maturity, with most organizations—over 86%—still in pre-adoption or early adoption phases, due to the lack of consistent governance and

---

[1] Alteryx. "Analytics Maturity Model." Accessed May 23, 2025.

[2] TDWI. "Analytics Maturity Model Assessment Guide." Accessed May 23, 2025.

integrated tooling.[3] This gap suggests why many content analytics initiatives stall: without standardized processes, clear roles, and investment in scalable infrastructure, their analytics insights will fail to translate into long-term growth.

On the other hand, Gartner's 2024 survey of digital marketing leaders found that companies with formal "analytics centers of excellence[4]" are able to cut their time-to-insight in half and achieve a revenue growth rate that's 1.8 times faster than those with ad hoc content programs.[5]

In this chapter, we'll chart the path from fragmented, reactive reporting to a mature, integrated content analytics practice. You'll learn how to establish core systems and processes, build the right team structure as you grow, and prioritize initiatives through a structured framework—transforming analytics from a tactical function into a strategic engine for your organization.

Establishing Core Systems and Processes

Building a scalable content analytics program begins with a solid foundation that includes developing a solid data infrastructure and establishing standardized taxonomies and governance. Let's look at all three.

---

[3] Wikipedia. "Big Data Maturity Model." Accessed May 23, 2025.

[4] A center of excellence (COE) is a centralized team that sets data standards, supports tool adoption, and fosters analytics best practices across the organization. It ensures consistency and shared learning.

[5] Graphable. "The 6 Stages of the Analytics Maturity Model." Accessed May 23, 2025.

Data Infrastructure Choices

Organizations typically select from three architectural models for their data infrastructure needs:

1. **Cloud data warehouse + ETL pipelines** (e.g., BigQuery, Snowflake). These platforms automatically pull in web analytics data (GA4), CMS exports, and CRM logs via scheduled ETL jobs, centralizing that data for flexible querying and analytics at scale.

2. **Customer data platforms (CDPs)** (e.g., Segment, Tealium), a centralized system that collects, integrates, and unifies customer data from various sources to create a single, comprehensive customer profile. CDPs are ideal for behavioral and causal analyses.

3. **Integrated marketing suites** (e.g., Adobe Experience Cloud), offering end-to-end tag management, dashboards, and A/B testing tools within a single ecosystem—speeding initial setup but often requiring heavy customization as your organization's needs evolve.

Each of these options supports different maturity stages: warehouses excel in correlational and predictive modeling at scale; CDPs allow for more robust user profiles, which makes causal experimentation more effective; and integrated suites are best at addressing challenges that call for descriptive and comparative insights.

The choice depends on your organization's needs and capacity, but it's also possible to layer these systems as your organization changes. Here are some guidelines for mapping the three options to your team's needs and experience:

- **Early Maturity**: Start with a cloud warehouse and ETL to give you the ability to centralize your data and control data quality and structure, while also enabling scalable querying and analysis as your needs grow.

- **Mid-maturity**: Layer on a CDP to unify customer data and enable initial segmentation and causal tests.

- **High Maturity/Activation Focus**: Adopt an integrated suite for end-to-end analytics, testing, and real-time personalization.

At any stage, however, it's just as important not to make the mistake of letting the tools be a substitute for strategy. Many teams invest in advanced tools before clearly defining their analytics goals. Choose platforms that match your strategy, not the other way around. Your business questions should always dictate your data architecture.

For example:

- *Are we trying to understand long-term behavioral trends across channels?* A cloud data warehouse may be best for scalable, historical analysis.

- *Do we need to personalize experiences based on real-time user behavior?* A CDP can unify customer profiles and support causal experimentation.

- *Is our priority rapid deployment of marketing tests and dashboards?* An integrated suite may offer the fastest path to activation with built-in tools.

While some organizations may move along the three phases of analytics maturity in anywhere from one to three years, others may never need to move beyond the early or mid-maturity stages. If your analytics are adequately meeting the business objectives of your organization, the best investment isn't more headcount—it's deepening capability and increasing impact.

One option might be to provide existing team members with additional training or certifications and encourage better team collaboration and cross-functional fluency—for example, helping data engineers understand UX or content strategists grasp SQL basics. Another might be to invest in workflow automation and other tools that reduce manual work and create opportunities for analysts to assume strategic roles that require more proactive problem solving—this can help position the team as a strategic partner for the organization, not just a service desk.

WHAT IS AN ETL PIPELINE?

An ETL pipeline is a data processing workflow that stands for Extract, Transform, Load. It involves three main steps:

1. **Extract**: Data is collected from various sources such as databases, applications, or external systems.

2. **Transform**: The extracted data is cleaned, formatted, and transformed to meet the requirements of the target system.

3. **Load**: The transformed data is then loaded into a destination system, like a data warehouse or database.

ETL pipelines are essential for ensuring data quality, consistency, and making data ready for analysis and reporting.

Standardizing Taxonomies and Event Schemas

Although we covered this in Chapter 4, it's important to underscore again—as you consider what growth could look like for your program—how consistency in naming conventions and metadata are critical components of that growth. The larger your program (and the more effective) it becomes, the more you'll need to rely on the quality of data you collect, and the more care you'll need to define a set of standards for the work you do. A shared content taxonomy guide for your team, like the one in Table 11-1, should define fields such as content type, topic, funnel stage, and campaign ID. Similarly, an event schema—a document listing each analytic event (e.g., page_view, video_start, form_submit) and its parameters—ensures that tracking implemented by developers, tag managers, and UX teams is uniform and auditable.

Table 11-1. Example event schema: marketing website

Event Name	Trigger Description	Parameters (Required/Optional)	Example Values	Notes/ Owner
page_view	Fired when any page loads.	page_url (req), page_title (req), referrer (opt), user_id (opt), device_type (opt)	/pricing, "Pricing", /blog/ post-1, user_42	Google Tag Manager (GTM)/dev
video_start	User clicks "Play" on an embedded video.	video_id (req), video_title (req), duration_sec (opt), location (opt)	vid_123, "Product Overview", 90, homepage	Dev/ content team
form_submit	User successfully submits a form.	form_id (req), form_name (req), submission_type (opt), page_url (req)	form_signup_1, "Newsletter Signup", email	Dev/UX

(continued)

Table 11-1. (*continued*)

Event Name	Trigger Description	Parameters (Required/Optional)	Example Values	Notes/ Owner
cta_click	User clicks a call-to-action button or link.	cta_id (req), cta_text (req), destination_url (req), page_url (req), cta_position (opt)	cta_demo_1, "Request Demo", / contact, hero	GTM/ content team
search_ query	User submits a search in on-site search.	search_term (req), result_count (opt), page_url (req)	"analytics platform", 12, / search	Dev/ analytics
download_ start	User starts a file download.	file_name (req), file_ type (req), page_url (req), user_id (opt)	ebook_v2.pdf, pdf, /resources/ ebook	Dev/tag manager
scroll_ depth	User scrolls to a defined percentage of the page.	page_url (req), depth_percent (req), device_type (opt)	/features, 75, mobile	GTM

For example, let's break down the page_view event:

- **/pricing → This is the page_url**: The specific URL path the user visited.

- **"Pricing" → This is the page_title**: The readable title of the page, often used in analytics dashboards

- **/blog/post-1 → This is the referrer**: The page the user came from before landing on the current one

- **user_42 → This is the user_id**: A unique identifier for the user (could be anonymized or hashed)

- device_type (not shown explicitly, but could be values like mobile, desktop, tablet)

These values help you understand which page was viewed, who viewed it, where they came from, and what device they used—critical for segmentation and behavioral analysis.

Ultimately, without this level of standardization, data silos and conflicting definitions will erode trust and hamper and compromise comparative and causal analyses.

The schema ensures naming consistency (e.g., always use page_url, not url); prevents data loss from incorrectly triggered or misconfigured events; helps nontechnical teams understand what's being tracked and why; and provides a single source of truth for developers, analysts, marketers, and designers.

Governance, Documentation, and Version Control

Governance policies establish who can request new metrics, approve changes to the tracking plan, and access sensitive data. A lightweight governance charter—outlining roles, responsibilities, and escalation paths—prevents ad hoc modifications that break dashboards or invalidate experiments.

Ideally, version-controlled repositories (e.g., Git or Confluence) should house all playbooks, tracking plans, dashboard templates, and data definitions. This practice supports effective change management, provides an audit trail for compliance (depending on what that means for your organization or industry), and accelerates onboarding for new team members.

By investing in robust infrastructure, clear taxonomies, and formal governance, you lay the groundwork that enables content analytics to scale from answering basic descriptive questions to powering advanced predictive and prescriptive insights across your organization.

Additionally, research has linked formal governance structures to significantly reduced time-to-insight and greater user trust in analytics.[6]

---

[6] Davenport, T. H., and Jeanne G. Harris. *Competing on Analytics: The New Science of Winning*, rev. ed. Boston: Harvard Business Review Press, 2017.

Staffing and Roles at Each Growth Phase

Growing a content analytics program requires evolving team structures that align with your organization's analytics maturity. As you move from ad hoc reporting to a center of excellence (COE), the skills you need—and the way you organize them—will certainly change. Table 11-2 illustrates a three-phase model adapted from a variety of industry maturity frameworks and organizational case studies.

***Table 11-2.** Three-phase analytics maturity model*

Phase	Team Composition	Core Responsibilities
1. Startup	• Analytics owner (generalist) • Part-time analyst • Content lead	• Manage basic reporting and dashboards • Translate business questions into initial KPIs • Maintain tracking plan and taxonomies • Provide ad hoc insights with minimal tooling
2. Growth	• Analytics manager • Data engineer • Full-time content analyst • UX/design specialist	• Build and automate ETL/data pipelines for structured and unstructured data • Develop self-serve dashboards and data models • Conduct experimental design for A/B and multivariable tests • Integrate qualitative and quantitative insights
3. Mature	• Center of excellence lead • Data scientists • Business intelligence developers • Domain-specific analysts (e.g., SEO, UX)	• Drive advanced predictive modeling and prescriptive analytics • Govern analytics strategy and data governance • Ensure cross-functional collaboration with marketing, sales, and IT • Champion organizational data literacy

MAPPING ROLES TO RESEARCH QUESTIONS

Descriptive questions ("What happened?") are typically managed by generalists in Phase 1 who set up foundational dashboards.

Comparative and **correlational** analyses ("Which performed better?" or "What patterns exist?") emerge in Phase 2 as teams add specialists who can automate data flows and segment audiences.

Causal ("Why did this change occur?") and **predictive** ("What's likely next?") require Phase 2–3 expertise, where data scientists and BI developers collaborate on experiments and forecasting models.

Research by the consulting group Deloitte highlights that hybrid organizational models—blending centralized analytical groups, or centers of excellence (COEs,) with decentralized analytics champions in business units—yield the fastest path to scaling insights and ensuring alignment with strategic goals.[7] In other words, companies can make the most of their data by combining two approaches to analytics:

1. **Centralized Teams (COEs—Centers of Excellence):** These are expert groups that establish best practices, set standards, and ensure consistency in data analysis across the organization.

2. **Decentralized Analytics Champions:** These are teams within different business units (like marketing, sales, or operations) that apply analytics directly to their specific needs and goals.

---

[7] Deloitte. "For Vanguard's CDAO and CMO, Partnership Is Part of the Job." Accessed May 23, 2025.

By using both instead of just one, companies can scale their analytics capabilities faster while ensuring that insights are aligned with overall business goals. The centralized team provides structure and expertise, while the decentralized teams apply analytics in ways that are most relevant to their specific areas.

Meanwhile, cloud-based business intelligence company Sigma Computing's maturity survey shows that companies with dedicated data engineers and business intelligence roles complete dashboard projects 1.7 times faster and report 45% greater user satisfaction with analytics tools.[8] This suggests that having specialized roles focused on data management and business intelligence significantly improves efficiency and user experience.

Note, too, that while Sigma's model may lead to faster execution and higher satisfaction, it could require more specialized hiring and higher costs. Deloitte's hybrid model, on the other hand, may offer greater flexibility and broader adoption but could face challenges in coordination between centralized and decentralized teams.

Prioritization Frameworks for Analytics Initiatives

Unless you're in the unusual position of having unlimited resources, you must choose which analytics projects to tackle first. A structured prioritization framework helps balance business impact, data readiness, and the effort required, ensuring quick wins without neglecting more strategic opportunities. Table 11-3 offers a simple 3×3 scoring matrix adapted from data engineering and analytics consulting company phData's maturity guidance and industry best practices.

---

[8] Sigma Computing. "The 5 Stages of the Business Analytics Maturity Model: Where Do You Stand?" Accessed May 23, 2025.

Table 11-3. *Scoring matrix for prioritizing analytics initiatives*

Criterion	Score 1	Score 3	Weight
Business impact	Low: Minimal revenue or engagement lift expected	High: Significant ROI or strategic value	40%
Data readiness	Poor: Data gaps, inconsistent taxonomies	Excellent: Clean, standardized data readily available	30%
Effort required	High: Complex engineering or cross-team dependencies	Low: Quick configuration, few stakeholders	30%

To use the matrix

1. **List** all proposed analytics projects (e.g., "Dashboard for hero image CTR," "Pipeline for email-to-form conversions," "Predictive model for lead scoring").

2. **Score** each project on the three criteria (1–3).

3. **Calculate** a weighted total:

   Priority Score=(Impact×0.4)+(Readiness×0.3)+((4–Effort)×0.3)

   (Note that Effort is inverted so that lower effort yields a higher contribution.)

4. **Rank** projects by descending score and select the top tier for the next 6–12 months' roadmap.

Example: Automating GA4 to CRM ETL

- Impact = 3 (directly ties content to lead conversions)

- Readiness = 2 (existing GA4 events but missing CRM joins)

- Effort = 2 (requires moderate ETL work and mapping)

- Score = $(3 \times 0.4) + (2 \times 0.3) + ((4 - 2) \times 0.3) = 1.2 + 0.6 + 0.6 = $ **2.4**

Projects scoring above **2.2** enter the roadmap for immediate execution; those between **1.8** and **2.2** become medium-term goals; those below **1.8** await further data readiness or smaller scoping.

Using this matrix ensures that your roadmap isn't just a wish list or a backlog but a strategically aligned plan. A *Harvard Business Review* study on project portfolio management found that organizations applying similar weighted scoring frameworks delivered 35% more projects on time and under budget, while also improving stakeholder satisfaction by 20%.[9]

Navigating Change: Embedding Analytics into Culture

Even with the right tools and the right team, there's no guarantee that your organizational culture will adopt an analytics mindset overnight. Effective change management is also an important bridge between intent and impact.

---

[9] Harvard Business Review. "Managing Your Innovation Portfolio." Accessed May 23, 2025.

To embed analytics into your culture, look for opportunities to make the change easy and gradual, to share a clear vision of the future with both your team and its stakeholders, to acknowledge and address the causes of obstacles and resistance, and to lead by example, not just dictate.

1. **Align on Shared Purpose:** Reinforce the "why" behind content analytics. Communicate business goals and show how analytics empowers rather than disrupts.

2. **Design for Low-Friction Adoption:** Choose tools and dashboards that align with how teams already work. Avoid over-engineering; instead, start with easy wins that demonstrate tangible value.

3. **Create Champions:** Identify internal advocates within editorial, product, and marketing teams who can interpret insights and evangelize their value.

4. **Use Narrative, Not Just Numbers:** Frame analytics insights as stories: "This campaign resonated with high-intent users at stage X." This builds emotional resonance and strategic clarity.

5. **Make Rituals Routine:** Institutionalize recurring touchpoints—monthly analytics reviews, quarterly roadmap updates, dashboard walk-throughs—so data becomes part of your organization's DNA.

6. **Manage Resistance Proactively:** Expect friction. Provide a forum for feedback, create incentives, and offer lightweight training (e.g., "data literacy lunch and learns"). Resistance often masks uncertainty rather than opposition, but it can also be caused by real problems that need to be recognized and addressed.

7. **Listen:** Seek out the naysayers, the veterans, and those who tell you it can't be done and understand their objections. Don't try to change your organization's culture until you've made the effort to understand why it is the way it is.

Ultimately, the goal is enthusiastic participation, not mindless compliance. Effective leadership and informed change management help transform analytics from a chore to the kind of challenge that brings new energy and purpose to your team's dynamic.

Case Study: Scaling Analytics at a Digital Publisher

When a media company launched its first analytics pilot, a single content analyst owned an ad hoc dashboard that reported page views and basic engagement metrics. Senior leadership praised the insights, but editorial and marketing teams complained that the dashboard didn't answer deeper questions like "Which series generate the most qualified leads?" or "How do our long-form and short-form assets work together?"

Phase 1: Pilot

- A lean team (generalist analyst + content manager) built descriptive dashboards in Google Data Studio, answering simple "what happened" questions about traffic and video completions.

- Editorial used these reports to tweak headlines, but conversions remained flat, highlighting the need to move beyond single-metric views.

Phase 2: Growth

- Hired a data engineer to build automated ETL pipelines from GA4, the CMS, and the CRM into a Snowflake warehouse, a cloud-based data storage and analytics platform.

- The analytics manager standardized a content taxonomy and event schema, enabling consistent "funnel stage" tagging across all assets.

- Introduced self-serve Looker dashboards for comparative and correlational analyses, so marketing could segment by campaign, format, and audience.

Phase 3: Maturity

- Formed a centralized content analytics center of excellence with data scientists who developed predictive models to forecast lead volume from upcoming content plans.

- Established a quarterly "Analytics Council" with reps from editorial, marketing ops, product, and finance; this forum prioritized analytics projects via the weighted scoring matrix and reviewed progress against roadmap milestones.

- Embedded real-time alerts and dashboards into Slack channels, so product and marketing teams received instant notifications when key metrics deviated from expected ranges.

Outcomes

- Ad hoc reporting requests fell by 40%, freeing the analytics team to work on strategic projects.

- Time-to-insight (how quickly data is converted into actionable insights) for campaign performance shrank from two weeks to under 24 hours.

- Lead generation content optimized through predictive scoring increased qualified leads by 28% year over year.

Key Takeaway

By evolving systems, roles, and governance in phases and by aligning analytics outputs directly to business questions, the company moved from reactive dashboards to a proactive, scalable analytics practice that drives measurable growth.

Workbook Exercise: Design Your Analytics Roadmap

Use Table 11-4 to translate your organization's goals and capabilities into a concrete, phased analytics plan.

Table 11-4. *Analytics plan template*

Step	Instructions	Your Response
1. List top business goals.	Identify three to five strategic objectives that content analytics should support (e.g., "Increase trial sign-ups by 20%," "Boost subscriber renewals").	
2. Inventory current capabilities.	For each goal, note existing analytics assets: dashboards, models, reports, and team skills.	

(continued)

Table 11-4. (*continued*)

Step	Instructions	Your Response
3. Brainstorm potential projects.	Under each goal, list three to four analytics initiatives (e.g., "Pipeline for GA4→CRM ETL," "Predictive lead-scoring model," "Content funnel dashboard").	
4. Score each project.	Use the prioritization framework: score Impact (1–3), Readiness (1–3), Effort (1–3). Calculate weighted totals.	
5. Set phases and milestones.	Assign top-scoring projects to Phase 1 (next 3 months), Phase 2 (3–6 months), and Phase 3 (6–12 months).	
6. Define roles and ownership.	For each project, assign an owner (e.g., analytics manager, data engineer, content analyst) and any supporting roles.	
7. Establish success metrics.	Specify how you'll measure each project's success (e.g., "ETL pipeline reduces report latency to <1 hour," "Predictive model $\geq$80% accuracy").	
8. Document dependencies and risks.	Note any resource constraints, data gaps, or technical blockers that could impede progress, and propose mitigation strategies.	

Save your completed roadmap in a shared workspace and review it with stakeholders. Update scores and timelines quarterly to reflect evolving priorities and new data capabilities.

Once your roadmap is defined, the next step is assigning the right people to carry it out, ensuring that everyone from data engineers to project sponsors is aligned on priorities and accountable for outcomes.

Integrating the Team

A sustainable content analytics program thrives on clear roles, shared ownership, and intentional collaboration. As your initiative scales, ensure every team member understands how their expertise contributes to the analytics lifecycle—from data collection to insight generation to action.

Table 11-5. *Key roles and responsibilities in the analytics lifecycle*

Role	Responsibility
Analytics manager	Owns the analytics roadmap, governance charter, and prioritization framework
Data engineer	Builds and maintains ETL pipelines, ensures data integrity across platforms and systems
Content/data analyst	Translates business questions into analyses, crafts dashboards, and drafts insight briefs
UX/design specialist	Designs dashboards, slide templates, and visualizations that maximize clarity and impact
Product/content lead	Frames the strategic context, validates that insights align with content strategy and goals
Project sponsor	Secures resources, removes blockers, and champions analytics initiatives at the executive level

Cross-Functional Squad vs. Centralized COE

As your team grows, it becomes more important to consider not just the individual team member roles but how your team, or teams, are organized based on how your organization is structured. The squad model is ideal for organizations that are more siloed or rely on ad hoc teams to tackle analytics projects, and the centralized center of excellence model is better for an organization with an analytics team that provides those services to its business units.

- **Squad Model:** Embed an analytics champion within each content or marketing team. This approach fosters domain expertise and rapid iteration but can lead to inconsistent methods unless overseen by a central curator.

- **Center of Excellence (COE):** A centralized analytics team governs standards, tooling, and methodologies, while providing self-serve support to business units. COEs accelerate best-practice adoption but risk disconnect if the business context isn't sufficiently represented.

Collaboration Rituals

Embedding rituals into your team's process not only streamlines your analytics operations but also cultivates a shared data culture where insights move seamlessly from one function to the next, ensuring content teams, data teams, and leadership are all moving in the same direction. It also creates an essential forum for team members to ask questions, offer ideas, and raise concerns that might otherwise get overlooked.

- **Analytics Storyboarding**: Before major projects, host a 60-minute kickoff to align on objectives, audience, and success criteria.

- **Weekly or Biweekly Office Hours**: Analysts make themselves available for ad hoc questions and mini-workshops, democratizing data access.

- **Quarterly Governance Forum**: The COE and business stakeholders review roadmap progress, reprioritize initiatives, and ratify any taxonomy or governance updates.

Budget-Friendly Ideas for Growing Your Content Analytics Program

Resource constraints should never stall your analytics ambitions. By prioritizing strategically and leveraging low- or no-cost solutions, even lean teams can build a foundation that scales.

- **Phase Your Investments**

  1. **Phase 1 (Foundational)**: Focus on core metrics and reporting: use free tools like Google Analytics, Google Tag Manager, and Google Data Studio to stand up dashboards and basic ETL via Google Sheets.

  2. **Phase 2 (Automation)**: Introduce a cloud data warehouse (BigQuery's free tier, Snowflake trial) and simple ETL scripts (Airbyte or Fivetran open source) to eliminate manual data pulls.

3. **Phase 3 (Advanced)**: Add lightweight machine learning tools (AutoML in BigQuery, Vertex AI) or low-code experimentation platforms (Google Optimize free tier) to support causal and predictive analytics.

- **Cross-Train Existing Staff**

  - Offer brief "analytics literacy" workshops for content creators and marketers, teaching them to interpret dashboards and basic query filters.

  - Pair a data analyst with a writer or editor on a weekly basis to co-author insight briefs, spreading skills organically.

- **Leverage Community and Open Source**

  - Tap GitHub repositories for dashboard templates (Looker Block Gallery, Google Data Studio Community Visualizations).

  - Join vendor user groups and forums (Databox, Supermetrics) to exchange templates, scripts, and tips, which can save weeks of development time.

- **Adopt Agile Reporting Cadences**

  - Replace larger quarterly reports with monthly one-pagers and weekly snapshot emails. Shorter, regular deliverables keep analytics top of mind without becoming a burden.

  - Automate distribution via Slack or email, using scheduled report exports from business intelligence platforms or simple scripts in Google Apps Script.

By sequencing your spending on new resources, upskilling internal talent, and tapping into the vibrant open source and user community ecosystems, you can deliver professional-grade analytics on even the smallest budgets, proving ROI and making a strong case for the value of future investments in the work you and your team are doing.

Final Thoughts

Building a content analytics program is a marathon, not a sprint. You've learned how to establish core systems, assemble the right team, and prioritize initiatives that balance quick wins with strategic impact. To sustain your momentum for the long run

1. **Iterate and Evolve:** Treat every dashboard, report, and model as a living artifact. Solicit feedback, monitor adoption metrics (dashboard views, slide downloads, ticket volumes), and refine both content and processes quarterly.

2. **Measure Your Maturity:** Use simple KPIs—time-to-insight, ad hoc request volume, roadmap execution rate—to track your progress along your team's maturity curve. Celebrate leveling up from descriptive to comparative, causal, and predictive capabilities.

3. **Champion a Culture of Curiosity:** Encourage all team members to ask "What if?" and "Why?" Host regular "analytics hack days" where cross-functional squads tackle small challenges using real data. Invite others in your organization to participate.

4. **Look Ahead:** As data volume and complexity grow, explore emerging technologies—real-time streaming analytics, generative AI for natural language insights, or behaviorally adaptive content delivery. Begin with small proofs of concept to assess fit and feasibility.

Your content analytics practice can become a strategic differentiator, fueling smarter editorial decisions, more efficient budgeting, and deeper audience engagement. By embedding robust systems, clear roles, and a disciplined roadmap, you ensure analytics isn't just an extra responsibility but a core pillar of your organization's success.

CHAPTER 12

Ethics, Privacy, and Responsible Data Use

Ethical stewardship and privacy compliance are no longer optional for organizations handling user data. Breaches of trust can incur heavy fines, erode brand reputation, and harm individuals. For organizations doing business in Europe, for example, under the European Union (EU)'s General Data Protection Regulation (GDPR), organizations face penalties up to €20 million or 4 % of global turnover for non-compliance, emphasizing the high stakes of data mismanagement.[1] Similarly, the California Consumer Privacy Act (CCPA) grants California residents the right to know, delete, and opt out of the sale of their personal information, with fines totaling up to $7,500 per intentional violation.[2] At the federal level in the United States, the Family Educational Rights and Privacy Act (FERPA) protects student records, imposing requirements on educational

---

[1] European Commission. "Data Protection in the EU." Accessed July 14, 2025. `https://commission.europa.eu/law/data-protection_en`

[2] California Department of Justice Office of the Attorney General. "California Consumer Privacy Act (CCPA)." Accessed July 14, 2025. `https://oag.ca.gov/privacy/ccpa`

institutions to safeguard personally identifiable information and empower students or parents to access and correct their records.[3]

More importantly, ethical analytics foster consumer trust, which in turn drives engagement and loyalty—critical assets for content-driven businesses. According to a 2016 study, MIT Sloan found that companies perceived as ethically responsible in their data practices enjoy higher customer trust scores and increased long-term revenue growth.[4] Moreover, as analytics capabilities advance from descriptive reporting ("What happened?") to predictive modeling ("What will happen?"), the potential for unintended harms—such as bias in recommendations or privacy intrusions—grows, making proactive ethical guardrails essential.

Embedding ethics in your content analytics program means going beyond mere legal compliance to embrace core principles that identify your organization as trustworthy and responsible: transparency (ensuring that your audience understands how their data is used), minimization (only collecting what's necessary), fairness (avoiding discriminatory outcomes), and equity (ensuring all groups are treated justly).[5] For instance, when running comparative or causal experiments, informing participants and obtaining their consent is critical, particularly when A/B tests could compromise sensitive personal attributes. Ethical reflection also guides which data segments to analyze—opting out of examining highly personal fields (e.g., health or ethnicity), for example, unless explicit, informed consent is obtained.

---

[3] US Department of Education. "Student Privacy Policy Office (FERPA)." Accessed July 14, 2025. https://studentprivacy.ed.gov/ferpa

[4] MIT Sloan Management Review. "Trust in Data: The Currency of Business." Last modified June 14, 2016. https://sloanreview.mit.edu/article/trust-in-data-the-currency-of-business/

[5] The Compliance Digest. "The Role of Ethics and Governance, Risk Management and Compliance." Accessed July 14, 2025. https://thecompliancedigest.com/the-role-of-ethics-and-governance-risk-management-and-compliance/

Industry leadership in ethical analytics can also create competitive advantages. For example, Microsoft implemented GDPR compliance before its enforcement, establishing itself as an industry leader in data privacy.[6] Additionally, surveys show that 78 % of consumers are more likely to engage with brands that demonstrate responsible data handling, while 67 % would switch providers after a single privacy mishap.[7] By positioning privacy and ethics at the heart of your content analytics practice, you not only protect stakeholders and comply with regulations, industry standards, or company policies, you also build the credibility needed to make analytics valuable not just to your company but to your consumers and stakeholders by making it possible to deliver more value more effectively.

Finally, there is also evidence that responsible and proactive corporate policies can reduce the risk of future regulatory action.[8] Companies that adopt proactive compliance measures tend to stay ahead of regulatory changes and even influence how future policies are shaped.

Key Legal Frameworks and Principles

Navigating the legal landscape of content analytics begins with understanding three foundational US and international statutes—GDPR, CCPA, and FERPA—and applying them through the lens of the concept of privacy by design (PbD).

---

[6] Corporate Compliance Insights. "The Future of Compliance: How to Lead the Way." Accessed July 15, 2025. `https://www.corporatecomplianceinsights.com/future-compliance-proactive-how-lead-way/`

[7] Alation. "Data Ethics Isn't Just a Checkbox—It's a Competitive Advantage." Last modified April 24, 2025. `https://www.alation.com/blog/data-ethics-competitive-advantage/`

[8] PwC. "Regulatory Compliance Risk in Transformation." Accessed July 15, 2025. `https://www.pwc.com/us/en/services/audit-assurance/digital-assurance-transparency/regulatory-compliance-risk-in-transformation.html`

GDPR: Lawfulness, Fairness, and Transparency

Even if you're not doing business in Europe, the EU's GDPR offers a model for ethical data use. It's seven core principles mandate that personal data be

- Processed lawfully, fairly, and transparently

- Collected for specified, explicit purposes

- Minimized in scope

- Kept accurate and up to date

- Retained only as long as necessary

- Secured against unauthorized access

- Subject to accountability measures[9]

These requirements translate into concrete steps for content analytics teams:

1. Documenting data processing activities

2. Mapping data flows

3. Publishing clear privacy notices

GDPR also protects certain individual rights—such as the right to access, rectify, or erase data—meaning analytics systems must support timely user requests without compromising reporting integrity.[10]

---

[9] European Union. "General Data Protection Regulation (GDPR): Key Principles." Accessed July 14, 2025. https://gdpr.eu/what-is-gdpr/#principles

[10] European Union, Regulation (EU) 2016/679 of the European Parliament and of the Council of 27 April 2016 (General Data Protection Regulation), arts. 15–17, Official Journal of the European Union L119 (May 4, 2016), Accessed April 23, 2026. https://eur-lex.europa.eu/eli/reg/2016/679/oj.

DO US BUSINESSES NEED TO BE CONCERNED ABOUT GDPR REGULATIONS?

Even if an American business doesn't have offices or staff in the EU, it can still be subject to GDPR if it

- **Targets or markets to EU residents**, including offering goods, services, or subscriptions

- **Monitors behavior** of EU visitors on its website or app (e.g., using cookies or analytics)

- **Collects personal data** from EU residents—even if only passively through contact forms or mailing lists

GDPR also has extraterritorial reach: it protects EU citizens wherever their data is processed.

How to Make Sure You're in Compliance

- **Audit User Data Collection:** Know where data comes from and who it belongs to.

- **Update Privacy Policies:** Make sure they reflect GDPR rights (e.g., data access, erasure).

- **Enable Cookie Consent:** Especially for behavioral tracking or marketing analytics.

- **Consider Adding a Data Protection Officer (DPO) Role to Your Team**: To demonstrate that you embrace proactive compliance.

CCPA: Control and Accountability for California Residents

CCPA grants California consumers rights to know what personal information is collected, to request deletion, to opt out of the sale of their data, and to non-discrimination for exercising these rights.[11] For content analytics, "selling" often encompasses sharing identifiers or behavioral profiles with third-party ad networks. That means analytics teams need to maintain opt-out mechanisms and update their consent records accordingly. CCPA's emphasis on "reasonable security" also requires implementing safeguards like encryption when storing analytics datasets that include any personal identifiers or when transmitting them—a step that can be easily overlooked when working with third-party vendors.[12]

FERPA: Protecting Educational Records

FERPA applies to any educational institution receiving US Department of Education funds and gives parents or eligible students control over disclosure of "education records" that contain personally identifiable information.[13] Analytics teams in higher education must anonymize or pseudonymize student data (i.e., replace personally identifiable information within a dataset with artificial identifiers) before including it

---

[11] Proofpoint. "California Consumer Privacy Act (CCPA): What You Need to Know." Accessed July 14, 2025. `https://www.proofpoint.com/us/threat-reference/california-consumer-privacy-act-ccpa`

[12] Deloitte United States. "CCPA Compliance: Implementing Reasonable Security Measures." Accessed July 14, 2025. `https://www2.deloitte.com/us/en/pages/risk/articles/ccpa-compliance.html`

[13] National Center for Education Statistics. "FERPA: Protecting Student Privacy". Accessed July 14, 2025. `https://studentprivacy.ed.gov/ferpa`

in dashboards or reports.[14] They also need to segregate access based on user roles. In other words, they need to grant users the minimum level of access they need to perform their jobs. For example, teachers might have access to students' grades and attendance records, while administrative staff might have access to enrollment and financial information. Analytics teams also need to implement audit logging (i.e., maintain records of who accesses the data they collect and when) to demonstrate compliance.[15]

Privacy by Design: A Framework for Embedding Ethics into Analytics

Of course, ethical practice is about more just complying with policies or the law. Content analytics teams should also be concerned with guarding against biased interpretations and inequitable outcomes. Research on big data ethics suggests implementing equity audits—examining whether models or content recommendations disproportionately disadvantage certain groups—and accountability measures such as third-party reviews or "Hippocratic oaths" for data practitioners.[16] Transparency in methodology (sharing code and parameter settings) further bolsters your team's credibility and aligns with best practices for reproducible, trustable analytics.[17] Altogether, measures like these will make it possible for your

---

[14] Pseudonymization replaces identifying information with coded placeholders (like hashed emails), while anonymization removes it altogether. Pseudonymized data can potentially be re-identified; anonymized data cannot."

[15] US Department of Education. "Best Practices for Data Privacy in Higher Education Analytics." Accessed July 14, 2025. https://studentprivacy.ed.gov/resources/best-practices-data-privacy-higher-ed

[16] McKinsey & Company. "Data Ethics: What It Means and What It Takes." Accessed July 14, 2025. https://www.mckinsey.com/capabilities/mckinsey-digital/our-insights/data-ethics-what-it-means-and-what-it-takes

[17] Research Studies Press. "The Importance of Transparency in Methodology and Data." Last modified January 24, 2025. https://research-studies-press.co.uk/2025/01/24/the-importance-of-transparency-in-methodology-and-data/

team to produce more effective results and can enhance the reputation of your brand in the marketplace.

One approach to incorporating these principles into your content analytics program is to adopt a framework like privacy by design.

Developed by privacy expert Ann Cavoukian in the 1990s and formalized as an international standard for ethical data use in 2009, privacy by design (PbD) prescribes seven foundational principles—most notably, the importance of being proactive, not reactive, and preventative, not remedial—and they recommend integrating privacy considerations at every stage of system design.[18] For content analytics, this means specifying data minimization strategies (only tracking metrics essential to your research questions), ensuring dashboards avoid exposing personal data, and designing consent flows into event-tagging implementations, which means

1. Obtaining explicit user consent before collecting data

2. Allowing users to have granular control over what data is collected

3. Enabling users to withdraw consent easily

4. Maintaining transparency about data use

5. Collecting only necessary data and securing it properly

PbD's emphasis on full lifecycle protection also drives automated data retention policies, which means that data should only be kept for as long as necessary for its intended purposes and securely deleting or archiving data that is no longer needed to minimize the risk of unauthorized use or access.

---

[18] Ann Cavoukian. "Privacy by Design: The 7 Foundational Principles." Information and Privacy Commissioner of Ontario. Accessed July 14, 2025. `https://www.ipc.on.ca/wp-content/uploads/resources/7foundationalprinciples.pdf`

Implementing Privacy by Design

While compliance is often treated as a checklist, ethical and privacy-minded analytics programs embed privacy directly into their systems, processes, and culture. A more proactive approach like privacy by design helps organizations avoid reactive fixes and future-proof their analytics against emerging regulations.

Start with Consent and Transparency

Consent is the cornerstone of privacy-centric analytics. This means users should

- Understand what data is being collected.

- Know why it's being collected.

- Be able to opt in or out at any point without penalty.

Designing clear, granular consent interfaces—such as cookie consent banners or pop-ups with toggles for analytics, marketing, and personalization—builds trust.[19] Especially avoid "dark patterns" like default opt-ins or vague language ("we may use your data to improve services") that manipulate users into consenting to data collection they might otherwise refuse. A 2020 study found that transparent consent banners significantly increased user satisfaction and reduced bounce rates compared with interfaces that were vague or unclear.[20]

---

[19] Alessandro Acquisti, Laura Brandimarte, and George Loewenstein, "Privacy and Human Behavior in the Age of Information," *Science* 347, no. 6221 (2015): 509–514.

[20] Christine Utz et al., "(Un)informed Consent: Studying GDPR Consent Notices in the Field," *Proceedings of the 2019 ACM SIGSAC Conference on Computer and Communications Security*, last modified November 15, 2019, `https://www.ftc.gov/system/files/documents/public_events/1548288/privacycon-2020-christine_utz.pdf`

And where possible, align your consent categories with your research questions. For example, if you plan to explore predictive behavior patterns using third-party tools, disclose this in your "advanced analytics" opt-in box.

Apply Minimization and Segmentation

PbD also calls for collecting only what you need and no more. This means designing data collection around your research question types:

- Descriptive questions might only require basic page view and session data only.

- Correlational or causal questions might need user-level interaction data, but it should be anonymized and time-limited.

Avoid capturing names, emails, IP addresses, or detailed device fingerprints unless absolutely necessary and only if your platform provides robust access controls and data segregation.

Segmentation techniques like using an algorithm to encode user IDs or bucketing users into behavior tiers let teams analyze patterns without being able to directly identify individuals. In fact, many compliance-friendly dashboards now operate on aggregated event models, which might show the total number of clicks on a particular button over a month rather than individual clicks. Strategies like this let your organization answer essential business questions without compromising the privacy of your audience members.

Secure the Full Lifecycle

Privacy by design also means planning for secure storage, responsible access, and timely deletion:

- **Data Retention Policies**: Define how long event logs, form submissions, and user IDs are stored. Use automated cleanup scripts or built-in platform tools (GA4 offers flexible retention settings).

- **Role-Based Access Control**: Ensure only designated personnel (e.g., analytics leads, not junior interns) can access sensitive datasets.

- **Audit Trails**: Keep a log of who accessed what data and when. This is especially critical under FERPA and for organizations handling EU resident data.

A 2021 PricewaterhouseCoopers study showed that organizations with mature data lifecycle policies were 60% less likely to suffer a privacy incident compared with those with no formal governance.

By implementing these practices, you create a system that doesn't just comply with regulations but also demonstrates ethical integrity, which helps you earn the long-term trust of your users and stakeholders.[21]

When Ethical Oversight Isn't a Major Concern in Content Analytics

While ethical compliance is fundamental to responsible analytics, not every situation demands the same level of rigorous oversight. Some teams' data use may pose only minimal risk to individuals or to an organization's regulatory obligations:

---

[21] PwC. "Data Risk & Privacy: Unlock the Value of Data in a Secure and Ethical Way." Accessed July 14, 2025. `https://www.pwc.com/us/en/services/consulting/cybersecurity-risk-regulatory/data-risk-and-privacy.html`

- **Aggregated, Non-personal Metrics:** Page views, bounce rates, and engagement signals that don't involve user identity

- **Internal-Only Dashboards:** Analytics confined to employee-facing content or intranet usage

- **Anonymized or Synthetic Datasets:** Data scrubbed of personal identifiers or generated for training/testing purposes

- **Open Source or Public Domain Sources:** Government repositories and pre-cleared research datasets

- **First-Party, Fully Opt-In Interactions:** Users knowingly providing data (e.g., surveys) with no third-party exposure

There are also a number of tools that can help make the task of ethical data use easier (Table 12-1).

Table 12-1. *Tools that minimize ethical risk*

Tool Type	Why It's Lower Risk
Basic web analytics (e.g., Plausible, Fathom)	Privacy-respecting, cookieless by default.
Heatmap tools with anonymization	Hide PII, don't store keystrokes or user IDs.
On-device analytics	Data doesn't leave the user's device.
AI models trained on synthetic or public data	No user attribution, no privacy violation.

No matter what kind of data you're collecting, though, it's best to think of ethical analytics not as an on/off switch but as a spectrum. Even in low-risk zones, clarity and transparency are always the key to earning your audience's trust.

Case Study: Navigating FERPA in Higher Education Analytics

A large public university wanted to improve recruitment outcomes by using content analytics to measure engagement with departmental landing pages, program videos, and virtual open-house recordings. The analytics team proposed tracking individual prospective students' interactions and correlating those with inquiry and application behavior.

However, when the project was reviewed by the university's data governance board and legal counsel, it became clear that the plan—without modification—could violate FERPA, the Family Educational Rights and Privacy Act. FERPA restricts how institutions collect and use personally identifiable education records, and any data linked to an applicant or student's identity must be protected as such.

The Challenge

The proposed system would have captured email addresses via web forms, joined them to CRM records, and then mapped behavior across multiple sessions and devices. Without adequate safeguards, this pipeline could

- Expose personal data in dashboards (e.g., "Jamie viewed three videos and downloaded a faculty profile").

- Allow unauthorized access to information that constitutes an educational record.

- Trigger a FERPA violation if shared with anyone outside the admissions team.

The Solution

The university's analytics and IT teams collaborated with their legal office and ethics committee to redesign the system with privacy by design principles:

- **Pseudonymization or Anonymization**: Instead of storing real email addresses in the analytics environment, the pipeline hashed identifiers and used a lookup table that only CRM admins could access.

- **Role-Based Dashboards**: Admissions counselors could view applicant-level insights, while marketing staff saw only aggregate trends by program or geography.

- **Event Annotations**: Events tied to key content (e.g., "download_program_pdf") included custom parameters marking content category but no user detail.

- **Governance Documentation**: The team created a "Data Use Protocol" defining who could access what, under what conditions, and how long data could be retained.

Outcome

The new system delivered actionable insights—showing which videos and pages drove conversions—while remaining FERPA-compliant. The approach also served as a model for other departments and was featured in the university's annual accountability report.

Key Takeaway

Even when your data-driven goals are legitimate, they must be pursued with thoughtful controls and cross-team collaboration. Privacy doesn't have to be an obstacle to innovation; often it's the catalyst that makes it possible.

While the stakes and regulations may vary across industries, this case illustrates how privacy by design can align stakeholder goals and prevent compliance failures.

Workbook Exercise: Conducting an Ethics and Privacy Audit

This hands-on exercise is designed to help your team evaluate and enhance your content analytics practices through the lens of ethics and privacy. By systematically auditing your data flows, you can identify potential risks and implement appropriate safeguards.

Step 1: Map your data flows

Begin by creating a comprehensive map of your content analytics data flows. Document

- **Data Collection Points**: Identify all sources where data is collected (e.g., web forms, cookies, third-party integrations).

- **Data Types**: Categorize the data collected (e.g., personal identifiers, behavioral data, demographic information).

- **Data Storage**: Note where and how data is stored, including databases and cloud services.

- **Data Access**: List who has access to the data and under what permissions.

- **Data Sharing**: Identify any third parties with whom data is shared.

Use Table 12-2 to map your team's data flow.

Table 12-2. *Sample data flow layout*

Data Source	Data Type	Storage Location	Access Level	Shared With
Website form	Email, name	CRM database	Marketing team	Email service provider
Analytics cookies	Browsing behavior	Analytics platform	Analytics team	None

Step 2: Identify personal and sensitive data

Review your data map to pinpoint personal and sensitive data elements. Personal data includes any information that can identify an individual, such as names, email addresses, and IP addresses. Sensitive data encompasses information like health records, financial details, and racial or ethnic origin.

Highlight these data elements in your map for focused attention in the subsequent steps.

Step 3: Assess risks

Evaluate the risks associated with each data element by considering factors such as

- **Data Sensitivity**: How sensitive is the data?

- **Volume**: How much data is collected?

- **Access**: Who has access to the data?

- **Storage Security**: How secure is the storage?

- **Sharing Practices**: Is the data shared with third parties?

Using the layout format in Table 12-3, assign a risk level (Low, Medium, High) to each data element based on your assessment.

Table 12-3. *Sample risk table layout*

Data Element	Sensitivity	Volume	Access Level	Storage Security	Shared With	Risk Level
Email	High	High	Marketing	Secure	ESP	High
Page views	Low	High	Analytics	Secure	None	Low

FIVE PRIVACY RED FLAGS IN CONTENT ANALYTICS

Keep an eye out for the following potential problems as you audit content or develop new analytics capabilities (Table 12-4).

Table 12-4. *Red flags in content analytics*

Red Flag	Why It's a Problem
Collecting emails in analytics tools	Exposes personally identifiable info
Tracking without user opt-in	Violates consent laws (GDPR/CCPA)
Sharing data with third-party ad networks without disclosure	Risks legal exposure
Retaining data indefinitely	Increases breach and misuse risks
Using inferred sensitive attributes (personal characteristics or information about individuals that are not explicitly provided but can be deduced from available data)	Can lead to ethical bias

Step 4: Define mitigation actions

For data elements identified as Medium or High risk, outline mitigation strategies, such as

- **Data Minimization**: Collect only necessary data.

- **Anonymization**: Remove or encrypt personal identifiers.

- **Access Controls**: Restrict data access to essential personnel.

- **Consent Management**: Implement clear consent mechanisms.

- **Regular Audits**: Schedule periodic reviews of data practices.

Document these actions and assign responsibilities to team members for implementation.

Integrating the Team

Effective ethics and privacy practices in content analytics require collaboration across various roles within your organization. Here are roles and responsibilities you can assign to members of your team to make sure they play a meaningful role in maintaining an ethical practice for your organization:

Legal/Compliance Advisor

- **Responsibilities:**

  - Interpret and ensure compliance with data protection regulations (e.g., GDPR, CCPA, FERPA).

  - Review data collection and processing activities for legal adherence.

- Provide guidance on consent mechanisms and data sharing agreements.

Data Steward

- **Responsibilities:**

  - Maintain data quality and integrity.

  - Manage metadata and data documentation.

  - Oversee data lifecycle, including retention and deletion policies.

  - Act as a liaison between technical teams and business units to ensure data governance policies are implemented effectively.

Analyst and Engineer

- **Responsibilities:**

  - Implement data anonymization and pseudonymization techniques.

  - Develop and maintain data pipelines with privacy considerations.

  - Ensure analytics tools and dashboards do not expose personal data.

  - Monitor data access logs and flag unusual activities.

Content Strategist and UX Designer

- **Responsibilities:**

  - Design user interfaces that clearly communicate data collection practices.

  - Develop content that informs users about their data rights and options.

- Collaborate with legal teams to ensure privacy notices are user-friendly and compliant.

- Incorporate feedback mechanisms for users to express privacy concerns.

By clearly defining these roles and fostering collaboration, your organization can build a robust framework that upholds ethical standards and can protect user privacy throughout the content analytics process.

Budget-Friendly Ideas for Ethical Analytics

Implementing ethical and privacy-conscious analytics doesn't require a large budget. Even small teams can make significant strides by focusing on foundational practices that prioritize user trust and data integrity.

Prioritize Data Minimization

Collect only the data necessary to answer your research questions. For instance, if you're exploring descriptive metrics like page views or time spent on content, avoid gathering personal identifiers unless absolutely required. This approach not only reduces privacy risks but also simplifies data management.

Utilize Free and Open Source Tools

Leverage available tools that support privacy-centric analytics:

- **Matomo**: An open source web analytics platform that offers data ownership and privacy compliance features.

- **Simple Analytics**: A privacy-first analytics tool that doesn't use cookies or collect personal data.

- **Google Analytics 4 (GA4)**: While not open source, GA4 includes features like data retention controls and IP anonymization.

Implement Basic Consent Mechanisms

Ensure users are informed about data collection practices:

- **Cookie Banners**: Use simple banners to inform users about cookie usage and obtain consent.

- **Privacy Notices**: Clearly state what data is collected, how it's used, and users' rights regarding their data.

Transparency fosters trust and aligns with regulations like GDPR and CCPA.

Schedule Regular Data Reviews

Even without advanced tools, periodic reviews can help maintain ethical standards:

- **Data Audits**: Assess what data is collected, stored, and shared.

- **Access Controls**: Ensure only authorized personnel have access to sensitive data.

- **Retention Policies**: Define how long data is kept and establish deletion protocols.

Regular reviews help identify potential issues and reinforce a culture of responsibility.

Foster a Culture of Ethics

Encourage team discussions about data ethics:

- **Training Sessions**: Educate team members on privacy laws and ethical considerations.

- **Ethics Committees**: Form small groups to oversee data practices and address concerns.

Cultivating awareness ensures that ethical considerations are integrated into daily operations.

Final Thoughts

As content analytics continues to evolve, integrating ethics and privacy considerations becomes more than just a legal obligation and a moral obligation; it can be a cornerstone in your brand's reputation and a competitive advantage in your marketplace. By embedding these principles into every stage—from data collection to analysis and reporting—organizations can build trust, remove obstacles from robust user engagement, and support the work of producing meaningful analytical insights.

Remember, ethical analytics is an ongoing journey:

- **Stay Informed**: Regularly update your knowledge on emerging privacy laws and ethical standards.

- **Be Transparent**: Clearly communicate data practices to users and stakeholders.

- **Engage Stakeholders**: Involve diverse perspectives in decision-making processes to ensure fairness and inclusivity.

By committing to responsible data use, organizations not only safeguard themselves against potential pitfalls and liabilities, contribute to a more equitable and trustworthy digital landscape, and create value for themselves and their customers.

In the next chapter we'll look at the future of content analytics, focusing on some of the most significant changes to keep an eye on, like the use of artificial intelligence, and on those aspects of analytics that will continue to need human input and oversight.

CHAPTER 13

The Future of Content Analytics

Today, whether we're content analysts or not, we find ourselves at the doorstep of a new era of data-enabled innovation, one driven not just by dashboards and KPIs but by the opportunity to innovate, expand, and accelerate everything we do.

More content is being published, and more data is being generated than ever before, but the user behaviors and experiences that data can describe are increasingly scattered and fragmented across devices, platforms, and media channels. Meanwhile, your audience continues to expect more content that's personalized, trustworthy, and instantly relevant. They also expect you, as a content developer, to understand their needs and the challenges they face, and they expect your content to be there when they need it. Fortunately, new tools are being created to make that work better and easier.

What will not change is the need to have a solid understanding of the science of content analytics. Having that under your belt will give you a solid foundation to build on and the confidence to understand how to assess the value of the new tools you'll encounter. It will also help you see how they fit into the bigger picture and how to implement them in an effective and meaningful way.

© Russ Bahorsky 2026

R. Bahorsky, *The Fundamentals of Content Analytics,*
https://doi.org/10.1007/979-8-8688-2601-6_13

In this chapter, we won't attempt to predict what the future will look like, but we will explore a way to prepare for that future—whatever it might be.

We'll explore how artificial intelligence, new data paradigms, evolving customer expectations, and ethical considerations are reshaping how content teams measure success. And we'll show you how to stay grounded: asking better questions, making informed choices, and knowing when to adapt your tools and strategy.

The chapters that came before this one focused on what's already working. This one looks forward, so your organization stays ready for what's next.

The bottom line is that while tools and platforms will continue to evolve, the fundamentals of good content analytics—clear questions, clean data, thoughtful interpretation—remain as important as ever.

Trend 1: AI-Generated Content and Analytics

Artificial intelligence is reshaping the entire content lifecycle, from creation and optimization to tagging, testing, and even analysis. For many content teams, AI has gone from buzzword to everyday toolset almost overnight. Here's what's changing:

- **Generative AI** (e.g., ChatGPT, Claude, Gemini) is being used to

    - Draft articles, emails, reports, and metadata.

    - Rewrite content for different segments or reading levels.

    - Generate summaries, headlines, and alt text at scale.

- **Analytics-focused AI tools** are now capable of

  - Extracting insights from raw content performance data

  - Clustering pages or audiences by engagement behavior

  - Automating tagging and classification for unstructured assets

For example, a university admissions team uses ChatGPT to summarize 500 student testimonials into key sentiment themes. At the same time, they use an AutoML tool to predict which content pieces correlate most with inquiries.

For content analysts this has a variety of implications:

1. **More Content Means More Measurement:** Teams using AI to scale production need to develop rigorous frameworks for evaluating quality and impact, not just quantity.

2. **Metadata May be Machine-Generated:** Auto-tagging and summarization introduce consistency but also risk introducing bias or inaccuracy if not checked by a human.

3. **Measurement Must Evolve:** Standard metrics like time on page or bounce rate may be less relevant in a future where content is modular, personalized, or conversational (e.g., chat-based interactions).

4. **Interpretability Matters:** As AI-generated content becomes harder to distinguish from human-crafted messaging, understanding why something worked—rather than just whether it worked—becomes critical.

However, no matter how good AI gets at generating content, it's still a good idea to focus on more than just click-throughs when you test it on your audiences. You'll also want to keep a close eye on how it affects audience sentiment, conversion quality, and downstream behavior.

And as you evaluate not whether but how these tools might have a place in your content analytics program, ask yourself these questions:

- What role should AI play in our content pipeline, and how will we track its performance separately?

- How do we ensure editorial oversight for automated content creation?

- What human feedback loops do we need to preserve insight, empathy, accessibility, and clarity?

If you haven't yet begun to integrate AI into your content analytics program, the time to begin experimenting and developing expertise in AI-assisted analytics and content development is now. Here are a few steps you should already be taking:

- **Invest in AI Tools:** Equip your team with AI-powered content creation and analytics tools to streamline processes and enhance productivity.

- **Let Your Team Explore:** Ensure your team is well-versed in using AI tools and interpreting AI-generated insights.

- **Balance Automation with Creativity:** While AI can handle repetitive tasks, creativity and storytelling remain irreplaceable and uniquely human. Use AI to complement, not replace, human input.

Ultimately, AI can support creative output and analytics insight but only if you treat it as a collaborator, not a shortcut. Research suggests that there are concerns about AI models generating inaccurate or fabricated data, especially when they lack sufficient training data,[1] so human oversight and validation will continue to be critical steps in your process.

WHAT AI CAN AND CAN'T DO FOR CONTENT TEAMS

AI can be a powerful tool for content analytics teams, but it's essential to keep its limitations in mind.

Table 13-1. *AI's limitations*

Can Help With ...	Still Needs Humans For ...
Drafting first versions	Final editorial judgment
Tagging and summarizing content	Defining what's relevant or audience-specific
Grouping similar content or users	Deciding what insight is worth acting on
Synthesizing survey feedback	Understanding emotion, tone, and context
Optimizing content for SEO	Assessing readability
Automating statistical testing	Defining the hypotheses and the appropriate data to test and applying good judgment to assessing the validity of the results

---

[1] Nicola Jones, "The AI Revolution Is Running Out of Data. What Can Researchers Do?", *Nature* 636 (2024): 290–292, https://www.nature.com/articles/d41586-024-03990-2

Trend 2: Predictive and Prescriptive Analytics

As analytics platforms grow more sophisticated, the emphasis is shifting from retrospective reporting to forward-looking insight. Instead of just asking *what happened*, content teams are increasingly asking:

- *What's likely to happen next?*

- *What should we do based on that forecast?*

This is the realm of predictive and prescriptive analytics. Predictive tools, like the ones we explored in Chapter 7, use historical data to model the probability of future behavior like

- Forecasting traffic to a resource library

- Estimating donation or conversion likelihood for a given audience segment

- Anticipating which visitors are likely to bounce based on early behavior

However, prescriptive analytics takes that one step further: it recommends actions based on the prediction, actions like

- Suggesting optimal send times for an email campaign

- Recommending content to repurpose or suppress

- Guiding budget allocation across formats or channels

For example, a SaaS content team might use an AutoML platform to suggest the best-performing blog format by user segment, which could save time and lead to increased conversions.

The tools these approaches use include both a variety of AI solutions and integrated marketing platforms that allow users to gain insight into their markets at the individual level.

- **AutoML platforms** (e.g., Google Vertex AI, BigQuery ML, DataRobot)

- **Marketing automation with predictive scoring** (e.g., HubSpot, Salesforce)

- **No-code AI builders** for audience segmentation and prioritization (e.g., MonkeyLearn, Akkio)

However, while these tools are powerful, they come with risks. As modeling capabilities become more powerful, so does the risk of overfitting, developing overly complex models that work well on historical data but fail in new contexts. Additionally, AI-based recommendations can lead to recommendations that may be difficult to interpret or challenge and may lead teams to act on predictions without understanding their risks or limitations.

When working with these tools, always ask: *What variables is the model using? How recent is the training data (and where is it coming from)? What margin of error should we expect?*

Trend 3: The Rise of Zero-Party and Consent-Based Data

As the use of third-party cookies becomes less common and as privacy regulations tighten, organizations are shifting toward the use of data that users intentionally share with a brand—also called zero-party data or consent-based data. It generally includes

- Preferences selected in a form

- Survey responses or voluntarily provided user profile information

- Chatbot conversations

- Voluntary responses to polls, chats, quizzes, or onboarding forms

When a university, for example, allows prospective students to indicate which programs interest them most, it can then use that data to personalize follow-up content and messaging. Zero-party data is ultimately more meaningful because it's

- **Voluntary**: It reflects what users choose to share.

- **Trust-Based**: It requires a clear value exchange.

- **Precise**: It often includes details you can't infer from behavior alone.

When it comes to analytics, the implication is that, even though users may generate less data, it's often more relevant and may help you shift your focus from understanding broad trends in your market or your audience to zeroing in on individual preferences.

The shift can be more effective for several reasons:

1. **Enhanced Personalization**: Zero-party data, which is proactively shared by consumers, allows for more accurate and effective personalization compared with data inferred from cookies.

2. **Improved Trust and Compliance**: This approach helps companies comply with privacy regulations and builds trust with consumers, as they have control over the data they share.

3. **Higher Data Quality**: Zero-party data tends to be more accurate and relevant because it is voluntarily provided by users.

4. **Future-Proofing**: With the phasing out of third-party cookies, zero-party data ensures companies can continue to gather valuable insights.

5. **Better Customer Relationships**: Collecting zero-party data fosters a transparent and respectful relationship with customers, leading to increased loyalty and engagement.[2]

Use zero-party data to enhance segmentation, inform content development, and trigger personalization, but don't overuse it. Respect for user autonomy should be part of your long-term strategy. Work closely with UX and content teams to design smart data capture moments.

Finally, as you're developing research questions in a zero-party data context, remember that user opinions and preferences are often very different from user behavior. When designing A/B tests based on user preferences, keep a close eye on how closely correlated they are (or aren't) to the outcomes they lead you to expect.

Trend 4: Content Analytics As Part of the CX and Product Stack

According to a recent study by the McKinsey group, companies today are moving toward creating end-to-end customer experiences that integrate products, services, and user environments. This approach is driven by the need to meet rising customer expectations for immediacy, personalization, and convenience. Traditional product companies are transforming into service providers, and service providers are incorporating products into

---

[2] Tim Glomb. "Say Goodbye to Cookies." Harvard Business Review. April 8, 2021. https://hbr.org/2021/04/say-goodbye-to-cookies

their offerings. This shift is part of a broader trend toward customer-centric strategies that focus on delivering value through integrated experiences.[3]

As the line between content, user experience (UX), and product continues to blur, content analytics is no longer a standalone function. It's becoming a critical input to broader customer experience (CX) strategy.

Ultimately, the shift is happening for a number of reasons.

- Content now exists inside apps, emails, platforms, and workflows, not just on landing pages.

- Content teams are responsible for more touchpoints (onboarding flows, help centers, microcopy).

- Users expect seamless experiences, not silos.

As a content analyst, you may find your content performance metrics blending with

- UX metrics (e.g., task success rate, satisfaction score)

- Product metrics (e.g., feature adoption, drop-off rate)

- Customer support signals (e.g., content viewed before contacting help)

For example, some SaaS companies now track how users interact with onboarding content inside their app, correlating content completion with trial-to-subscription conversion.

If you're faced with making a shift toward greater cross-organizational integration, you may need to consider how to expand your reporting efforts to include other functional units within your organization. And if you haven't already incorporated journey mapping or cohort analysis

---

[3] McKinsey. "The Expanding Role of Design in Creating an End-to-End Customer Experience." Accessed June 18, 2025. https://www.mckinsey.com/capabilities/operations/our-insights/the-expanding-role-of-design-in-creating-an-end-to-end-customer-experience

into your analytics, it may be time to do so. Under this kind of business model, success is not about traffic; it's about retention, activation, and lifetime value.

As part of your efforts to integrate analytics into the culture of your organization, advocate for content to be included in CX conversations, and make sure your team has access to product analytics when relevant.

Trend 5: Ethics, Fairness, and Algorithmic Transparency

As analytics tools grow more powerful—and more automated—the ethical implications become harder to ignore.

It's one thing to report on content performance. It's another to deploy machine learning models that predict behavior, segment users, or determine which messages people see (and which they don't). With greater capability comes greater responsibility.

A public health campaign, for example, used a segmentation model to target messages but failed to realize it was underserving rural communities due to incomplete historical data. As you evaluate your own program for its ethical implications, here are a few things to consider:

- **Bias in Data = Bias in Outcomes:** If your training data overrepresents one group or excludes another, your predictive models may reinforce inequities.

- **Opaque Logic Can Erode Trust:** Stakeholders (and users) may not understand how a model makes decisions or what assumptions it relies on.

- **Automation Can Obscure Accountability:** If a personalized experience backfires, who's responsible? The content team? The tool?

Ideally, you'll need to involve your legal and public relations teams in these conversations. Prepare for those meetings by reviewing your program's

- **Auditability**: Can someone outside the analytics team trace how decisions were made?

- **Transparency**: Are stakeholders aware of when automation is being used and how?

- **Equity**: Does the analysis consider how different groups may be impacted differently?

Use a bias-auditing checklist (see Appendix E); segment your audience by race, age, region, or other equity-relevant categories to look for disparities; and make sure you and your team are carefully reviewing any automated personalization or scoring systems.

With your legal and crisis management experts, make sure you have a damage control plan in place for each red flag you see. It's much easier to do this before a problem occurs.

Finally, remember that ethical analytics is a design challenge, not a compliance exercise. The goal is to build systems that are *useful, fair, and trustworthy* by design.

What Won't Change

For all the change happening in platforms, tools, and expectations, the core principles of content analytics remain remarkably consistent. If anything, they're becoming more important as that complexity increases.

Even though the tools and resources may change, you and your team will still need a good blueprint and these fundamental skills to make those tools work for you and your organization:

- **The Creativity to Ask Clear Questions:** The ability to frame a focused, decision-driven research question will always be more valuable than the ability to run a complicated analysis.

- **The Insight to Measure What Matters:** Choose metrics that reflect business goals and user value, not just what's easy to track.

- **The Ability to Interpret in Context:** Numbers don't speak for themselves. Great analysts understand the content, audience, and environment they're measuring.

- **The Willingness to Collaborate Across Roles:** Content analytics is not the job of one person. It requires input from content creators, marketers, analysts, UX designers, and leadership. It's also about creativity and recognizing opportunities to be innovative.

- **The Power to Communicate with Clarity:** Turning insights into action is a storytelling skill. Good analytics isn't just about the math or the technical skills; it's about using the right tools to persuade and improve.

Final Thoughts

The future of content analytics isn't just about AI, personalization, or predictive scoring. The key is to build a data-informed, learning-centered approach to how we measure and improve the stories we tell.

Yes, tools will evolve. Platforms will shift. Privacy laws will change. New benchmarks will emerge. But the teams that thrive in this future won't be the ones that can afford the latest tools and technology; they'll be the ones who

- Frame strong questions.

- Collaborate across disciplines.

- Focus on their audience.

- Interpret results in context.

- Learn and adapt.

To be future-ready, you'll need to

- **Develop Habits, Not Just Reports:** Build rhythms for testing, debriefing, and iterating.

- **Make Space for Experimentation:** Don't wait for certainty. Test small, learn fast, and refine continuously.

- **Document What Works:** Build a knowledge base your team can draw from.

- **Invest in the Process, Not Just the Tools:** Tools will change. The ability to create a focused research question won't.

And remember, the human aspect of the equation will continue to matter. Even in a world of machine learning and predictive platforms, your most powerful asset is still human judgment. Analytics will tell you what's happening, but only your team can decide what it means, why it matters, and what to do next.

So, whether you're running simple page-level reports or piloting an AI-powered content scoring system, the goal remains the same: use data to tell smarter stories, serve your audience, and create more purposeful communication.

Ultimately, you don't need to know what the future holds; you just need to be the kind of team that has a clear goal in sight and is open to finding the best way to get there.

APPENDIX A

Event Tagging Using Google

Understanding how users interact with your website is essential for making informed decisions, and that process starts with tracking the right events. Whether your goal is engagement or lead generation, setting up event tagging in Google Analytics 4 (GA4) and Google Tag Manager (GTM) allows you to capture meaningful data tied directly to your business objectives. This appendix walks you through a simple, step-by-step process for identifying key actions, configuring your tools, and validating your setup.

Step 1: Decide what events matter

Start by tying events directly to business goals. Don't just tag everything; focus on actions that reflect progress toward your objectives. For example:

- **Engagement Goals:** Scroll depth (50%, 90%), video completions

- **Conversion Goals:** Sales, brochure downloads, form submissions, registrations

- **Partnership Tracking:** Outbound link clicks

If the goal is *brand awareness*, prioritize video views and page depth. If it's *lead generation*, focus on downloads and form fills.

© Russ Bahorsky 2026
R. Bahorsky, *The Fundamentals of Content Analytics*,
https://doi.org/10.1007/979-8-8688-2601-6

Step 2: Set up the tools

You'll need two free tools:

- **Google Analytics 4 (GA4):** Stores and reports events

- **Google Tag Manager (GTM):** Controls when events fire

Make sure GA4 and GTM are installed on your site. This requires a small script in the header for each, but otherwise, no coding is required—most events can be configured in GTM's interface.

Step 3: Create tags and triggers in GTM

- Tag = what you're sending (e.g., "download_whitepaper")

- Trigger = when it fires (e.g., when a user clicks a PDF link)

Example: Whitepaper download

- **Trigger**: Click URL that contains .pdf

- **Tag**: GA4 event → event name = download_whitepaper

- **Parameters**: Filename, page URL (optional)

Always test in GTM's Preview Mode before publishing.

Step 4: Confirm in GA4

Check that your events are firing:

- **GA4 ➤ Admin ➤ Events** (list of custom events)

- **Reports ➤ Engagement ➤ Events** (performance over time)

Mark important ones (like form submissions) as conversions.

Step 5: Review and refine

Audit monthly:

- Are events firing consistently?

- Do they still align with business goals?

- Could you capture more context with parameters?

Event Planning Worksheet (Quick Version)

To help translate goals into measurable actions, use Table A-1 to map out key events, their names, and any useful parameters you'll want to track.

Table A-1. *Event planning worksheet*

Goal	Key Action	Event Name	Useful Parameters
Drive brochure downloads	Clicks "Download Brochure"	download_ brochure	file_name, page_url
Boost video engagement	Watches 75%	video_75_ percent	video_title, video_ duration
Capture inquiries	Submits contact form	inquiry_form_ submit	page_url, form_id

Extra: Cross-Domain Tracking

If your users move across multiple domains (e.g., university.edu → apply. university.edu)

1. Ensure all sites use the same GA4 property.

2. In GA4, open the relevant data stream, go to Configure Tag Settings, and add your domains under *Cross-Domain Tracking*.

3. Test in Debug View to confirm sessions aren't broken.

Caution

- Keep names consistent (all_lowercase; underscores, not spaces).

- Don't over-tag. Only track what supports your strategic goal.

- Never send PII (names, emails) in events.

Pattern Hunting with Excel

A correlation matrix is a powerful tool for uncovering relationships between multiple metrics in web content performance, like page views, time on page, bounce rate, and conversion rate. By showing how strongly each metric is related to the others, you can identify patterns, spot potential redundancies, and prioritize areas for optimization. In Excel, building a correlation matrix is straightforward and requires only a well-organized dataset and the use of the CORREL() function. This appendix outlines the steps to create one and interpret its results in the context of content strategy and performance evaluation.

How to Create a Correlation Matrix

Step 1: Gather your data

Export your performance data from Google Analytics 4, your CMS, or business intelligence tool. You'll need a table like Table B-1, where each row is a content item (e.g., blog post, video) and each column is a metric (e.g., time on page, bounce rate, conversions).

© Russ Bahorsky 2026
R. Bahorsky, *The Fundamentals of Content Analytics*,
https://doi.org/10.1007/979-8-8688-2601-6

Table B-1. *Sample content metrics table (input data)*

Page	Page Views	Time on Page (sec)	Bounce Rate (%)	Conversion Rate (%)
Page 1	1,000	140	50	1.8
Page 2	950	135	52	1.7
Page 3	1,100	160	48	2.2

Step 2: Create a matrix

On the same worksheet or on a different tab, create a table like
Table B-2 with the presented column and row configuration (your metrics
may differ, of course).

Table B-2. *Sample matrix table layout*

	Page Views	Time on Page (sec)	Bounce Rate (%)	Conversion Rate (%)
Page Views				
Time on Page				
Bounce Rate				
Conversion Rate				

Step 3: Populate the matrix with the CORREL function

In an empty cell use the following formula: =CORREL(range1, range2).

1. range1 and range2 are the two columns you want to
   compare.

2. For example, =CORREL(B2:B4, C2:C4) compares
   Page Views and Time on Page.

Table B-3. *Populated matrix table*

	Page Views	Time on Page (sec)	Bounce Rate (%)	Conversion Rate (%)
Page Views	*	.961	−.973	.959
Time on Page	.961	*	−.967	**.997**
Bounce Rate	−.973	−.967	*	−.969
Conversion Rate	.959	**.997**	−.969	*

Step 4: Interpret the results

Each cell shows the correlation coefficient between two metrics:

- A metric compared with itself will equal 1.00 (noted in Table B-3 as "*").

- If the correlation is positive, the metrics increase together.

- If the correlation is negative, one increases, while the other decreases.

- If the value is near 1, there is a strong relationship.

- If the value is near 0, there is little to no relationship.

Example

- A correlation of **+.997** between conversion rate and time on page suggests that users who spend more time on your page are more likely to convert.

- A correlation of **–.967** between bounce rate and time on page suggests that when users bounce, they're spending less time (no surprise).

How to Use It in Content Analytics

Keep in mind that correlation does not equal causation. Just because two metrics move together does not mean one causes the other, but the matrix can help you generate ideas worth testing by

- **Identifying Signal Pairs:** Which metrics might be related in a meaningful way?

- **Spotting Tradeoffs:** Are high page views correlated with high bounce rates? That may signal low-quality traffic.

- **Prioritizing Tests:** Focus your optimization efforts on the strongest positive correlations with conversion or engagement.

Calculating RMSE in Excel

RMSE (Root Mean Squared Error) measures how far, on average, your predictions are from actual results. Lower RMSE values mean your model is more accurate. It's widely used in forecasting because it translates prediction errors into a single, easy-to-interpret number.

Think of it as the "average distance" between what your model predicted and what actually happened.

Step 1: Set up your data

- **Column A**: Actual values

- **Column B**: Predicted values

Step 2: Calculate errors

In **C2**, enter

=A2-B2

Fill down for all rows. This gives the difference between actual and predicted.

Step 3: Square the errors

In **D2**, enter

=C2^2

Fill down. Squaring ensures all errors are positive and magnifies larger mistakes.

© Russ Bahorsky 2026
R. Bahorsky, *The Fundamentals of Content Analytics,*
https://doi.org/10.1007/979-8-8688-2601-6

Step 4: Average the errors

In a blank cell (e.g., **E2**), enter

=AVERAGE(D2:D6)

This calculates the mean of squared errors.

Step 5: Take the square root

In **F2**, enter

=SQRT(E2)

This is your RMSE—the average prediction error in your data's units.
Table C-1 offers data for use in this example.

Table C-1. *Example table*

A (Actual)	B (Predicted)	C (Error)	D (Squared Error)
100	110	−10	100
200	190	10	100
150	160	−10	100
130	140	−10	100
180	175	5	25

Step 6: Calculate the RMSE

Average Squared Error (E2): =AVERAGE(D2:D6) → 85RMSE (F2): =SQRT(E2) → 9.22

Step 7: Interpret the results

- RMSE = 9.22 means that, on average, the predictions deviate from the actual values by about 9.22 units.

- Since the actual values range from 100 to 200, an error of 9.22 is relatively small, suggesting that the model is performing reasonably well.

Tips

- **Use Hold-Out (Test) Data:** Don't calculate RMSE on the same data used to build your model.

- **Watch for Overfitting:** If your RMSE on test data is much higher than on training data, it signals the model is too tightly fitted to past data and may not perform reliably.

- **Clean Your Data:** Remove blanks or text before calculating.

Basic Statistical Tests

This appendix provides a practical guide for using Excel to perform common statistical tests. These include calculating standard deviation, running t-tests and z-tests, and interpreting p-values to evaluate statistical significance. These tools help you determine whether differences you see in content performance between results from an A/B test are real or just random noise.

Calculating Standard Deviation in Excel

A standard deviation shows how spread out your data is from the mean. It's a quick way to measure the consistency of your results and how reliable they are as a basis for effective decision-making.

Steps in Excel

1. Enter your data in a column (e.g., A1:A10).

2. In an empty cell, type =STDEV.S(A1:A10), or use STDEV.P if you're analyzing the entire population instead of just a sample or subset.

© Russ Bahorsky 2026
R. Bahorsky, *The Fundamentals of Content Analytics*,
https://doi.org/10.1007/979-8-8688-2601-6

Interpretation

- Low SD = consistent performance (most data points are reasonably close to the average).

- High SD = variable performance (data points widely spread and may be poor indicators of future performance).

- As a rule of thumb, values outside Mean ± 1 SD are unusual and may warrant further investigation. For example:

- See if the dataset includes any unusually extreme values and exclude them.

- Recheck the data for errors.

- Look for clusters of values that might suggest the need for segmenting the data by user type, time, location, or some other relevant criteria.

Understanding Statistical Significance

A statistically significant result means the difference observed is unlikely to be due to random chance.

- The key value is the p-value.

- If $p < .05$, the result is usually considered statistically significant (less than a 5% chance the result is random).

Understanding statistical significance helps you determine whether a result is likely due to chance or potentially reflects a real difference. Once you've grasped the concept and the importance of the p-value, you can use Excel to test for statistical significance in your own data.

To do this, Excel offers tools for running common statistical tests like t-tests and z-tests, which help you compare groups and evaluate whether differences are meaningful. Here's how to get started.

Choosing Between a T-Test and a Z-Test

Use Table D-1 when deciding whether a T-test or a z-test is more applicable to your needs.

Table D-1. *T-test vs. z-test*

Test Type	Use When	Examples
T-test	Use this when you're comparing the averages of two groups, especially if you have a small sample size or you don't know the overall population's standard deviation.	Comparing engagement between two blog formats, evaluating A/B test results for headlines
Z-test	Use this when you're comparing proportions or averages and you have a large sample size and you know the population's standard deviation.	Comparing bounce rates to industry benchmarks, testing conversion rate changes after a major redesign or email open rates against historical data

Running a T-Test in Excel

Steps in Excel

1. Enter the scores for version A (your control) in column A and version B (your test) in column B.

2. In an empty cell, enter =T.TEST(A1:A10, B1:B10, 2, 2).

- A1:A10 captures the control data.

- B1:B10 captures the test data.

- The fourth argument "2" tells Excel to assume equal variance between the two groups (if you're not sure whether the groups have similar variation, you might use 3 instead, which assumes unequal variance).

  - **When Equal Variance Might Be Reasonable**

    - The two versions are very similar (e.g., minor wording changes).

    - The sample sizes are equal or nearly equal.

    - You've run similar tests before and found consistent variance.

  - **When You Should Be Cautious**

    - The two versions differ significantly (e.g., layout vs. content change).

    - One version gets more traffic or engagement than the other.

    - You notice that one group has more extreme values or outliers.

Interpretation

- The output is a p-value.

- If $p < .05$, the two versions differ significantly.

Running a Z-Test for Proportions in Excel

Steps in Excel

1. Compute the expected standard deviation using the following formula: =SQRT((p*(1-p))/n) where p = baseline proportion (0.10) or your control rate of response and n = your sample size.

2. Compute the z-score: =(p_observed - p_expected) / stdev (e.g., (0.12 – 0.10) / stdev).

   - p_observed = your new conversion rate (e.g., 0.12)

   - p_expected = your baseline rate (e.g., 0.10)

   - stdev = the result from Step 1

3. Convert the z-score to a p-value: =2*(1 - NORM.S.DIST(ABS(z), TRUE)).

   - z = the result from Step 2

Interpretation

- If $p < .05$, the new campaign's improvement is statistically significant.

- This means the result is unlikely to be due to chance.

Bias Audit

Review these questions regularly with your team to identify and mitigate systemic biases in the way you collect, interpret, and act on content data.

- **Quarterly:** To audit data sources, tools, and reporting practices

- **At Project Kickoffs**: To confirm KPIs and methods reflect true objectives

- **During Project Reviews**: To challenge team assumptions and ensure multiple perspectives are considered

1. **Audience Coverage Bias**

   - Do our data sources reflect the full range of our audience or only the most digitally visible (e.g., frequent site visitors, social media users)?

   - Are underrepresented or hard-to-measure groups (e.g., offline users, low-bandwidth regions, non-English speakers) being overlooked?

   - Do our segmentation practices unintentionally privilege some demographics over others?

© Russ Bahorsky 2026
R. Bahorsky, *The Fundamentals of Content Analytics*,
https://doi.org/10.1007/979-8-8688-2601-6

2. **Measurement and Metric Bias**

- Are we relying too much on "easy-to-measure" metrics (page views, clicks) while neglecting harder-to-capture outcomes (satisfaction, learning, trust)?

- Do our chosen KPIs reflect organizational goals or just what's available in analytics tools?

- Are we weighting metrics fairly across channels or preferring one because it's more trackable?

3. **Tool and Algorithm Bias**

- Are third-party analytics tools introducing algorithmic biases (e.g., attribution models that over-credit last-click behavior)?

- Do our dashboards reflect national/regional/cultural assumptions about content use that could bias our observations?

- Are we aware of how recommendation systems or SEO algorithms shape the data we see?

4. **Team and Process Bias**

- Does our analytics team include diverse perspectives when interpreting findings?

- Do decision-makers review negative as well as positive results, or do our reports overemphasize wins?

- Are we regularly auditing tagging schemas, taxonomies, and categorization to avoid interpreting data that reflects only the perspective of one segment of our audience?

5. **Interpretation and Reporting Bias**

- Are we ensuring that reports don't cherry-pick data to justify prior decisions?

- Do we present uncertainty (confidence intervals, limitations, risks) clearly, or do we only highlight strong effects?

- Are alternative explanations for findings being considered, instead of just the convenient one?

6. **Strategic Bias**

- Are we checking for confirmation bias in strategic decisions, or are we only looking for data that supports an existing campaign or approach?

- Do we revisit earlier assumptions when new evidence arises, or are our strategies and decisions locked in prematurely?

- Are executive requests shaping analyses in ways that compromise our objectivity?

Glossary

A

A/B testing – A method of comparing two versions of content (such as headlines, layouts, or emails) to determine which performs better with a target audience.

Accessibility – The practice of ensuring content can be used by people of all abilities, including those with disabilities, often by following standards such as WCAG.

Accountability – The responsibility of organizations and individuals to ensure their data practices and analytics are ethical and transparent.

Algorithms – Sets of rules or formulas that process data to generate outputs, such as ranking search results or personalizing content recommendations.

Anonymization – The process of removing or altering personal identifiers in data so that individuals cannot reasonably be re-identified.

Audience segmentation – Dividing users into subgroups based on characteristics, behaviors, or needs to tailor content and measurement strategies.

Audits – Structured reviews to assess the quality, accuracy, fairness, and compliance of content and data practices. Common types include bias audits, content data audits, ethics audits, and privacy audits.

AutoML (automated machine learning) – A branch of artificial intelligence in which systems improve performance on tasks through experience and data, often applied in predictive analytics.

© Russ Bahorsky 2026
R. Bahorsky, *The Fundamentals of Content Analytics,*
https://doi.org/10.1007/979-8-8688-2601-6

B

Balanced Scorecard – A framework that connects organizational strategy to measurable outcomes by evaluating performance across four perspectives: financial, customer, internal processes, and learning/growth.

Bias – Distortions in data collection, analysis, or interpretation that lead to misleading conclusions. Common types include confirmation bias, measurement bias, and systemic bias.

Bounce rate – The percentage of users who leave a site or page without engaging further, often used as an indicator of relevance or user experience quality.

C

CDP (customer data platform) – A system designed to automatically collect, unify, and activate customer data across channels. CDPs create persistent user profiles that connect marketing, content, and behavioral data.

CTA (call to action) – A prompt asking a user to take a specific next step—such as "Apply now," "Subscribe," or "Download the guide."

CCPA (California Consumer Privacy Act) – A California law that grants individuals rights over their personal data, including the ability to access, delete, and opt out of its sale or sharing.

Click-through rate (CTR) – The ratio of users who click a specific link compared with the total number who view the page, email, or advertisement.

Comparative analysis – An approach that evaluates performance across different content assets, audience groups, or time periods to identify strengths, weaknesses, or patterns.

Competitor analysis – Reviewing competitor content and performance to benchmark positioning, messaging, and strategic opportunities.

Content analyst – A professional who uses data to evaluate how content performs, understand audience behavior, and support strategic decision-making.

Content attributes – Structured descriptive elements used to catalog and analyze content (e.g., audience, format, funnel stage, tone, length).

Content governance – Policies, workflows, and decision-making structures that ensure content is planned, created, maintained, and measured consistently.

Content lifecycle – The stages content moves through—from planning and creation to publication, evaluation, updating, and eventual retirement or archiving.

Consent management – The process of obtaining, recording, and managing user permission for data collection and processing, often required by privacy laws.

Content scoring – A system of assigning quantitative values to content pieces based on performance indicators, allowing teams to prioritize and optimize content.

Conversion rate – The percentage of users who take a desired action (such as completing a form, making a purchase, or subscribing) out of the total who view the content.

Correlation – A statistical measure of the relationship between two variables, indicating whether and how strongly they move together.

CRM (customer relationship management) – Software that manages interactions with audiences (prospects, customers, donors) and tracks their engagement history.

CX (customer experience) – The full set of interactions and perceptions a user has with an organization across channels and touchpoints.

D

Data dictionary – A centralized reference document that defines the data fields, tags, metrics, naming conventions, and classification rules used in an analytics system.

Data governance – The framework of policies and procedures that ensure data is accurate, consistent, secure, and used responsibly.

Data hygiene – The practice of cleaning and maintaining data to ensure accuracy, consistency, and reliability for analysis.

Data minimization – Collecting only the data necessary for a specific purpose—and retaining it only as long as needed.

Data quality – How accurate, complete, consistent, and reliable data is for use in analysis and decision-making.

Data steward – A role responsible for maintaining data accuracy, consistency, privacy, and quality across systems.

Data visualization – The use of charts, graphs, and other visuals to communicate insights from data clearly and effectively.

Data warehouse – A centralized storage system that houses large volumes of structured and semi-structured data from across the organization.

Descriptive analytics – Analysis focused on summarizing past events and identifying what happened, often using metrics and reports.

E

Event (analytics) – A measurable user action captured by analytics tools such as GA4 (e.g., click, scroll, form submission, video play, file download).

Event tagging – The process of adding code to content or platforms to track user interactions, such as clicks, video plays, or form completions.

F

FERPA (Family Educational Rights and Privacy Act) – A US law that protects the privacy of student education records.

Frameworks (strategic) – Structured approaches for aligning analytics with organizational goals, such as Balanced Scorecards or Objectives and Key Results (OKRs).

Funnel – A model describing the stages users pass through—from initial awareness to conversion, retention, and advocacy.

G

GA4 (Google Analytics 4) – The current version of Google's web analytics platform, emphasizing event-based tracking and cross-device measurement.

GDPR (General Data Protection Regulation) – A European Union law governing data protection and privacy, with requirements for consent, transparency, and user rights.

Google Tag Manager (GTM) – A tool that enables teams to manage website tracking tags and events without altering code directly.

H

Heatmaps – Visual representations that show where users click, scroll, or hover on a web page, highlighting patterns of attention and engagement.

I

Impressions – The number of times content, ads, or posts were displayed to users—regardless of whether they interacted. Impressions are an indicator of reach and visibility, not engagement or interest.

Interpretation bias – A tendency to draw conclusions that confirm expectations rather than objectively reflecting the data.

J

Journey mapping – The process of visualizing the stages and touchpoints a user goes through when engaging with content, from discovery to conversion and beyond.

K

Key performance indicators (KPIs) – Metrics selected to measure progress toward specific business objectives.

L

Lifecycle policies – Rules governing how long data or content is retained, how often it must be reviewed, and when it should be archived or deleted.

Lift – The improvement in performance attributable to a specific action, test, or intervention (e.g., "email B increased conversions by 12% vs. A").

M

Measurement bias – Systematic distortion in data caused by flawed tools, methods, or assumptions.

Metadata – Descriptive information about content (such as author, date, keywords, or tags) that helps organize, manage, and analyze it.

N

Net Promoter Score (NPS) – A metric that gauges customer loyalty and satisfaction by asking users how likely they are to recommend an organization.

O

Objectives and Key Results (OKRs) – A goal-setting framework pairing qualitative objectives with measurable key results, reviewed regularly to track progress.

P

Persona – A fictional but research-based profile representing a segment of the audience, used to guide content design and strategy.

Predictive analytics – The use of historical data, statistical models, or machine learning to forecast future outcomes, such as user behavior or conversion likelihood.

Pseudonymization – The process of removing or altering personal identifiers in data so that individuals cannot reasonably be re-identified.

Q

Quality assurance (QA) – Processes used to verify that content, data tags, systems, or analysis outputs meet required standards before release.

R

Recency bias – Overweighting recent events or behavior when evaluating performance or predicting future outcomes.

Regression analysis – A statistical method used to examine relationships between variables and determine the degree to which one variable predicts another.

Reporting (analytics) – The communication of data and insights, often through dashboards, one-pagers, or narrative briefs designed for stakeholders.

Return visit rate – The percentage of users who return to a site or content within a defined period—a signal of sustained interest or loyalty.

S

SaaS (Software as a Service) – Subscription-based software delivered via the cloud (e.g., HubSpot, Salesforce, Canva).

Scroll depth – A measure of how far users scroll down a page, often used as an engagement metric.

Segmentation – The process of dividing data or audiences into subsets for targeted analysis or content delivery.

Search engine optimization (SEO) – The practice of optimizing content and websites to improve visibility in search engine results.

Sentiment analysis – The process of using language models to identify the emotional tone behind audience comments, messages, or reactions.

Share of voice – A measure of how much attention or visibility a brand, topic, or message earns relative to peers in media, search, or social channels.

SMART criteria – A framework for setting goals that are Specific, Measurable, Achievable, Relevant, and Time-bound.

Social listening – Monitoring social media platforms for mentions, conversations, and sentiment related to an organization, brand, or topic.

Social media analytics – Measurement and analysis of engagement, reach, sentiment, and performance across social platforms.

Standardization – Creating and enforcing consistent processes, taxonomies, and definitions so data can be compared and trusted.

Statistical significance – The likelihood that a result or relationship observed in data is not due to chance, typically measured using p-values or confidence intervals.

Survivorship bias – Drawing conclusions from data that only includes successful or visible examples—ignoring those that failed or didn't appear.

T

Taxonomy (content) – A structured system for categorizing and tagging content, improving discoverability and analytics.

Trend analysis – Examining data over time to identify patterns, shifts, or emerging topics of interest.

U

User experience (UX) – The overall experience of users when interacting with content or systems, shaped by usability, design, and accessibility.

UTM parameters – Short tags added to URLs to track the performance of campaigns in analytics platforms. The term, short for Urchin Tracking Module, was created by the analytics company Urchin, which later became Google Analytics.

V

Vanity metrics – Numbers that look impressive (such as page views or follower counts) but do not directly align with business objectives or outcomes.

Z

Zero-party data – Information users intentionally and proactively share (preferences, interests, needs)—distinct from inferred or observed data.

Index

© Russ Bahorsky 2026

R. Bahorsky, *The Fundamentals of Content Analytics*,
https://doi.org/10.1007/979-8-8688-2601-6

L

M

N

O

GPSR Compliance
The European Union's (EU) General Product Safety Regulation (GPSR) is a set
of rules that requires consumer products to be safe and our obligations to
ensure this.

If you have any concerns about our products, you can contact us on

ProductSafety@springernature.com

In case Publisher is established outside the EU, the EU authorized
representative is:

Springer Nature Customer Service Center GmbH
Europaplatz 3
69115 Heidelberg, Germany